HOLD

FAST

By Lindy Gligorijevic

Chapter 1

December 1996

Shea Reed decided against valet parking her Mustang. She had two weeks' worth of dirty laundry and her service 9mm handgun in the trunk. She turned off the engine, took a last look in the rearview mirror and got out of her car. Her tight maroon silk dress had ridden up on her hips and she dragged it back down to its intended length.

She was not looking forward to this Los Angeles Police Department Valley Division Christmas party. Shea had no date, and sitting at a table with her colleagues in the homicide unit would normally be fun; however, the men she would dine with tonight would bear no relation to the men she actually worked with. They would be with their wives and therefore on their best behavior. And the poor wives—they were trotted out once or twice a year like migrating birds to look good and try not to fall asleep while they pay homage to their husbands' occupations.

There was an inordinate amount of pressure for every detective and officer to attend the Christmas party. A formula of measuring morale and esprit de corps was based on how many employees the captain of a division could convince to attend the event. Judging by the cars in the parking lot, Shea guessed the captain's strong-arm tactics had worked. It was nearly full.

This year the party was held at the Odyssey, a hillside restaurant overlooking the San Fernando Valley. After Shea locked her car door, she took a moment to gaze out over the glittering expanse of lights of the Valley and she made a silent bargain that she would be nice to her boss's wife, her partner's wife, and whatever twit Vaughn Powers brought as his date. On cue somebody grabbed her waist from behind, startling her with a squeeze that felt like borderline misdemeanor battery.

"Nice try, Vaughn, but I smelled your Aqua Velva before you got here," Shea said, in as bored a tone as she could muster to cover her surprise, and pulling away quickly.

"I haven't worn Aqua Velva since 1977."

"I think the *boys* aren't wearing cologne these days, old man." She sniffed his neck. Vaughn was right, it wasn't Aqua Velva, but it was a cloying smell that made her think of smoking jackets and Penthouse Pets.

"I was right behind you driving up the hill. I could tell you weren't too thrilled to be here. Now I see why, dateless." Vaughn tipped his head to the right and eyed her.

Vaughn was Shea's "training officer" when she first came to the homicide unit, exactly eighteen months ago. He had the good looks of an aging television news anchor and all of the annoying qualities of an un-neutered male cat. Despite the fact that she half expected him to lift his tail and spray one of her car tires, she knew he would never make a serious pass at her.

"Where's *your* date? Misty? Bambi?"

"Oh, you mean Candy. She couldn't make it." He shrugged.

"No other strippers to cover her shift?"

"What about you? Lieutenant Wonderful's wife wouldn't let him out to play tonight?"

"Touché." Shea quickly changed the subject. "Can we just head in to this torture chamber?" The men in her unit didn't know the identity of her boyfriend, but somehow they knew his rank.

"You know, people will think we came together if we walk in together. Hey, what do they call the woman who is seen with a guy to cover that he's gay? A beard? I'll be your beard," Vaughn said as they walked towards the restaurant. Shea pulled a sheer shawl over her shoulders.

"That makes no sense. I'm not gay."

"But you're banging a married man, which is supposed to be a secret, so I think it's an accurate comparison."

A group of young female police officers Shea barely recognized were gathered outside the restaurant. One of them had dropped the contents of her purse on the pavement and the others were helping her gather up various lipsticks and other beauty items. Vaughn gallantly swooped down on them.

"Allow me."

Shea just kept walking, shaking her head. Vaughn may have come to the party alone, but he wouldn't leave alone.

Shea smiled and exchanged greetings with familiar faces as she moved through the bar, looking for the conference room reserved for Valley Division. She noticed a sign on an easel announced, "LAPD Valley *Holiday* Party." The LAPD stopped referring to Christmas parties as "Christmas parties" years ago. They were now "holiday celebrations," with non-denominational decorations—and after Sergeant Westin's performance last year as a Kris Kringle on death row, even Santa Claus was off- limits.

The captain approached Shea with an extended hand and a bright smile. She had not bothered to learn his name; he was the third captain through their division in a year.

"Happy holidays, Detective Reed. How are you?" He asked with rank-enhanced bedside manner.

"*Merry Christmas*, Captain," Shea said.

"Well, I do hope you have a good time tonight. And by the way, good job—and I mean *good job*—on solving that triple homicide. Amazing work. Amazing. How you get those homeboys to talk to you is just amazing." He was smiling, shaking his head in wonderment.

"Yeah…well." She looked over his shoulder and into the crowded room. Did he actually say "homeboys?"

"No, seriously, I took a class in interrogation once, and I'm just amazed at your skill level. You should teach it. But maybe it comes naturally to women."

Shea's eyebrows rose a little at that last comment, but she decided to just smile and shrug. No matter anyway, the captain was already extending his soft hand to people behind her. She walked into the party and quickly found the table where her unit was sitting.

Her boss, Curt "Boots" Anderboot was holding court as usual. Empty beer bottles were lined up like soldiers in front of him. Shea looked at her watch. How late was she? She figured about a half an hour, but Curt had consumed four beers already. She knew from experience he probably had a flask of the hard stuff in his jacket pocket. His long-suffering wife, Nancy, was fingering the leaves on the centerpiece and not listening to the conversation around her. Nancy wore that badge of annoyed tolerance well. She would sigh and smile resignedly tonight, making sure everyone felt like the juvenile delinquents she thought they all were.

Seated next to Boots was Shea's partner of six months, Jack Rainier and his pretty wife, Samantha. Samantha was five months pregnant with their second child. Jack draped his arm around the back of Samantha's chair and played with the curls that fell over her shoulder. Just as Shea was about to take her seat, Vaughn grabbed her around the waist again and this time she did jump.

"Oh, are you two *together*?" Nancy Anderboot cooed.

"Not yet, Nancy, but you know she wants me." Vaughn kissed Nancy's hand, causing her to giggle and blush.

"Yeah, I just don't want to stand in line with the rest of the girls. Hi everyone." Shea sat down next to her boss.

Curt had picked a good table. It was way in the back, next to the wall and with a good view of the dance floor. After Vaughn was done kissing and hugging everyone's wives, he sat down next to Shea.

"Okay everyone, no shoptalk tonight!" Nancy said.

That narrowed the possibility of acceptable topics to a minimum for this group, Shea thought. Nancy then turned to Samantha and engaged her in pregnancy talk. Shea grumbled to herself that pregnancy talk *was* shoptalk for Samantha and Nancy.

The group of young women who delayed Vaughn earlier slipped into the room. The woman who had dropped her purse looked over at Vaughn, but Vaughn was feigning interest in second trimester updates.

The three girls were officers from mid-PM watch. Shea was

familiar with them from her crime scenes, though they were barely recognizable tonight. They were making concentrated efforts to highlight their feminine wiles. Shea understood that. She remembered what it was like to be seen only in a bulletproof vest and unflattering uniform, with your hair tied and pinned back like a librarian's. So tonight the hair was down, the breasts were displayed like hood ornaments, and the slits in the gowns were precariously near their waists, revealing long, silky legs. Shea was ten years further down the road and she didn't have it in her to dress up like a show pony anymore.

"I thought the short one was married," Curt said to Shea. Her boss was watching the same group.

"The only time you reference women by height and *not* by breast size is when Nancy's within earshot," Shea whispered. "Yeah, the short, flat-chested one's married."

"The *tall* one, in black, wasn't she on Vaughn's last crime scene?" Curt smiled at the word "tall."

"I think she was on Vaughn, not the crime scene. The dead body was just the conduit."

Curt laughed conspiratorially and before tipping his bottle

back said, "I live vicariously through that ol' boy."

"Then I'd have myself checked for virtual STD's if I were you," Shea said.

Nancy leaned in and asked, "You two aren't talking shop are you?"

"We're only talking about the people who work *in the shop*," Shea said sweetly.

"So, Shea where's *your* date tonight?"

Shea grimaced. At least Nancy did not wonder aloud why such a pretty girl couldn't get a date, like she did at the last party.

"He's home banging his wife," Curt said.

"Curt! That's just rude." Nancy shook her head.

"He couldn't make it, he's –" Shea said.

"Banging his wife," came a choir of Vaughn and Curt. Only her partner, Jack, did not join in.

"Shea! You aren't really involved with a married man are you?" Nancy's eyes were wide. It was as if this made all of the husbands at the table suddenly vulnerable.

"He's separated. They're getting divorced."

"Shea, you want a beer?" Jack stood up. "Anyone else?"

"I'll come with you." Shea pushed her chair back and leaped up. She followed her partner as he moved through the crowd and found the bar. Shea leaned into the bar and asked for two Miller Lites from the bartender.

"I can't make anymore small talk," Shea said. "Curt's wife's driving me nuts. She monitors every conversation and makes sure we don't discuss the one thing we all have in common."

"You mean the fact that we don't like her?" Jack said. The bartender delivered their beers and Jack paid him.

"No!" Shea laughed for the first time that evening.

"Even Curt doesn't like her," Jack said. "Besides we've got more in common than just work. When we're *at* work we manage to talk about stuff other than work."

"Yeah, but then we aren't stuck in these stupid clothes, off duty, and at a *holiday* party."

"Speaking of stupid clothes, Lieutenant Wonderful's missing out tonight." Jack smiled and pointed his beer bottle towards Shea's dress.

"That almost sounds like a compliment," Shea said. Jack was like the brother who would only acknowledge begrudgingly that his tomboy sister was really a girl.

"Looks good, but same salty, unappealing personality."

They stayed at the bar, gossiping about their colleagues back at the table. Jack and Shea felt like they were the underdogs, with the least amount of time in the homicide unit. But what they lacked in experience they made up for in tenacity. They solved every murder they were assigned to investigate in the last six months and accumulated more overtime than anyone in the detective squad.

Shea imagined people speculated that they were sleeping together, just as they did when she worked with Vaughn. Essentially, every man she had ever shared a black and white with, or talked to in the parking lot, was speculated as a potential lover. She could cry foul, but one rumor about her was actually true — her affair with a married lieutenant.

Despite any gossip, her partner Jack was a faithful husband who loved his wife and his young family exclusively. He did attract his share of female attention. He was unremarkably handsome, until he smiled. When he smiled, his cheeks would accordion back to his ears, giving him long dimples. His sandy brown hair always looked like he had just run in from centerfield.

Jack was speculating about retaliation between two rival factions of the same gang when Shea's pager began to vibrate. She pulled it from her purse and looked at the phone number. It was from her boyfriend using some numeric code that meant he loved her or he wanted her. She got the codes confused.

They gathered up the fresh beer bottles they ordered and turned to make their way back to their table. The "short, flat-chested" female officer, who had attracted her boss's attention, bumped into Shea. Jack was unaware that Shea was hijacked and continued through the crowd.

"OhmyGod, Detective Reed, where's your babe partner?" she asked breathlessly with stale beer breath.

"On his way back to his babe wife," Shea told the young woman.

"OhmyGod, I'm sooo embarrassed. But, you're like, major lucky." The officer slurred as she stroked Shea's free hand.

"Yeah, yeah he's dreamy." Shea unclasped the women's hands and followed Jack back to the table.

The dinners had been served while they were away and Shea sat down to an overcooked plate of chicken. She took a gulp of her beer and began to pick at her meal. The conversations floated around her. No shoptalk, only nondescript chitchat ringing in her ears. She opened her evening bag, which was just big enough for her two-inch revolver, lipstick, and pager. She checked the number again and tossed it back in the bag, snapping it shut.

"Excuse me," Shea said to no one in particular and headed out to find a payphone.

The DJ announced the dancing would begin shortly and the music went up a couple of decibels. Shea passed a table where the entire gang unit was sitting. They yelled out salutations and asked her to join them. Only one of these young bulls brought a date. The woman looked like she might be a cop herself, but Shea didn't recognize her. The girl gave her a look which read she already marked her territory at that table.

The woman's date started telling her how Shea and Jack Rainier solved a triple homicide last week. Not only that, he was telling her, but Shea had made one of the gangsters cry. Another officer handed Shea a drink that smelled of pure alcohol and told her she was the best-looking homicide detective he had ever seen, even on TV. She thought it was a mediocre compliment considering the lack of women in the homicide units across the Department, but when he added TV, she thought that was pretty sweet.

The woman at the table had heard enough. She grabbed her date before any further damage could be done and dragged him out to the dance floor. Shea talked with the remaining gang officers for a while. When their attention became diverted to some shenanigans on the dance floor, she slipped away to find a phone.

In the lobby of the restaurant, she dialed her boyfriend's pager number and waited for the recording of his voice to come on the line.

"Hi. I got your message. I hate being here alone. I feel…" Shea paused. "I feel like an idiot." She hung up the phone. Shea considered getting in line for the bathroom line, but grimaced at the prospect of small-talking her way through a half-hour procession of drunken rookies and cop's wives.

A passing waitress must have read her mind and stopped long enough to tell her there was an additional bathroom outside the restaurant.

"Just follow the lanterns," the waitress said as she breezed by Shea.

Shea walked outside. It was still uncharacteristically warm for the second week in December. She followed the lanterns, passing a group of detectives who were smoking and commiserating. She nodded at them, and in return she received a brief acknowledgement. This group was the old guard—detectives with thirty or more years on the job. Every one of them passed over for promotion, and each one certain this injustice was due to affirmative action.

Shea was the first woman in this particular homicide unit, but she wasn't the first woman in the city to work homicide. Women had been in homicide units for years, just not in the San Fernando Valley. This was where aging white men went to pasture—a pasture she now roamed as well. She watched them as she walked by. They were like bored dinosaurs, rambling around smoking and grumbling, smoking and blaming.

Shea found the restroom empty and blessed the waitress for keeping her out of the line inside the restaurant. She raked down her pantyhose and sat down on the cold toilet seat. After she was done, she sat still with her head in her hands, lost in her thoughts. She heard a pair of women come in, heels clicking on the tile and a waft of perfume. The women were only there to touch up their make-up, and based on their conversation Shea figured they were real estate

party revelers from one of the other parties at the restaurant, not

cops. After they left, Shea came out to wash her hands. She looked at

herself in the mirror. *God, I looked tired.* She realized she had put on

too much make up, in a wasted attempt to look more awake than she

felt.

As Shea reached for a paper towel, she noticed a familiar-

colored smudge near the dispenser. She leaned over to get a better

view. It looked like a bloody fingerprint. Not enough to get any

ridges, she surmised. She looked on the floor underneath the

dispenser and saw one small, perfectly formed drop of blood. Shea's

eyes swept the floor for more blood, but she didn't see any. She

pushed open the second stall door with her shoulder. She wouldn't

have been surprised to find a fetus in the toilet. Shea took a piece of

toilet paper and opened the lid, but the only thing in the water was a

floating cockroach.

She dropped the lid and looked around the small bathroom

again. Nothing else appeared out of the ordinary. The trashcan was

filled with damp, discarded paper towels and a couple of tampon

wrappers. Probably someone just had their period or picked a scab.

She chided herself for how quickly her mind went to murder and mayhem. She chided herself again for being disappointed there was no bloody evidence in the toilet bowl.

When she left the restroom, Shea saw Curt smoking a cigar with the same old guard she saw on her way in.

"Shame," Curt called to her drunkenly. It was his clever take on her name. Sometimes it was "What-a-Shame Shea" or "Shea Stadium" or the dreaded "Shea-mus."

"Hey boss, can I talk to you?" Shea pulled him away from the other detectives who chuckled and speculated until she walked him out of hearing range.

"Listen, I just found a bloody fingerprint in the women's restroom-"

"Don't your people bleed?" Curt grinned around his cigar.

"Yeah, but…it was in an odd place for that kind of accident." Shea waved a cloud of smoke from her face.

"You're off-duty. Let's go in and dance." And then Curt said one of his tried and true phrases, "If there's a problem, it'll turn up on its own."

Shea smiled. He was always telling her in one way or another not to go looking for trouble because it would find her. Most of the time he was right.

Chapter 2

The evening moved along as Shea expected. She sat sandwiched between Vaughn and Jack at the homicide unit's table. Curt was pulled up on stage and roasted by a mediocre comedian.

"Just like the song says, 'Boots' was made for walking, but he's so old, his wife has to push him around in a wheelchair."

Vaughn raised his beer in a toast.

After Curt's affair, the community relations sergeant raffled off prizes, and the DJ announced karaoke would be the next order of business. A group of civilian employees dragged a clerk typist up to sing.

Out of the corner of her eye, Shea spotted a uniformed police officer duck into the room and make a beeline for captain's what's-his-name's table. The officer squatted next to the captain to tell him something. It must have been important; the captain's hand froze midair with his drink inches from his mouth. His eyes swept over the room until they landed on the homicide table. *Uh-oh*, she thought. But that was strange, because a neighboring homicide unit was covering for them tonight. When the captain started walking directly towards their table, she assumed it was just to notify Curt.

The captain leaned down and whispered in Curt's ear. Shea watched as her boss sobered up before her eyes. It never ceased to amaze her how he was able to do that. She reached under her chair and grabbed the heels she had kicked off earlier. Curt looked around the table and said quietly, "I don't want to ruin everyone's evening, but I need to talk to…"

Everyone stopped talking and looked around to size each other up.

"Hey, I'm sober," Vaughn said. "Sober-ish."

"Yeah, boss, I'm straight." Jack kissed his wife's head as he got up. "Lemme just see what's up, honey."

Shea grabbed her purse and followed her unit and the captain to the event manager's office. Once everyone was assembled in the small room Curt began.

"Captain Sanchez just got word of a…situation we need to assist with."

"How come Devonshire isn't handling it?" Jack asked.

Curt raised his hand and Shea began to feel instinctively that this was not an ordinary, garden-variety drive-by shooting.

"We have a homicide," Captain Sanchez said. "It's in the

hills right next to the restaurant…this is our jurisdiction; however, Robbery Homicide Division will also be rolling. I'm going to notify them." The captain wiped his brow before he continued. "The officer says it's a woman in a black party dress…maybe one of our officers. Gunshot wound."

"What?" Jack's mouth dropped open.

"How did the call come out?" Vaughn asked.

"911. A man walking his dog. I guess from those condos at the bottom of the hill. Ironically, he walked to the restaurant to make the call. He didn't know we were all here, of course." Captain Sanchez was rattled. They didn't cover dead female officers at holiday parties in his leadership classes.

Curt, however, looked right at home. As soon as his young superior officer was done with the summary Curt began to work out the logistics.

"Ok, well, we don't even know what we've got yet, Captain, so let my team take a look at the scene and get the witnesses organized. We've got to give it up to RHD if it's a murder of an officer because that falls in their shop. Captain, you better let our party know they can't leave. Vaughn, make announcements at the other two parties being held here, I think Coldwell Banker's and something else. I'll take care of the general customers. Shea and Jack - take a look at the scene and make sure it's locked down. Let me know what you find. This might be a suicide, maybe just making a point by doing it here." Curt paused as everyone nodded. "Captain, just inform our people there's a possible homicide on the grounds, it's a crime scene, etcetera…but don't tell them you think it could be one of us."

"Right, of course." Captain Sanchez nodded. "Well, I better get in there."

After the captain left, Curt looked at his unit.

"Are you guys okay to work this? We're going to get a major second guessing from downtown for doing any police work here tonight, especially if we're in the bag."

"No, we're all good, boss. We're just gonna get this thing contained for the downtown boys anyway, right?" Vaughn said.

"You know those swinging dicks'll have us doing interviews of 200 drunken real estate agents while they process this scene…" Jack groaned.

Curt cut in before the conversation got out of hand, "Ok, we

can bitch about them later, let's see what we can do in the meantime.
The cavalry's going to be notified. The captain's going call the
bureau chief in the next 80 seconds."

As they left the office, Shea saw the young uniformed officer
in the front lobby. The partygoers were beginning to notice his
presence also. She could feel a buzz moving through the crowd.
Shea grabbed him by the arm and told him to lead them to the dead
body. The young man looked at Shea's heels and shook his head.

"Ma'am, it's down a hillside."

"Just take us to the body," Shea said.

They walked to the corner of the parking lot where she saw
two black-and-whites with their amber lights on. No crime scene
tape had been put up.

"When did you get the call?" Jack said.

"Just about twenty minutes ago. We were just finishing
Code-7 at the Denny's restaurant down the hill, so we got here pretty
quick. We're on loan to your division from Foothill. I guess your
whole morning watch went to your Christmas party. Anyways, I did
my probation here, so when the call went out, I got us here right
away."

"What's your name?" Shea said.

"Officer Collier, ma'am."

"Okay, Officer Collier, get two more units here. Get a crime scene log started immediately. I want a unit at the driveway at the bottom of the hill; you know where the driveway comes in? I want tape across it and no one gets in, unless they're here for this scene, okay?" Officer Collier nodded. Shea continued, "I want another unit at the top of the hill and no one leaves. People are going to try. No one leaves." Officer Collier nodded again. "I want someone writing down every vehicle license plate in this parking lot as well, clear?"

"Yes, clear."

"Okay, hand me your flashlight and point us toward the body," Shea said.

"She's just about 20 feet down the embankment there." The officer keyed the microphone on his police radio, "Partner, give me a light—the detectives are on their way down."

His partner responded with two flicks. Jack took the flashlight from Shea and started down the hill.

"I need to go first for a change. You could trip in those heels."

Shea couldn't argue with him on that one and she followed him down a clear trail, probably a jogging or hiking path. She concentrated on not tumbling into her partner's back as she navigated the ruts in the path. When they reached the second officer he was standing with his arms crossed, wearing a "if I've seen one murdered woman, I've seen a hundred" expression.

"She's right around here." The officer pointed his light at a scrub bush.

Two high-heeled feet protruded behind the bush. The flashlight's beam caused her legs to look ghostly white against the black night.

"Were paramedics down here?" Jack said.

"Yeah, but we beat 'em here, so we walked down with them. They declared death at 2355 hours." The officer checked his notes.

"It was you and your partner and how many firemen? I need to know in case I find footprints. How many people were down here?" Jack said.

"Yeah, ah, just us and two paramedics. Only one worked on her. All the footprints are right where we are and on the left side of her body. We had them walk out the same way they walked in, so anything else you see, it wasn't us."

"Ok, good job." Jack moved around the bush. Shea followed him and stopped short when he illuminated the body. The victim was on her stomach, but her long blonde hair and the black dress told Shea exactly who she was.

"That's, it's – " Jack fumbled for the victim's name.

"The one who dropped her purse." Shea leaned over the body trying to get a look at her face.

"What purse? Isn't she on mid-PM watch? She has a Hispanic last name…" Jack shined the light on her head. "Oh shit, watch the blood."

Blood was pooled around her head. Particles of dirt encroached on the edges, little specks floating on the outskirts of black puddle.

"We thought maybe she was just drunk, you know, and fell," the officer said. "But the paramedic started to turn her over and we saw the gunshot wound to her temple. He felt for a pulse…then he just put her down the way we found her. He didn't disturb much. Her dress was like that."

The victim's long dress was bunched up around her thighs.

Shea hovered over the woman's body like a magician's assistant. She could see just a portion of her face in the dirt. The woman's hands were under her body.

"Chloe Diaz," Shea said. "Her locker is next to mine."

"Yeah, that's right. Do you think she was raped?" Jack said.

"I don't know. It's definitely RHD. We know it and we've got to get out of their crime scene," Shea said.

"Yeah. Shit. She was nice." Jack shook his head.

"Officer, will you go back to your car and grab me some paper and a pen?" Shea gestured to her dress and added, "Obviously, I wasn't prepared for this."

"Oh, yeah, sure."

The officer left them alone with the body. With the tiniest tips of her fingernails, Shea pulled up Officer Chloe Diaz's dress. She wasn't wearing underwear and dirt was smeared across her upper thighs.

"No underwear," Shea said. "But that doesn't mean anything. She might not have worn any tonight. No pantyhose either…but then she's still in her heels."

"Maybe she didn't want any panty lines," Jack offered. Shea

looked at him skeptically, causing Jack to add, "I know about panty

lines, Shea. I *have* a wife."

"I didn't say you didn't know about panty lines, Jack." Shea

stood up. "There's a divot in the dirt between her legs, it makes me

think he might've taken them off after she was dead. Maybe took

them with him."

"How did our suspect get away? Down the hill? Back up to

the parking lot?"

"RHD's suspect, not ours." Shea knew they'd be reduced to

witnesses themselves and get their information from the same rumor

mill the rest of the dead officer's watch would.

"We need to find out who she came with, Shea. Shit, what if

her date did it? What if it's a cop?" Jack whispered.

"She was with two other girls from mid-PM watch. She

didn't come with a date - "

"Oh, she was dancing with the other girls. I saw them

dancing together." Jack thought for a moment. "Do you think

they're-"

"No, they aren't gay, you idiot. The short one, Kristie or

Crystal, she tried to hit on you tonight...wanted to know where my *babe* partner was."

"You're kidding."

"No, I'm not. I don't see a gun. It doesn't feel like suicide," Shea said.

Shea took a step away from the body and nearly lost her balance. She glanced around the dirt. More than anything, she wanted to process this crime scene. After six gang homicides in a row, she was ready for something interesting. The possibility of working a case with something more than three casings in an intersection and no witnesses was tantalizing.

But the dust had finally settled from the OJ Simpson case and RHD was more possessive of their cases than ever before. Having been publically embarrassed and blaming most of it on West LA Detective Mark Fuhrman, they weren't going to have any interloping, Mayberry RFD- divisional homicide detectives mucking up their scenes again. The paranoia and resentment for Robbery Homicide Division from divisional detectives were second only to the collective mistrust of all municipal police departments for the FBI and Shea was no exception.

"No one shoots themselves down the hill outside a restaurant with a huge party going on. Either you'd want to be discovered or not."

"Let's pretend this was ours, just for a minute. What would we do first?" Shea asked.

"Well, get a light truck here so we can see. Get some guys to canvas this area—shit, I wish it was ours. Something interesting for a change," Jack said. "Hey, I gotta get back and tell Boots. Do you want to look around some more?"

"When I went to the bathroom tonight, I saw a bloody fingerprint on the wall. And some blood on the floor." Shea began the trek back up the hill, her ankles wobbling in her heels.

"You're kidding. He had to have shot her here though, so it wouldn't be her blood. The killer's blood? In the women's bathroom? Maybe the killer is a woman?"

"Well, the bathroom is the one outside the restaurant and a man could go in there. I gotta get back up there and see if it's still there. It may be a good print," Shea said. "It's not a cop, Jack. A cop isn't going to shoot a colleague, then go back to the bathroom and clean up and leave a print."

The second police officer met them at the top of the hill and gave Shea a notebook and a pen. She thanked him and Jack returned the flashlight.

"No one goes down there, not sworn or civilian, no one. Only RHD detectives, OK?" Jack said to the officers.

Jack and Shea started walking back to the restaurant. People were milling around at the entrance, trying to get a look down the parking lot. More squad cars had arrived and officers were talking to the two valets. It was no longer an "incident" and it was no longer a secret.

"I'm going to find Boots and then see if I can let Sam drive home. She wasn't feeling real good tonight."

"Okay, I'm going to go check on the outside bathroom."

Shea didn't make eye contact with anyone in the crowd outside the restaurant as she walked quickly down the corridor to the bathroom. She pushed open the door and flicked the lights on.

The blood on the floor was gone, as was the fingerprint on the towel dispenser on the wall. She looked in the trashcan, but it was empty. She checked the toilet stalls. Nothing. She turned in a circle and surveyed the room. It must have been cleaned. Shea leaned against the bathroom wall and pictured the last time she had seen Chloe Diaz in the locker room. Shea was changing out of her workout gear and Chloe and a couple of other women were getting ready to start their shift. Chloe had pulled off her shirt and Shea remembered seeing a large tattoo on her shoulder. Was it a bird? Or a cat?

Shea didn't feel connected to this generation of female officers. She couldn't get used to not being the only woman in the locker room before a shift. She couldn't get used to their tattoos or sorority girl attitudes. They didn't use kit bags for their gear anymore, but rollaway suitcases, like stewardesses—that image boggled her mind. But the men dragged luggage behind them as well; maybe it wasn't a female thing, but a generational thing. She just remembered not wanting anyone to think for a nanosecond that she wasn't strong. Carrying three radios, two shotguns, and a kitbag slung on your shoulder was just what you did to help that image along.

Shea remembered Chloe was also one of those officers who had pictures taped to the outside of her locker, another thing that annoyed her. It was like walking into a scrapbook every day. Shea couldn't remember what was on Chloe's locker. In fact, there was very little about Chloe that she remembered. A tall, slim blonde. A

big flirt. Probably dating a couple guys on her watch. Nothing

remarkable. Until now.

Chapter 3

Shea walked back toward the restaurant. She saw the short, dark- haired friend of Chloe's in the middle of a small crowd, crying, with big chest-heaving sobs. Clucking hens were patting her back and stroking her hair. An older woman was trying to take charge, calling out instructions for water, a jacket, and tissue. Vaughn was in the crowd as well. He caught Shea's eye and intercepted her before she reached the group.

"Krista Tanner. She's one of Chloe's friends. I was talking to her when a uniform walked up telling someone about the murder. Krista was already asking about Chloe, so she put two and two together and just broke down." Vaughn shrugged. "I got the Coldwell real estate people buttoned down. No one's leaving."

"Where's the other girl, the one with the long brown hair?" Shea asked.

"I don't know. I haven't seen her."

"We've got to get Krista out of here."

"RHD. We can't interview."

"We're getting her out of here." Shea walked purposely into the group and removed the older woman's hand from Krista

Tanner's shoulders.

"Officer Tanner," Shea said sharply. The word "officer" resonated in the girl's intoxicated brain. She looked up, mascara running down her cheeks. "I'm Detective Reed. Come with me."

"You're Detective Rainier's partner," Krista mumbled, allowing herself to be led away from the group.

"Where's your other friend?" Shea said.

"Ann? Annie? She was here…" Krista looked around.

"We're going to find a quiet place inside." Shea guided Krista with a firm grip on her elbow. She turned to see Vaughn following behind. "Find the brown-haired friend, Vaughn. Her name is Ann."

"Shea, you can't do this," Vaughn said.

"Just because this isn't our deal does not mean we let it go to shit on purpose, right?" Krista was softly crying as Shea talked to Vaughn. "I'm just going to pull a major witness away from everyone else."

"And if she happens to give you a statement, oh well," Vaughn said and waved her off.

Krista Tanner tumbled into Shea as they walked to the event

manager's office.

"Hi, I need to use this office," Shea said to a woman she assumed was the event manager. The woman looked up at Shea, one eyebrow raised and hung up the phone. Shea hoped the phone call she was not to the news media.

"I'm sorry, I really need my office. There's an employee lounge if your friend needs to lie down," the woman said through pursed lips.

"I'm a police detective. There's been a crime. I need a place to put this witness," Shea said in a voice that did not match her slinky slip dress and three inch heels. The woman picked up some papers from her desk and huffed out of the room, closing the door behind her.

Shea sat Krista down in a chair and yanked some tissue from a box on the file cabinet. She leaned against the desk and waited as Krista blew her nose. Krista was thin and without her makeup she looked too young to be a police officer.

"It's Chloe, right? The officer said there's a murder." Krista wouldn't look up at Shea.

"When was the last time you saw her?" Shea said.

"When? Tonight?" Krista blew her nose again. Shea knew Krista was stalling. Her nose sounded dry.

"Yes, Officer Tanner," Shea said.

"I don't know."

Shea let a minute pass. Suddenly she was in interrogation mode. She felt that familiar kick of adrenalin as she pulled the manager's chair from around the desk to sit in front of Krista Tanner. She pulled herself knee to knee with Krista. Shea reached over and pulled Krista's hands down from her face.

"Sober up, Krista," Shea said gently. "When did you last see Chloe?"

"She, I can't believe..." Krista mumbled.

"Krista, are you afraid of something?"

"What?" Krista looked at her for the first time. She looked startled, but not frightened.

"Is it about you? Or Chloe? Did you lose track of her because of something you were doing? Or something she was doing?"

"Ah, I saw her about an hour ago. She said she had to go to the bathroom," Krista said. "Where were you guys when she told you that?"

"In the bar."

"Who else was there?"

"I don't know, a bunch of people." Krista shook her head.

"Cops?"

"I guess." Krista was looking down and Shea could barely hear her.

"Krista, why are my questions such a big deal? I'm just trying to get a time line of what Chloe was doing." Shea wanted to add "before she was murdered," but she knew Krista would take that opportunity to start crying again.

"I don't want to get anyone in trouble." Krista ripped at the wet tissue in her hands. "I've been on the job like less than two years and I've been interviewed ten times on misconduct stuff and you guys always want to know who else is there, so you can burn them too." Her tone touched on defiance.

"I'm not internal affairs. I'm a homicide detective. You could be shooting heroin for all I care. I just want to find out who killed your friend." Shea took Krista's hands in hers. Krista started to cry again.

"Krista." Shea sighed. "Do you know that people lie to me all day long? Some witness will lie about smoking marijuana and they'll risk being accused of murder just so they don't have to admit to a stupid misdemeanor."

"I didn't murder Chloe!" Krista dropped the tissue remnants and they fluttered like confetti to the floor.

"Of course you didn't, but what are you worried about? What don't you want to talk about?"

"It's just like…so much. It's crazy. My best friend was killed tonight." Krista gripped her stomach.

"Who would want to hurt Chloe?"

"I have no idea," Krista said. "I think I'm going to be sick."

Krista grabbed a trashcan and bent her head into it. As she was retching, the door opened slightly, just enough for the detective from RHD to peek his head in. Shea had met him at the last city-wide homicide meeting. He mouthed, 'can I talk to you?' Shea felt her stomach sink.

"Hey. Steve Lancaster, RHD." He extended his hand as she came out of the room.

"Yes. We've met." She shook his hand.

"Shana, right?"

"Shea Reed," she said. "The best friend." Shea nodded back at the office. Shea shut the door behind her. After someone was murdered, everyone in their life was reduced to titles: "the mom," "the husband," "the best friend."

"Have you established a rapport with her?" Detective Lancaster sounded pleasant, but Shea translated that into, "you haven't been interviewing my witness, have you?"

"No, not really. I just wanted to get her away from everyone for you guys."

"Thanks, thanks. I understand you saw the body."

"Yup. My boss wanted to make sure this wasn't a suicide, before we called you guys." Shea knew she sounded defensive.

"I'll need you to write a statement."

"Right."

"Did you – "

"Disturb anything?" Shea felt her cheeks flush and she leaned slightly into Detective Lancaster's space.

"I'm sure you didn't, but I gotta ask, you know."

"No, we didn't disturb anything." Shea felt absolutely ridiculous standing in a cocktail dress talking to Detective Lancaster;

she might as well have been naked and wrapped in a towel.

Lancaster pulled out his small notebook from the inside pocket of his

sports coat.

"What's your serial number?"

Shea recited her serial number and folded her arms. She was

officially reduced to being a witness.

"Hey, if I need some female back-up with the best friend, do

you want to sit in?"

"No, you won't have any problems with her," Shea said. She

gave him her office phone number and excused herself.

Shea found Jack, Vaughn, and Curt in a group with Captain

Sanchez, the bureau deputy chief, and the captain from RHD. Curt

made room for her to join the group. The captain from RHD was

explaining he had an entire squad en route, but possibly they could

use the on-call Devonshire detectives to interview all of the guests

from the various holiday parties. He was sure they would be short,

non-informative interviews, but they had to be done.

"Yeah, my crew can help with that," Curt offered.

"Well, it's important that no one who is impaired by alcohol

conduct any of these interviews, no matter how insignificant," the deputy chief said.

"Trust me, Chief. We're all very sober," Curt said.

"Let's get this started, so we can start cutting people loose," Captain Sanchez said.

"I want my people interviewing any and all law enforcement. If *your* people get any good information from any of the civilians at the other two parties, we need to be immediately notified," the RHD captain said sternly.

As the group started to disintegrate, Curt grabbed the RHD captain's arm. "Hey, Mark, do me a favor and start your guys off with my unit's wives, so they can get home. Jack Rainier's wife's pregnant."

Captain Mark whatever-his-last-name-was surveyed the male detectives. And, as if he was a king granting a wish, he nodded and motioned for one of his detectives to come to him.

"Boss, this is just taking a bunch of FI's for the most part," Vaughn grumbled, referencing thee small index sized cards, "Field Identification," which patrol officers routinely filled out during nearly every encounter they had with someone.

"Yeah Vaughn, I know. But it has to be done, so let's get

this started. Jack and Shea, why don't you guys start with the real estate group. Vaughn, do the other one, MKG or whatever they are, and I'll start in the restaurant. Meet me back in there when you finish up," Curt said.

Shea liked the fact that Curt always counted himself in on thankless tasks.

Shea and Jack made their way back to the conference rooms. She noticed the easels for party announcements and on the one for LAPD in the Bear Lodge room, the word "Bear" had been crossed out and "pig" was scrolled across the poster. Shea pointed it out to Jack.

"Hmm. Maybe people aren't thrilled with not being able to leave."

"I guess we should point that out to RH and D," Shea said.

"Shea, they're far better detectives then we are - just ask them. They'll find it on their own," Jack said with a grin. "Come on, let's get this over with. Mr. and Mrs. 'I-don't-know-anything, I-didn't-see-anything, when-can-we-leave,' are waiting."

Shea had to smile and she followed her partner into the real estate reveler's Christmas party.

For the most part, Jack was right. No one saw anything or heard anything, and there were a few people who questioned the legality of being detained. Some questioned whether Shea was really a cop at all. She looked "too pretty" to be a real detective. She would smile, break out her identification, and move on with the interview.

One man had seen Chloe. He remembered a tall blonde in a black tight gown. She was "talking to a bus boy or a valet," and he thought she was probably leaving. He said he finished his cigarette and went back inside. Shea asked him what made him remember seeing Chloe.

"She was like that song, 'a long cool woman in a black dress.' I thought she looked like trouble," the witness said.

It was nearly four in the morning before they had completed identifying all the people at the restaurant and the Christmas parties. Shea turned her notes over to a RHD detective who was coordinating the paperwork. She suppressed the desire to ask if the valets and busboys had been interviewed and if they remembered the "long, cool woman in the black dress." Most of the police officers were gone as well. In the corner of the parking lot the coroner's van has arrived and was backing up to the edge of the parking lot. RHD detectives gathered at the edge of the hill in a little pow-wow.

"How about I buy you guys some breakfast?" Curt stretched his arms over his head.

"Do you think they'll let us go? We haven't been officially interviewed," Vaughn said.

"Yeah, aren't we suspects, slash witnesses, slash detectives?" Shea asked.

"I think we have actually managed not to piss anyone off for a change." Curt looked pointedly at Shea. "Let's just see if we can get out of here without that happening."

"I'll go get my car," Vaughn said.

"That's right, the wives took our cars." Jack looked at his watch.

"I'll get mine." Shea hurried up to walk with Vaughn. "So what do you think?"

"About what?" Vaughn jammed his fists into his suit pockets. As dawn neared, it was getting colder.

"Mmm, the dead officer?" Shea crossed her arms across her chest and walked briskly next to him. She was cold, too.

"I think this is a big mess. I think those dumb assholes are all standing around not wanting to get dirty. Do you know that no one has searched the hillside yet?"

"Maybe they're waiting for it to get light."

"Yeah, I'm sure the killer appreciates the head start." Vaughn shook his head.

"Jack and I were talking about that. We would've got a light truck up here."

"See, I taught you well."

"Yes, you did. I heard that we can use the sheriff department's bloodhound on crime scenes now."

"Yeah, I know some guys in 77th Division who tried that. It was a lot of red tape to get the dog out, but he led them right to the suspect. Holed up in an attic."

"Hey, Vaughn," Shea said as they reached their cars. "Did you know the victim?"

"The dead girl? Of course. We all knew her." Vaughn unlocked his car door.

"I meant – "

"I know what you meant, Shea. No, I hadn't fucked her. I might've, eventually. I was thinking I might've tonight. She asked me if I dated younger women."

"And you replied, 'exclusively?'"

"Something like that." Vaughn chuckled.

"Remember what you told me, we'll always be partners, Vaughn. Partner loyalty, partner rules," Shea said. "I'm just saying-"

Vaughn turned from his car and smiled at Shea. He shook his head and pulled her over to him and hugged her.

"I'm fine, Shea. I didn't fuck anyone, I didn't kill anyone and you're very cute when you're concerned." He kissed the top of her head and got in his car.

Chapter 4

Under the overhead lights in the Denny's they looked especially tired. Shea thought the men looked like the prom dates from hell.

Curt took off his glasses for the third time during the meal to rub his eyes.

"Now, you know I'm going to tell you guys to stay the fuck out of this. And it's going to be next to impossible. There's going to be rumors and bullshit all over the station. We cannot, in any way, get involved. If you get a lead, any lead, you gotta let me know and then RHD."

"You say this like you don't trust us, boss," Vaughn said.

"Well, we've got our own murders to solve. We don't need to get diverted and mixed up in something that's only going to be a fucking cluster fuck."

"Where was the entrance wound?" Vaughn asked Jack and Shea.

"It looks like the entrance was in the side of her head, a little high to call the temple. I couldn't see an exit wound. Probably small caliber," Shea said.

"No way it could be suicide?" Curt said.

"It doesn't make sense, the angle, you know?" Shea positioned her right hand next to her temple, like a gun. She realized what that must look like to the other patrons in the restaurant and dropped her hand.

After breakfast, they divvied up who would drive whom home. Shea volunteered to take Jack while Vaughn took Curt.

Jack lived in Stevenson Ranch, a suburb within the suburb in Santa Clarita, a community north of Los Angeles. The overpriced tract home communities twenty miles out of the city were home to more police officers and firefighters than any other place in the surrounding area. Shea drove through the labyrinth of twists and turns into the three-year-old housing development where the houses were different shades of beige. Every street she passed had the word ridge attached to it. Eagle Ridge, Flower Ridge, and inexplicably – Cliff Ridge.

"Do you ever get the wrong house when you come home late at night?" Shea turned down Jack's street.

"That happened to my next door neighbor. He and I were the first families to move in on our block, when these were built. He came home late one night and walked into the house right behind his own and got all the way into the kitchen before he realized it was the wrong house."

"He's lucky he didn't get shot. Isn't everyone a cop or a deputy out here?"

"Yeah, in fact, he's a Glendale cop. But the house he walked into wasn't occupied yet." Jack pointed to a dark beige house at the middle of the block. "That's my house."

"I'm so tired. Why'd we have a Christmas party on a Thursday anyway? Probably cheaper. Hey, don't forget we're on-call this weekend."

"You're kidding me. Oh shit." Jack leaned his head against the window. "Sam and I are going to a big dinner for my brother."

"Which one?"

"Eddie. He's getting some award. Firefighter of the year or something."

"What'd he do? Save some kittens? An old lady?"

"Nothing special. According to him, it was just his turn in the barrel. I guess his captain gets to nominate a different guy from the station once a year. I don't know. I just know we have to drive all the way to the Harbor for this shindig."

"I suppose your dad's going," Shea said. Jack's father was a battalion chief and his other brother was also a firefighter.

"My Dad, my brother Casey, wives, children. A whole Rainier civil servant festival," Jack said. "I've got court on an old robbery otherwise I'd take a day off today. Maybe I'll take an early-out this afternoon."

Shea pulled in front of his house. His vehicles made it impossible to park in the driveway.

"Doesn't this place have rules about parking in your driveway? Don't all the cars have to be in the garages?"

"This homeowner's association is a bitch. I got a citation last week. I gotta get the boat out of the garage. I think I'll store it at Eddie's. But then he'll feel the need to clean it. I don't keep anything as clean and pristine as my brothers and Dad." Jack pulled at his tie. "It's a fireman thing. Everything's cleaned with a toothbrush and elbow grease. Anyway, thanks for driving me home. I know it's the opposite way for you."

"No worries, mate. I'll see you before nine, then."

"Yeah. You okay to drive now or do you want to come in and

get a cup of coffee?"

"I'm fine. I'll stop at Starbucks on my way home."

Shea drove south on Interstate 5, out of Santa Clarita and into the rough-and-tumble San Fernando Valley. The sun was officially up and her eyes burned. She didn't have her sunglasses, when she left her house last night; it was to go to a party she assumed would be over long before sun came up. She turned on KFI talk radio and rolled down her window, but she could feel her eyelids growing heavy. She willed herself to stay awake as she drove across the Valley to the Hollywood Hills.

Shea's Mustang snaked up the road to the house she shared with her older sister since the earthquake in '94. Her condo in Chatsworth had been hit hard enough to be condemned and subsequently torn down. Twenty months later she was still living in the studio apartment burrowed into hill beneath Shannon's house.

The tiny apartment had a separate entrance from the rest of the house and enough of a kitchen to accommodate a heated up TV dinner and a six pack of beer. The shower in the bathroom was better suited for auto mechanics cleaning up before going home from the shop, but Shea couldn't complain. The rent was cheap and her sister was kind. Shannon was a personal assistant, a job that she had not yet been able to adequately describe to Shea. Shannon was currently in England for a month with a record executive, who she was currently "personally assisting."

After Shea pulled into the drive way, she didn't bother going down to her apartment. She knew had Shannon's three hungry cats waiting for her. The cats were named after Fleetwood Mac songs. In fact, the newest addition, an orange stray, was named after Stevie Nicks herself. The trio greeted her enthusiastically and Shea felt guilty. Not only was she supposed to feed them and clean their litter box, she was required to spend quality time with them. She defined "quality time" as attending to the first two tasks. As she became lost in thoughts of blood drops and fingerprints, Rhiannon slid like a slinky through her legs and Sarah snagged her pantyhose with her claws.

After Shea fed the cats, she ate some of her sister's granola cereal and sorted through the mail. When she finally made it down to her apartment, her telephone was ringing. Kicking off her heels, Shea cradled the phone between her cheek and shoulder and tried to unzip the back of her dress, "Hello."

"Finally you're home." It was the low voice of her mostly-married boyfriend.

"Hi, Andrew." She flopped down on her unmade bed, where Andrew had spent many hours, but never an entire night.

"Did you get my messages?"

"No, I just walked in the door. I'm sure you heard about what happened at our party last night."

"Of course. I'm already at my desk," he said. He always spoke at a low volume. Shea read that Jackie Kennedy did the same thing, in order to get people to lean in to listen to her. She thought maybe Andrew did that because he was concerned about being overheard.

"I need to take a shower and then I'm going back to work."

"Did you know the victim?"

"Yeah, sort of. Hi-bye sort of thing," Shea said. She pulled off her pantyhose and threw them into the trash.

"She was interviewed a month ago by my team. Remember the OIS in your division where the cop got his ear shot off?" Andrew was the officer-in-charge of the Officer Involved Shooting section of Robbery Homicide Division.

His entire unit was devoted to the *administrative* aspect of an officer firing his or her gun. The divisional detectives were responsible for handling the *criminal* aspect of the case against the suspect who the officer shot at. But, if the officer was accused of a crime, then that aspect of the case went to a third place, Internal Affairs. Shea often thought it would be good to have an air traffic controller at the scene of a shooting, so all the interested parties could be coordinated.

"Yeah, of course. I remember the shooting."

"Well, she was his partner. She didn't get any rounds off at the suspect."

"I didn't know she was the partner officer. For some reason I thought it was this other girl on mid-p.m. watch," Shea said. "Well, it doesn't matter. Your boys came in and took over."

"They're not *my* boys. I keep telling you that. You should just apply at RHD and work with them yourself and then I won't have to listen to you lambaste them every other day."

"First of all, you and I both know they'd never take a woman in Homicide Specials, and secondly, I only have a year-and-a-half of experience."

"Those 18 months are like dog years in your division. You know you've personally handled more homicides this year then all of RHD combined."

"But they'll be the first to tell you that they get the complicated, high profile ones. My gang-drug-domestic violence murders are simple." Shea coughed a bitter little laugh.

"It's neither here nor there. You wouldn't apply anyway. You'll be working for Boots until he retires," Andrew said. "Did you have a good time before all of this happened last night?"

"No. I wish you would've come with me. People actually thought I was Vaughn's date because we walked in together."

"Oh no." Andrew chuckled. "Tell me he wasn't able to lure you back to his bachelor pad for a dip in his hot tub."

"Yeah, I just got back from there. Bacon and eggs, six stewardesses, and two Bloody Mary's later."

"So you want to come downtown for lunch today?"

"I doubt it. Are you coming over tonight?"

"Melissa is in a play and I said I'd go." Melissa was his oldest daughter with his current wife. Andrew had two twenty-something-year old daughters with his first wife.

"Okay."

"Hey, we'll talk later."

"Yeah, I hope so." Shea paused. "I'd like to be able to call you."

"You know you can call me on my City cell phone."

"Right. I guess I just want confirmation that you don't actually live in the same house as your wife does, Andrew. I guess I'd like to know for sure that you're actually legally separated."

"I can't get into this right now, Shea. I'm sitting at my desk."

"I know. And I know that whole office is empty and I know that if you wanted to talk to me about this or anything else you could."

"You know this is complicated, Shea."

"Uh-huh."

After almost a minute of silence, Shea hung up the phone. She unplugged it from the wall. Not because she thought he would call back, she just didn't want confirmation that he wouldn't.

After a hot shower and half a pot of coffee, Shea was on her way back to work.

The route to her division was lodged deep in her middle brain and she was on autopilot on her way to work. Her mind was preoccupied - not with murder, but with her two-year love affair. She had no desire for a husband and white picket fence she imagined came with one. But after a year, they began talking about a future together. The acknowledgement that the relationship was something more than hot sex with no strings attached changed everything. The second year was marked by a series of break-ups, days of lonely silence, and then more promises of a vague future together—someday soon.

Andrew Thorpe was one of those men who entered a woman's life like a bullet to the chest. Shea met Andrew twelve years ago when she was in the Police Academy. He was a SWAT team member and was involved in the tactical portion of recruit training, taking place at the end of the academy. Her class was at the Universal Studios back lot for situation simulation training. The SWAT team had set up four different scenarios for her class to go through. All designed to get them killed, in theory, but probably more to get them to revere the magnificence of the most elite unit in all of law enforcement. And the SWAT guys were pretty magnificent.

When it came time for her squad to begin their scenario, she was nervous. She waited her turn to tackle an unknown situation. Her classmates were paired up and assigned a patrol car, with a SWAT team member in the backseat. The cars would drive off down the make believe street and eventually the remaining recruits would hear simulated gunfire and shouting. Shea assumed this was probably some kind of ambush scenario. They just received an hour-long lecture on driving into the "kill zone." In other words, if you are being fired upon, drive directly into the source of the gunfire. This was just one of many lessons that defy human nature, but become second nature to police officers.

When it was her turn, the SWAT team member assigned to them looked her up and down and told her to drive. Her partner was a fellow recruit, who was shorter than she was and a year younger. Shea slid her shotgun in the rack against the front seat and climbed in.

"Ok, you guys got a radio call of a 415 man with a gun. Drive straight down this street," the SWAT officer told them cryptically as he got in the backseat. "I'm not in play, I'm just here to monitor you and let you know where you fucked up."

She had driven less than two blocks into this make-believe city when they heard gunfire. It was coming from an upstairs window of a building on an arrowhead-shaped corner she was driving directly toward. She hit the gas, drove directly to the building, and parked right in front of it. She threw open her door and told her partner to slide out on her side. He grabbed the shotgun and crawled to the rear of the police car. She took cover behind the engine block and saw a man in a lime green t-shirt exit the building. He was shouting that he didn't have a gun. She yelled at him to get his hands up, which he did, but he continued to yell and walk towards her car. For some reason she looked over her shoulder and saw another bad guy/SWAT officer running across the street directly towards her with a gun in his hand—ready to shoot her full of blanks.

Shea drew down on him and pulled the trigger on her empty pistol. The SWAT officer stopped in his tracks, acknowledging she had shot him. She whipped back around, instantly aware she had taken her eyes off the original suspect. He was reaching into his waistband for his gun, only a few feet from her. She pulled her trigger again, sending make believe bullets to the imaginary ten ring of a chest.

"Scenario over," the SWAT officer who had been in the back seat called out.

Shea stood up, prepared to be yelled at for taking her eyes off the first suspect, for not communicating with her partner, or for ever thinking she could be in law enforcement. The SWAT officer she shot first came barreling up to her. She braced for a verbal assault. He grabbed her hand and pumped it hard, "Out-fucking-standing, recruit. What's your name?"

"Recruit Officer Reed, sir," she said when she could find her breath.

The first suspect came around the car and clapped her hard on the back. "Well done."

The SWAT officer from the backseat opened his notebook and began writing. He looked at her partner and told him to take the black-and-white back to the starting point. Her partner barely mumbled a "yessir" and drove away. Shea stood in the street looking at the three of them.

"You have no idea what you did, do you recruit?" the monitoring officer asked.

"No sir, hopefully what you told us to do. I took my eyes off the first suspect. I know I shouldn't have," she said.

They started to laugh.

"Okay, Recruit Officer Reed, you're going to stand here and watch your classmates," the monitor told her as he led her over to an alcove near the middle of the intersection.

She watched as three sets of classmates completed the scenario. Not one drove into the kill zone. They all stopped short. The second officer on each scenario was successfully taken hostage by one of the SWAT officers, and the guy in the lime green shirt convinced each remaining partner to give up his gun in exchange for not shooting his or her partner.

Shea stood watching, aghast. She tried to understand. She had simply done what she was told. She did not feel particularly brave, knowledgeable about tactics, or tenacious. She followed instructions. However, she knew she would never give up her gun. She had read *The Onion Field* long before she had ever thought about being a police officer. The relinquishment of an officer's gun caused his death in an onion field outside of Bakersfield.

"Pretty sorry, huh?" The SWAT officer in the lime shirt

asked her after she watched the last scenario. "You and your class DI were the only two that survived this scenario. You're going to be okay in the field."

"Thank you, sir." Shea liked being put in the same category as the class drill instructor.

"Have you had your self-defense test yet?"

"Yessir."

"Where did you finish?"

"Fifteenth, sir."

"Out of how many?"

"We have 52 in our class, sir."

"I assume you were the top female." He surveyed her again and she felt her cheeks burn.

"In self-defense, but not in PT, sir. Recruit Officer Brown was the top female."

"Black, right? She can run, huh?"

"Ah, yes sir." Shea smiled and looked him in the eyes for the first time. He was not much taller than she was. He had coal black hair and dark brown eyes. He may have been the most handsome man she had ever seen.

"I'm Andrew Thorpe. I teach hostage negations. You'll get that class next week."

"I...okay."

"I'm going to give you some advice...no, not advice, I'm going to give you a peek into the future. When you're on probation, your training officer's going to tell you that you're the best female boot he ever had. When you get off probation and when you're a patrol officer, your partners are going to begrudgingly tell you that you're the best female partner they ever had. Maybe someday you'll be the best female sergeant anyone ever worked for. When someone tells you that you're the best partner he ever worked with, and he doesn't put the word 'female' in front of it, trust *that* guy and nobody else." Andrew winked at her and told her to go back to her classmates.

Shea saw him again when he came to her class and instructed them on hostage negotiations. He didn't appear to notice her and she didn't see him again until three years later. She was working Rampart Division and a SWAT call-out brought Andrew Thorpe back in her path. She watched him changing into his uniform behind his undercover sedan. The trunk was open and he was pulling his uniform shirt over a tight white t-shirt.

"I remember you," she said. By that time she was the lone female on a ballsy mid-p.m. watch, and she wasn't intimidated by anyone.

"Yeah." He looked at her for a long time. "You've gained some weight." His partner busted into peals of laughter and for a second time he made Shea's face burn.

"It's the vest," she said.

"I know. So they call you 'Jane Wayne' here?" he asked. Shea was officially reduced to a bug on his windshield.

"I've only heard that name when they're looking for you," she said and walked away. His partner started laughing again.

The next occasion was when she was a new detective in Hollywood Division. Andrew had been promoted and was the lieutenant watch commander for patrol's day watch. She ran into him in the records room when she was trying to find a report. She knew him immediately, but he didn't recognize her. Of course, she was in a business suit. She had her hair down, and she was ten years older.

"You used to work SWAT," she said.

"I did. Andrew Thorpe." He shook her hand.

"Shea Reed. I work sex crimes."

"You look familiar to me."

"Yeah, I think I impressed you briefly in 1984 and then we traded insults in the parking garage of Rampart station in 1987."

"Oh, I remember you. I do. My partner called me Jane for three weeks. I called you to apologize, but you never called me back."

Shea looked at him skeptically. It was possible. That was the age when a message was taken by a malcontent officer at the front desk, and then—if he chose to write it down—it might on a pink memo pad paper in an alphabetized recipe box under R.

"So, did you just make detective?"

"I did. I transferred here last DP." Shea said using the slang for a deployment period, LAPD's version of calendar months. Transfers, promotions, everything related to a schedule was based on the thirteen DPs in a year.

"Do you like it?" He leaned against the file cabinets.

"So far. Yeah."

"Somehow I didn't picture you going the detective route. I

pictured you in the field. Maybe even Metro."

"All from one scenario in a make-believe city?" She pulled out a cabinet drawer and began to look for her report.

"That and I asked around about you in Rampart. You were well-respected."

"For a female," Shea said. She was flattered he had asked about her. "Why were you asking about me?"

"I think we were recruiting females in Metro then. You fit the bill. Tall, muscular. You could take a joke." He seemed to be looking through her suit at her, trying to size up if she still fit that bill.

"Well, that ship has sailed. I went, as you put it, the detective route." She shut the drawer, not finding the report.

"Actually, I was probably looking for you to ask you out," he said. "I was single then…"

Shea looked at the ring on his left hand.

"Another ship that sailed." She looked him directly in the eye. "Nice seeing you again, Lieutenant Thorpe."

Chapter 5

When Shea got to work that morning, she saw that Curt was already at his desk, his telephone locked between his shoulder and his ear as he jotted down a note. She threw her bag under her desk and sat down. On her desk was a copy of the *Los Angeles Times*. A red arrow was drawn to a grainy picture of the coroner's van. Her own subscription to the Times was delivered with only occasional regularity so more often than not, she read it at work.

The headline read, "Murder Mystery at Cop Party." Shea checked the byline. It was Isabella Anton. A couple of months ago, Shea put her on the list of reporters she wouldn't talk to. Isabella was just another LA Times reporter with an agenda.

After Rodney King and OJ Simpson crossed paths with the LAPD, a new breed of beat reporter had emerged. Breaking a story on a serial rapist wasn't nearly as coveted as getting the scoop on an LAPD scandal. If a police officer was involved in anything that made the news, the *LA Times* went straight to their circulation department to see if the fool was a subscriber. They would then drive to his address and start talking to his neighbors. Before he made it home, the world would know how often he mowed his grass and if he took his trashcans in.

Shea was looking through the messages left on her desk when Curt got off the phone and leaned on her partition.

"You aren't going to believe this." Curt ripped the top sheet of a pink memo pad and dropped it on her desk. In his chicken-scratch writing was an indistinguishable name.

"Let's see, do I get to guess? RHD found the killer?"

"No, not yet. But they're coming down here today. I talked to Steve Lancaster, the lead on this case. He's sending down some light-duty guy to go through her locker. He wants you to be there."

"Be where?"

"Are you going to be purposely dim-witted all day?" Curt looked over his glasses at her. "The victim's locker. Where'd you think? He needs a female detective in there with him."

"What am I going to do, identify Tampax for him? Who is this guy?"

Curt looked at a piece of paper he had dropped on her desk.

"Walter Smith. He's a D3 down there. I guess he's permanent light-duty. According to Lancaster, they've sent this guy to Quantico and he's got all kinds of specialized training in profiling.

He doesn't go in the field anymore. He just analyzes things—diaries, notes, shit like that. I knew a Walter Smith when I walked a foot-beat in Central, but he was a hundred years old when I was there, so it probably isn't him."

"When is Walter the profiler gonna be here? I do have things to do," Shea said primly.

"No you don't. Smith said he'd be here in the next hour."

"I've got to get prepared for the *Rosales* pre-lim. And I thought you said we weren't supposed to get involved in this case."

She followed Curt as he ignored her and walked back to his own desk.

"Seriously, it's not like RHD would drop everything to help out a divisional detective. Remember the Moreno case? I needed-"

"You know, you're a real pain-in-the-ass today. If you don't want to stand by while this Walter Smith looks through a locker for ten damn minutes, I'll go round up some female from the domestic violence unit to help him," Curt said. He sipped coffee from a mug with a logo that read, "Our day begins when yours ends."

"No, I'll do it. I just would've rather had nothing to do with this case, instead of being on the sidelines watching. Plus, it feels like I've been called in to do a strip-search of a female suspect. It's the only thing you guys need female officers around for."

Shea sat down in a chair sandwiched between Curt's desk and the waist-high carpeted wall.

"Ah, yes. Sure. If the Supreme Court would only let us search female suspects, we could do without your kind entirely. Now, if you and the chip on your shoulder could leave me alone, I *do* have work to do."

Shea remained seated next to him as he began to drag reports out of his in-box.

"Remember to turn in overtime for last night," he told her as he sifted through the paperwork. Under his blotter was a montage of pictures of his wife and children. It was a virtual time capsule of soccer games, fishing trips, graduations, and pets. Smiling, sunburned kids were reminders of something beyond the murder reports that were now covering their faces. Taped to the bottom of his desk lamp were four uniform buttons.

"Did you have to buy new buttons for the inspection next week?" Shea asked.

"No. Those are standby buttons."

"Stand by for what?" Shea said.

He put his glasses on his desk and turned his chair towards her. "When you retire, you have to turn in 30 rounds of ammunition, all your gear, including exactly four buttons."

"Are you retiring?" *Who would replace him?* Shea immediately felt of bit of panic set in. She knew the Detective III in charge of the burglary table was always sniffing around trying to take Curt's job.

"No, probably not. I've got 29 years on, Shea. There just might be a straw one day that finally breaks my back. I want to be ready with my four lousy buttons when that day comes." Curt put his glasses back on and picked up his paperwork. She hoped he'd stay well past the usual 30 years most detectives put in.

Shea sighed something between relief and fatigue and watched the squad room start to fill up. Detectives who attended the party were huddled with detectives who hadn't, filling them in on their firsthand knowledge of what happened last night. Shea imagined very little work would get done today. The detectives who went over to file their cases at the DA's office would gossip with attorneys. The officers who booked suspects would share what they knew with the jailers. The captain's secretary would call the secretaries at the other divisions to let them know her take on what had happened.

"Shea, are you going to sit here all day? Is there something you want to talk about?"

"No. Do you know if RHD had criminalists go through the bathroom where I saw the blood?"

"I'm sure they did. I saw criminalists heading that way when we left," Curt said. "Are you beating yourself up over that blood being gone? What could you do? Did you have a crime scene kit in your little evening bag? Did you have a camera? Plus, and I'd like to emphasize this, *there was no crime* at the time you saw that. It may not even be related."

"I know." Shea sighed again. "I just can't get motivated this morning."

"Try."

Three older detectives approached the cubicle. What did Curt know? What had he heard? Is it true the dead P2 was naked?

Shea returned to her desk. Unlike her boss, Shea had no family photos on her desk. She used to, until she came in for a homicide at midnight one night and found six gang member witnesses sitting at all of their desks. One officer was guarding them, but he was using Vaughn's phone and not paying attention. Several hours later that night, after everyone had been interviewed, she sat down at her desk and saw that someone had scratched filthy comments and gang monikers on her plastic blotter. Vernacular for female genitalia was scratched over a picture of Shea and her sister on vacation in Hawaii. After that, Shea pulled everything personal off her desk.

One side of her desk was now jammed with reference books, *Gray's Anatomy*, books on ballistic evidence and crime scene procedures. She also had a signed copy of *His Name was Ron* on her desk by the family of Ron Goldman. A rather morbid collection of comical miniature toy skeletons hung and stood in the spare real estate of her desk. A Costco-sized container of Tums took the place of friendly people's candy dishes. She wondered what the profiler would say if he analyzed her desk for clues to her psyche.

Shea pulled out the *Rosales* murder book. The preliminary hearing would probably get continued for a third time, but she had to be prepared in case it wasn't. She opened it to the witness statements portion and started to review her notes.

In the next half-hour, Jack arrived in a blur of motion, in a hurry to get to court. He gathered up his reports and searched his desk for his subpoena.

Jack nodded as Shea told him her big plan for the day was to babysit a locker. Shea realized he was not listening to her so she sat back down at her desk and began clearing out the numbers on her pager.

"I've got to get to court. If the DA calls tell him I'm on my way." Jack shoved his reports into a manila folder.

"Who's the DA?" Shea asked.

"Younger. I'll call you at lunch, maybe you can meet us somewhere."

"Yeah, maybe. I might be busy though. I'm a very busy person."

"Fine. Stay here and get a burrito from the roach coach. I'm taking our car. I don't have time to scrounge up another one."

Shea noticed someone who was probably the light-duty RHD detective enter the squad room. He was in his late forties, tall and thin, with skin was so white it was almost translucent. He wore small, wire-rimmed glasses. Shea thought he looked like a pharmacist. He asked someone to direct him to the homicide unit. Heading in the right direction he bumped into Curt precisely at Shea's desk.

"Detective Anderboot?" His voice seemed to evaporate in the air.

"You must be Walter Smith. Welcome to Valley Homicide."

"Thank you."

Shea stood up and introduced herself. When she shook his hand she was startled by the slight man's grip.

"I hope I'm not taking you away from anything too vital," he said pleasantly. "Short notice is never good for a homicide detective."

Shea didn't come across too many "gentleman" detectives. He glanced at her desk and she wished she had scooped the skeletons into her desk drawer.

"If you're ready, I'll take you up to the locker room." She picked up several empty evidence bags from her desk and led him away from the homicide unit. "We should have it all to ourselves. Day-watch roll call just ended."

Shea and Detective Smith walked upstairs to the second floor of the station. After checking to make sure the locker room was empty, she told him to come in and he followed her down the aisle to Chloe's locker.

"Would you like an explanation for why I needed you for this search?" Detective Smith opened a burgundy-colored leather notebook and took a fancy pen from his shirt pocket. Shea didn't know a Monte Blanc from a Bic, but it looked expensive.

"I assumed it's because you're going to collect some evidence, you needed a witness and it's a female locker room." Shea shrugged, "I assumed you were killing two birds with one stone."

"Do you do that often?" He scanned the pictures taped to the outside of the locker.

"What?" Shea sat down on the bench in front of the locker.

"Assume."

"Probably." Shea could recognize the beginning twinges of irritation in her voice.

"Admitting it…is the first step to curing it. Good for you," Walter said.

"Do you work at a 'twelve step' meeting off-duty?"

"No. How long have you been in homicide?"

"Eighteen months. How long have you been in RHD?"

"Ten years." He was writing some notes in his notebook.

"Why are you light-duty?"

"How did you know I was light-duty?" He looked up from his notebook.

"Someone told my boss."

"I have a heart condition," Walter said. "So, if we're done sparring, I requested you to be here for the reasons you assumed. However, I also wanted an experienced female officer's take on the contents of this locker. I've sorted through a few male officers' lockers and it's not difficult for me to tell what is incongruous; however, I've never opened a female police officer's locker."

Shea just hated the word *female* when it was associated with "police officer." It was as if men were referring to Panda bears or something. Then she remembered Curt pointing out the chip on her shoulder this morning. She took a deep breath and vowed to be a better person—or at least to act like one.

"I notice many of the women have pictures on the front of their lockers. Interesting." He looked at the collages.

"Men don't do that?"

"No. You may see a subpoena taped to a locker, but the personal pictures are inside." Walter Smith was looking back and forth between Chloe's pictures and the pictures on a nearby locker. "Things have changed over the years, of course. Due to the sensitivity for sexual harassment, gender bias, hostile work environments and the like, there is less Playmate-type stuff in men's locker rooms and lockers."

Shea swept her hand across several lockers. "As you can see, it's usually women's kids or if they're young and single there's friends and parties, classmates from the academy, pets, that sorta thing. There's a woman who works morning watch who is way too attached to her Yorkshire terrier, in my opinion."

Walter chuckled. "Officer Diaz appears to fit the bill for young and single. Do you know any of the women in these pictures?"

Shea got up and peered over his shoulder. There were half-a-dozen pictures of women with their arms around each other taped to the locker. A few of the pictures were from the Sheriff Department's annual mud run. Chloe was in the middle of four other young women, all covered in mud and laughing. There were also pictures of her graduation from the academy, and pictures of a party that was probably to celebrate the completion of her probation.

"Well," Shea said as she pointed to the muddy picture. "I think these girls work on mid-p.m. watch. And I would assume--" she stopped herself. "*Guess* that these other women are classmates. I think Diaz was divorced and I heard her father was a retired deputy chief."

"I didn't know that."

"I heard he died before she came on the job."

Walter spun the dial with the locker combination he must have obtained from the captain. He checked the numbers on his notebook. After a false start, the locker opened.

Shea was half expecting a dramatic gasp, but it was anti-climatic. At first glance, the interior of Chloe's locker was as unremarkable as the outside. She had two fresh uniforms hanging up, still draped in the dry cleaner's plastic. A worn uniform hung from one of the hooks. The rest of her gear, her Sam Browne belt, baton, and boots were at the bottom of the locker. Shea noticed her 9mm was not in the holster.

On the inside of the locker door, Chloe had hung a plastic shoe storage unit. Shea had one just like it in her locker. It worked well to hold nameplates, buttons, hairspray, and just about any other small item one might need. She winced for Chloe as Walter sifted through her tampons, Midol, Summers Eve feminine-odor wipes, and used panty hose. He moved the shoe holder off the locker door and it revealed more photos. Shea drew closer. These pictures were different than the ones on the front of the locker. These were of men.

"Wow," Shea said. Her eyes moved across the pictures. The photos were of men in provocative poses. Shirts off, lying across a bed, sitting on a motorcycle, a good-looking black officer with his uniform shirt unbuttoned and his hand in his pants.

"Same question," Smith said. "Do you know these men?"

"Yeah, yeah I do. Some of them. Wow."

"Why the 'wows'?"

"Well, you can write this down from my *experienced female officer* perspective, I've never seen anything like this in a woman's locker."

"I've seen this sort of thing in men's lockers, essentially a trophy wall. Bragging rights."

"But women don't do this. I mean, who brags about quantity?"

"Their placement may be significant," Walter said. He pulled a small camera out of his suit pocket and took a picture of the locker door. He took one of the pictures down and put it in an evidence envelope. Shea recognized the model for that picture as a training officer in the gang unit. He was sitting on the edge of a bed, with a beer in his hands. He was in his briefs and smiling.

"Did you look at the back of the picture?" Shea said.

"No." Walter said. He retrieved it from the envelope and flipped over the picture. In loopy, girlish scroll, the words "little dick" were written.

"That's not what I expected," Shea said.

The second picture was of a sergeant who had transferred out of the division several months ago. He looked less comfortable than the gang officer. He was nude from the waist up, with his arms crossed. Shea could tell he was trying to push out his biceps with his unseen hands. Walter flipped the picture over and in the same writing was, "didn't get it up."

"Oh wow." Shea laughed uncomfortably. "Man, if these guys

only knew what she wrote they'd kill her."

Walter reached for the next photo.

"I'd like to think that a lack of sexual prowess or diminutive endowment were not grounds for murder. Or blackmail," he said.

"Of course," Shea said.

"A fellow I worked with in Southeast Division, he had a list. No pictures, but a list of female employees…clerk typists and the like…with what they did well in bed. It was taped to the inside of his locker. It was a little disconcerting to have a records clerk, who according to this officer preferred a particular sexual position, run warrants for you."

Walter pulled the third photo down. Shea didn't know this man. He flipped it over and Shea read the words 'tiny balls.'

"This's weird," Shea said. "I don't remember ever hearing her talk about these pictures or anyone mentioning them in here."

"In your experience, do women share these kinds of details with each other?"

"I suppose with your girlfriends, but not in a locker room, not with people you work with. This really surprises me. Not that she screwed around, but that she took the pictures. I mean how do you even get a guy to pose like that for you?"

"Do you think she kept the observations on the back of the photos private?"

"I'd have no idea, but I think if a woman was passing around something like that—the watch commander not being able to get it up or something—it would've got around." Shea shook her head. She sat quietly as he went through ten more photos.

Walter had to squat down to pull the last photo from the bottom of her locker door. When he did, it revealed a photo underneath. Shea leaned over, instantly recognizing it as different from the rest. He held it so she could see it. It was a Polaroid photo taken at a crime scene. Curt and Jack were standing together outside the yellow caution tape. Inside the tape, Vaughn was bending over the body. Shea was not in the picture, but she knew where she was at the very moment the photo was taken; she had walked out of the crime scene and was looking in a gutter where she thought she saw a casing.

"This is my unit. This is Vaughn Powers' last homicide. A drive-by. It happened at the end of watch, that's why we are all there."

"How long ago?"

"Uh, about ten days ago," Shea said.

"Do you remember if Officer Diaz was there? Perhaps she took this picture?"

"Yes, I do remember her being there. We were just talking about her – " Shea stopped a minute before she could add, "flirting with Vaughn." Shea stared at the picture.

Walter turned the picture over and Shea was relieved to see it was blank. But her next thought was disappointment. She wouldn't know why Chloe Diaz took the photo.

Walter stood up and began to look through the papers shoved on the top shelf of the locker. He began separating things on the bench. Subpoenas were placed in one neat pile. Police reports in another. Stacks of overtime receipts were placed next to the subpoenas. Business cards were sorted and documented. Walter sifted through the pink message notes, reading them quickly and not making any effort to share them with Shea.

As he pulled papers from the back of the shelf, a dried rose fell onto his shoulder and then onto the floor. Shea retrieved it and held it in her hand. Someone had cared enough to hand this girl a flower at some point. And the girl who wrote such crude things about men on the back of the photographs was sentimental enough to it. Shea ran her fingers over the paper-like petals and thought of the dried rose corsage she kept pressed in a big dictionary from 1979.

Walter was looking at a calendar he found on the top shelf. Shea could see that Chloe had a doctor's appointment today. She couldn't make out the last name, but she saw "DR." in front of it. She thought it should be a psychologist. The girl certainly needed it. She unfolded a wad of crumpled-up newspaper articles that had also fallen from the top shelf. It took her just a few moments to see that these were all related to the shooting Chloe Diaz and her partner were in a few months ago.

"From the shooting?" Walter asked as he leafed through the calendar.

"Yeah, all the articles are about the shooting," she said.

She vaguely remembered the details of the officer involved shooting. She was not called out on this particular OIS, it had been Vaughn's case. She scanned the article for the facts.

Patrol officers, Officer Chloe Diaz and her partner, Officer Ornelas, had attempted to pull over and cite a vehicle. Before Officer

Ornelas could make his way to the driver's side window, he was being fired upon. The only round to hit him was the first one. It sheared his right ear off, and he fell to the ground. Officer Ornelas drew his gun from his holster and fired one round in the vicinity of the open driver's side window, but the vehicle was pulling away. Officer Diaz was on the passenger side of the vehicle and didn't get a round off before the vehicle sped away.

It was a fairly uneventful shooting, except, of course, for the two officers involved. This was probably why Shea hadn't paid much attention to it, that and the fact that she and Jack were working 18-hour days during that time period.

"Don't discuss the contents of the locker with anyone," Walter said. She appreciated that he didn't try to hide his admonition with some weak, "I know I don't have to tell you this, but…"

"I won't." Shea folded the newspaper articles.

"I would be interested in your take on this."

"Ha! I'd be interested in yours." Shea handed him the articles. "You can have my take on why gang members yell, 'Where you from?' That's my area of expertise."

"My take is…" Walter sat down next to his envelopes. "She

was manipulative and angry for a start."

"Yeah," Shea said. "But why'd she have this stuff here? Why not keep it at home? Have you been to her house?"

"They went last night. I wasn't there. She still lived with her ex-husband. She had a separate bedroom apparently," Walter said.

"What does the ex do?"

"He is…" Walter chuckled. "A photographer."

"Hmph. How'd he take the news?"

"He appeared devastated. And he had an alibi for last night."

"You know, I saw blood in the bathroom last night."

"I read your statement before I came here."

"You wouldn't be able to tell me if they did a presumptive test for blood in the bathroom and if they found anything, would you?" Shea asked.

"I *would* tell you." He smiled. "But I don't know. What was your take on the best friend?"

"Just what was in my report."

"You wrote that you found a secure location to place the witness for interviewing by RHD personnel. She was intoxicated and physically ill."

Shea shrugged.

"What was your take on her?" Walter pressed.

"That she was hiding something. Maybe something insignificant, but she didn't want to get anyone in trouble," Shea said. "I'm not doing a Mark Fuhrman on you guys; I'm not holding anything back." Detective Mark Fuhrman was the divisional detective who accompanied RHD detectives on the search of OJ Simpson's house. Apparently, Mark hadn't shared all of his notes with RHD personnel because of their haughty attitudes. Or that was the official gossip, anyway.

"I'd like to think we're having a private discussion," Walter said.

"Well, then, I'll tell you this. Men, seasoned detectives or not, are lousy at interviewing women. You know why? They're so used to being lied to and bullshitted by their wives, mothers, and girlfriends that they can't spot it in the women they have to interrogate. I used to laugh when a partner would ask a woman for her height and weight, like for an FI or a ticket. Women lie by 20 or even 40 pounds and men never question it. I think you guys probably think women are all 5'7 and 115 pounds."

"And they're not?" Walter smiled.

"No. And that's just an example. But I guarantee the friend probably cried and cried and the detective couldn't wait to dispatch with that interview. Men who could break down a hardcore con will flee the room once a woman starts blubbering," Shea said. "I will say this, though… maybe her friend just knew about the pictures or who she was sleeping with, but her friend was determined not to cooperate completely. She likened the questions about when she last saw Chloe to an internal affairs interview. I thought that was really odd or overly dramatic."

Shea stopped talking when she heard two female voices coming through the first door of the locker room. They burst through the second door and into the locker room. It was the brown-haired officer from Chloe's little group last night and another woman Shea recognized as an employee defense representative.

"What are you doing?" the officer asked, her hands on her hips.

"This is Detective Smith from RHD and he's collecting evidence from Chloe's locker."

"Do you have a warrant?" The defense rep asked. She was

5'1, about 40 pounds overweight and hadn't worked the field in five years.

"As a matter of fact I do. It's on your captain's desk. And you two are--?"

"I'm LaShonnda Williamson. I'm a rep, and I've repped Chloe in the past, and this is Ann Gross. She was one of Chloe's friends."

"I have stuff of my own in that locker," Ann said, her hands still anchored on her hips.

"Were you coming to retrieve it?" Walter asked kindly.

Ann exchanged a hard look with LaShonnda Williamson.

"Is there a law against that?" Ann asked.

"Today there is." Walter shut Chloe's locker and placed a new padlock on it, spinning the dial. "At some point any property that is not deemed the victim's, will be made available. We'll contact you, Ann." He began to write in his notebook. "Is it Gross?"

"Yes, yes it is. I've already been interviewed."

"Of course. I'm just making a note that you advised me that you have property in the locker. Please tell me what it is."

Shea watched as Ann exchanged another look with

LaShonnda.

"It's not important," Ann muttered.

"Evidently you were coming here to get it out, hours after your friend's murder," Walter said. "That sounds important to me."

"I didn't say that was what I was doing." Ann set her jaw.

"She's not required to answer any of your questions, Detective," LaShonnda blustered.

"Hmm." Walter turned to Shea. "Uncooperative."

"I don't mean to be uncooperative." Ann fell in a heap on the bench and began to sob. LaShonnda rushed to her side.

"I just lost my friend. I've been interviewed all night, and I don't know what happened to her and I just-- I just can't understand what's going on."

"This is kind of what you were just talking about, correct?" Walter looked at Shea with a twinkle in his pale blue eyes.

Shea nodded.

"Well, Officer Gross. I'm sorry this happened to your friend. We're trying to find out who did it." Walter picked up all of the envelopes and walked over to her. She peeked at him through her hands as she sniffled. "Do you have any reason to think that *you* might be in any danger?"

The officer withdrew her hands and stared up at him, suddenly dry-eyed. "Why?"

"I don't know. I'm just asking you the question."

Ann shook her head and looked at Shea, "You mean, like, Chloe wasn't the only target?"

"I have no idea. If you think of something and you don't feel comfortable talking to the guys downtown, perhaps you might talk to Shea, here. She's a good listener and she's always right downstairs." He put his free hand on Ann's shoulder, "And I am sorry about Chloe."

Ann started to cry again. Walter and Shea left the locker room. Once they got into the stairwell, he told her, "Maybe you'll get something from her. She was definitely coming up to clean something out of that locker."

"Wait, Detective Smith. My boss has already made it clear that I have to stay out of this."

"Detective Reed, we don't have any female detectives in RHD. We have a dead woman with female friends, and I wasn't kidding when I said I'd like your perspective. This is *your* division.

If people talk to you, I'm sure you know how to tape record the conversation and pass it along to the detective in charge of the case."

"That Lancaster guy would be incensed he was notified after the fact. You know that, for Pete's sakes," Shea said.

"I do know that. But I think after today you may be working with us in a more official capacity on this case."

"No, no, no. Don't do this to me." Shea grabbed his arm and he stopped walking down the stairs. "I don't want to go on loan to RHD. I don't want to work a case in my own division. I have two trials coming up, and a new case my partner and I are working on. I don't have the time to do 'female' stuff for you guys. I'm not a consultant for all things female. Jesus!"

"You have already been recommended by people who outrank either one of us, so let's make the best of the inevitable. I will share your reluctance though." Walter continued to walk down the stairs with Shea trailing behind him.

"This is *not* going to work," she mumbled, wondering just who had recommended her and for what.

Chapter 6

Shea was on her knees, elbow deep in the bowels of the copy machine as she tried to remove a jammed piece of paper from a hidden roller. She gave the piece of paper a solid yank, ripping it into pieces. Her palms were covered in ink and she wiped her forehead with the back of her hand as she cursed under her breath.

"There you are." She heard her partner's voice behind her. She stood up and slammed the copy machine door and pressed start. It still showed jammed.

"Goddamnit. Since I didn't have a partner all day, I decided to run off copies of the Diaz murder book for discovery. You can see I only got to page 201."

"You didn't bate stamp the blank pages." Jack flipped through the stack of papers.

"I wrote 'blank' on them. That should be enough. I have only so much time to waste on nonsense. How'd your case go?" Shea opened the copy machine door and Jack bent down to take a look.

"Held to answer. Of course, the dipshit eye witness pissed backwards on the stand, but Younger did a good job," Jack said. He methodically ran through the steps of clearing a jam as he told her about the case.

"Hey, you wanna go over to Humphrey Park, see if we can track down Diablo?"

"Ah, no. It's Friday night. It's five minutes to EOW. I'm going to go home like a regular person. You should try it sometime."

"Going home on time feels like going home early."

"Well, that's what I'm doing. Have a good weekend. Hopefully I won't see you until Monday." Jack pressed the start button and the printer began to hum with activity. "I don't know why you can't operate a copy machine." He gave her a smile and walked over to the sign out sheet. Shea finished her copying duties and was the last detective to sign out on a Friday evening.

The traffic on the way home was reminiscent of the copy machine. Start and stop. Jammed. The 20 mile commute to her home took almost an hour. She sat on the freeway thinking about how it was the great equalizer. No matter your position in life, the type of car you drove, you were wedged in between cars crawling down the freeway. Television executives, in their BMW's, sat behind gardener's in their pick-up trucks.

Exiting the freeway and creeping onto Ventura Blvd, she

drove past a ratty Christmas tree lot. It dawned on her she hadn't even bothered with any Christmas decorations. Shannon would be in London until the first of the year and she was the official keeper of anything that remotely resembled normal traditions in their family.

A compact car, with an oversized Douglass Fir strapped to roof, barreled out of the Christmas tree lot. Shea slammed on the brakes. The driver waved to her as if she planned to yield for him. Shea gave him an exaggerated "after you" sweep of her hands and tailgated the merry driver all the way to Laurel Canyon.

This wouldn't be the first Christmas without tinsel and garland. The apartment where she grew up never had a string of lights in the window. Their father was a 'single dad' before there was a catchy term for a man's wife bailing out on him. Four years into their mother's escape, she died of cervical cancer.

Liam Reed was too busy with his own life to consider the impact a little Douglass Fir might have in their dingy living room. He was a philosophy professor at Valley Junior College, where recent high school graduates went to vegetate before realizing their futures didn't lie in higher education. It was probably the same for her father, his future in academia didn't exist past the community college level. He was popular with the students, perhaps because he shared their fatalism.

Watching the Christmas tree strain against the twine on the car in front of her, Shea remembered the one attempt to purchase a Christmas tree the Reed family ever made. William Shea, her father's best friend, had come over with a fifth of Cabin Still and a tree hunting plan was hatched after the two were halfway through the bottle. That evening they squeezed into William Shea's old Vega, and he drove them to a Dale's Junior market parking lot. Shea sat in the backseat with her bored teenaged sister, hoping this Christmas would be different.

As the two men drunkenly perused the trees loudly running down commercialism, capitalism, and the nonsense of religion, Shea held back, hoping no one would notice she was with them. Shannon followed behind them, wearing her signature faraway stare. Shea ducked into a tight row of trees and breathed deeply. Dusty from traffic and San Fernando Valley smog, she could still smell the promise of nature in the branches. She watched as a mother and father allowed their little boy to pick out a giant Noble Fir. His father picked him up and the boy stretched to touch the top of the tree. The mother snapped photos, the flash cube making a little chemical pop and sizzle as the boy laughed.

When Shea reappeared from her hiding spot in the trees, her family was heading into the market. Shea waited by the car for a long time. Maybe they were looking for her in the store? They returned carrying paper sacks with bottles clanking, Shannon trailing behind with her nose in a Tiger Beat magazine. No one mentioned the tree, or asked where she had been. Back at the apartment, William and her dad celebrated Christmas Eve by planning the revolution, same as any other booze-soaked night.

That was the last even tacit acknowledgement of holidays in general (with the exception of May Day). Shannon and Shea forged through their teenage years like young roommates who were occasionally visited by a wayward landlord. Shea took over the household chores and made sure their father set aside enough money so she could pay the bills. Shannon made sure they were stocked in Tab and Fritos.

By the time Shea was a sophomore in high school, her sister was gone nearly as much as their father. The cupboards stayed stocked with junk food, but Shannon was rarely home to share a TV dinner with Shea. She spent most nights at the Starwood nightclub in Hollywood. Shea remembered sitting on the brown plaid couch, watching her sister lie on the floor to zip up her pencil-thin Jordache jeans. Shannon would strap on her four inch wedgies and with barely a wave, be gone for days.

Like a neighborhood cat, she would eventually return with stories of nearly famous rock bands, encounters with everyone from producers to police, and then would sleep for two days before starting all over again. Shannon married a drummer from a popular band in the early 80's. She inherited the house they now lived in after he overdosed a year into their marriage.

Shea pulled up to the dark house, picked up the newspaper off the drive way and fed the cats. She walked down the stone steps to her own apartment and her eyes went to her answering machine as soon as she unlocked the door. No blinking red light. Andrew hadn't called.

Shea tossed a bag of popcorn in the microwave and got a beer out of the refrigerator, turned on the television and kicked off her shoes. She wished Jack would have wanted to go hunting for

Diablo. She would have burned off her restlessness searching for a gangbanging witness instead of flipping through TV channels.

Shea woke up Saturday morning with renewed energy from a decent night's sleep. She took off for a two-mile run through the narrow streets in her sister's neighborhood. This was a perk of living with her sister. She could get a challenging run in without having to drive anywhere first. She ran by sweet bungalows, next to million-dollar modern atrocities, bordering houses that could be home to the next Kool-Aid drinking cult.

When she got back to her sister's house, she picked up the Saturday's newspaper on the way in. Shea cleaned the cat litter box and took a shower in her sister's bathroom. She threw on her sister's robe and she poured herself a cup coffee and stretched out on the couch with the paper.

She wasn't surprised to see Chloe Diaz's academy picture on the front page of the Metro section. She read the article carefully. It was another article by Isabella Anton. There were plenty of quotes, including one from Chloe's ex-husband, Mario Diaz. He described Chloe as a dedicated police officer and loving woman who cherished her friends and family. He went on to say that he never wanted her to be a police officer and was certain her occupation played a part in her death. Diaz said he was frustrated with the lack of communication from the police department and was considering hiring an attorney and a private investigator.

Shea flipped through the rest of the Metro section. She didn't see anything about Vaughn's homeless victim from earlier that week. She had written a press release about him, but it didn't make the paper. His anonymous life and death were not nearly as interesting to the editors or the readers as Chloe Diaz's.

Shea tossed the paper and headed downstairs to her own studio apartment. She had no idea what she was going to do with her day. She had some Christmas shopping to do, namely for Andrew's present. She would probably end up buying him an expensive tie. Maybe some cuff links. It was the type of gift his wife might think he purchased for himself.

Shea loved the extra-starched French-cuffed shirts Andrew wore. Men's fashion typically did not make it to law enforcement for several years after a trend was popular. Shea could always spot a detective without having to see his gun belt and badge. They might own three sports coats, at the most, and two suits for jury trials, in shades of gray, blue and brown. But really, when you think about planning your day, what do you wear to an autopsy? The service of a search warrant? The clothes had to be functional, but also fall under the category of "business attire" as delineated in Volume III of the Department Manual.

Andrew was different. He wore tailored suits and edgy ties. He wouldn't wear a tie clip of replica handcuffs or the police union's logo. Shea remembered how he dropped an expensive suit jacket on the ground during their first kiss. It seemed careless and sexy at the time, but dropping a jacket turned out to be far simpler than dropping a marriage.

Shea filled her tiny kitchenette sink with lukewarm water. While she was on a roll of completing her obligations, she might as well wash out her stained coffee cups and wine glasses. She lost herself back in the memory of her hands moving across Andrew's crisp starched shirt right before he kissed her.

The kiss came after six solid months of flirtation. After the encounter in the records office, Shea always found an excuse to land herself in patrol's watch commander's office. She'd search for a report or ask for the printout of a radio call, basically any excuse to find herself in Andrew's line of sight. She watched him giving even-toned orders over the radio, one hand on the radio and the other signing his name to a report, while checking out an arrestee some officers had pulled in. Then, in the midst of all the chaos, he'd meet her eye and give her a direct look.

Shea finished her chores and she put on a pair of jeans and sweatshirt and was looking around her apartment for her car keys when the telephone rang

"Detective Reed?" It was an unfamiliar female voice. *Shit – a murder notification.* For some reason it was easier to get out of a warm bed in the middle of the night than it was to get called out on a Saturday morning.

"Yes," Shea said, stepping up the search for her car keys. It was going to be a retaliation murder stemming from last week's drive-by.

"It's Krista Tanner," the woman said. *Who?*

"Okay."

"You talked to me the night Chloe was killed," the woman went on, maybe sensing that Shea could not place the name.

"Oh, of course, how are you doing?"

"Okay. Ann told me I should call you." Shea remembered Ann from the locker room. Walter had suggested to Ann that she call Shea. She apparently delegated this duty to Krista.

"Good," Shea said.

"I got your phone number from the watch commander's office...I hope it's okay."

"Yeah, of course it is. Are you at the station? I can drive in."

"No, I don't really want to talk at the station. Can we meet somewhere?"

"There's a Starbucks on Ventura...near Laurel Canyon." Shea searched through a pile of dirty clothes as she talked. She pulled out a pair of dirty jeans and looked through the pockets for her keys.

"I know which one you're talking about, on the south side of the street?"

"Yeah."

"Ok, how 'bout in an hour?"

"I'll see you there."

"Can this be confidential?"

"We can discuss that in person."

"Okay, see you there." Krista hung up.

Shea abandoned the search for her keys. She looked through her bag for Walter Smith's business card. She was sure she wrote his home number on the back of it. She dumped half of the contents out on her bed and sifted through them. She vowed to become more organized if it killed her. She wasted a lot of time looking for things. Shea finally found the card, secreted in a small compartment, as if a responsible person had placed it there. She always had to consider looking in the proper place for things, because sometimes she surprised herself and actually put things where they belonged. With that in mind, Shea looked on the key hook by her front door, but the keys were not there.

Shea dialed the number on the back of the card. It was a 310 area code. That might mean West Los Angeles. Shea wondered if Walter had more money than the average detective.

"Hello," a woman's voice answered on the first ring.

"Good morning, I'm Detective Reed from Valley Homicide. Is Detective Smith there?" Shea asked in a formal sounding voice. Shea learned from Curt's wife how annoyed spouses get when a woman calls and asks for their husband by first name, without identifying themselves. It does come across a little salacious, Shea conceded; besides, it was rude.

"Just one second, he's in the garden." Shea waited for a few minutes and then she heard Walter's voice.

"Shea, how are you?"

"Good…in the garden, huh?"

"Yes, you should see our roses." She heard him washing his hands in the background.

"I'm sorry to bother you. One of the Chloe's friends called me. Krista – "

"Tanner?"

"Yes. She said Ann, that's the one from the locker room, said she should call me."

"Very good."

"So, here's the problem. She wants to meet me and she wants it confidential."

"What did you tell her?"

"That we'd discuss it when we met."

"That was wise," Walter said.

"Okay, so what do you want me to do? I don't have a tape recorder at home."

"What would you do if this was just one of your regular murders?"

Shea laughed. What a concept, a *regular* murder.

"I'd meet with her, see what she has to say, explain that I can't keep facts relevant to the murder a secret, but I sure don't have to tell anyone she's cheating on her taxes. I'd write up the statement and then at a later date get an official statement on tape."

"I think that's how you should handle this. Treat this like you would any other investigation. I realize the fact that this has occurred in your division and you know all of the parties makes it difficult."

"Detective Smith, you've been in RHD for ten years, so you're like Rip Van Winkle as far as my world's concerned. Officers live in absolute fear of getting personnel complaints. If she tells me something that amounts to misconduct I'm required, *required*, to notify my supervisor."

"Please, call me Walter. What's your rank?"

"Detective I."

"I'm a Detective III, and for purposes of this investigation only, I'm your supervisor and you will report any misconduct to me. By the way, you're a peer counselor, correct?"

"How'd you know that?"

"I pulled your package. You have some discretion in what you report, correct?"

"Oh brother, that's a stretch. But, I like the idea that I can report to you. Can I assure her though, that if it's just stupid shit you aren't going to do a personnel complaint?"

"I'm interested in criminal behavior not misconduct," Walter said.

"Okay then. Well, should I call you after I'm done with this?"

"That would be nice. Good luck."

"Thank you," Shea said and hung up.

She threw her long hair into a pony tail and didn't waste time on make-up. She hoped the casual appearance would put Krista at ease. She snapped her beeper on her waistband and threw her notebook and pens into a backpack. She slipped on her running shoes and headed upstairs to find a spare set of car keys she kept in her sister's junk drawer.

Shea drove quickly down the hill into the Valley, hoping Krista Tanner had something important to say.

<u>Chapter7</u>

Shea beat Krista to the Starbucks. After ordering a latte, she grabbed a discarded New York Times and found a table near the back of the coffee shop. After brushing away crumbs, she sat down, facing the door. She opened her paper and tried to read an article about the Speaker of the House, Newt Gingrich and the ethics panel, but a raspberry smear obliterated too many paragraphs. She searched for the movie section and found a review for Jerry Maguire and was half way through when her pager vibrated with Andrew's car phone number.

Shea looked around to see if Starbucks had a public phone. The barista told her the nearest payphone was across the street, behind the drug store. With a quick look at her watch she did the math, by the time she made it across the street, dialed the number, and argued with him for several minutes, her witness would probably arrive and change her mind. Tossing her calf across her thigh, her foot bounced with reticular motion, followed by her fingers tapping on the front page photo of a snowy Central Park.

Krista Tanner pushed through the glass door and gave Shea a little wave before placing her order. Wearing a white t-shirt and jeans, it was evident she just finished her shift. If Shea she pulled up Krista's pant legs, she'd probably see ugly black socks. The severe bun on the back of her head was in a losing fight with gravity and was on the verge of unraveling.

After Krista retrieved her drink, which looked suspiciously like a malt, she sat down across from Shea with a bit of a thud.

"Hi. I'm not much of a coffee drinker, but these things taste like shakes to me." Krista looked around the nearly vacant coffee shop.

"I never drank coffee either, until I went to homicide. Now it's a bad habit."

Maybe a little small talk would help ease Krista in to the deep end of the pool, Shea thought as she checked out Krista's bitten fingernails.

"I'm sorry about not being very cooperative that night."

"Well, it's pretty understandable."

"I don't know who killed Chloe or why." Krista's eyes started to tear up.

"Okay."

"But there's some stuff that needs to be explained…you

looked in her locker?" Krista said.

"Yeah."

"I want to be anonymous."

"That probably isn't possible in the way that you're thinking." Shea explained what Walter Smith had told her. "I'm giving you my word, Krista, if you tell me something and it leads to her killer, I will figure out every way possible to keep you out of it."

"I don't think what I've got to say will lead you to a killer. It's about those stupid pictures." Krista shook her head and looked down. She shoved the straw in and out of her frosty drink.

Shea looked down at the Central Park picture, quietly waiting for Krista make up her mind about talking.

"Ann was going up to the locker to get those pictures. She didn't want Chloe's memory trashed and obviously the guys don't know what Chloe said about them. It'd embarrass everyone."

"What's the deal with those pictures?"

"Okay." With a deep exhale blown through chapped lips, Krista began her story. "It started when Ann, Chloe and me were on probation in Rampart. We didn't know each other, Chloe and me. We were on different shifts. Anyway, there's this thing called the

Rampart Gazette in the men's bathroom."

"I worked Rampart. I'm familiar with the Gazette. Third stall in the downstairs bathroom off the men's locker room, right?"

Krista's looked Shea directly in the eyes for the first time.

"Well, I appeared on it, of course," Shea said, answering the unasked question of how she knew. "I had a partner who told me my name was on it, and he took me in to see where all the assholes I thought were my friends had written things about me. Although, I have to say, it was nice to see that I had some rebuttal comments to the crap that had been put up there."

"What'd they write?"

"I'd just made P3. There weren't too many women training officers back then. It was the usual, I wore kneepads and that's how I got the job. The really shitty one said that I was unsafe in the field. That one bothered me more than all the blow job comments." Shea shrugged. Krista nodded, her shoulders dropping a fraction from up around her ears.

"I didn't know that went on back then."

"Oh please, first of all it wasn't *that* long ago, and some of the same assholes who wrote about me were probably the same ones writing about you guys."

"Uh-huh. Well, someone was writing about Chloe and it was really bad stuff. Everyone was talking about it. It seemed like it was one guy and he was writing that he had sex with her and …" Krista hesitated. "He wrote awful stuff. That she…"

"Go on."

"I hate even repeating this shit. That she smelled. That she like to be fucked in the ass. It was beyond gross. I heard about it before I even knew who she was. Anyway, I was EOW one morning, taking off my gear and Chloe was coming onto her shift. She was sitting in the locker room and she just-just started like…crying. Normally I wouldn't've said anything…I mean I didn't know her," Krista said.

"What happened next?"

"I just sort of, walked past her, you know? And I saw that she had her back-up gun in her hands. It wasn't like she was putting it in her holster or anything. I thought…well, I didn't even know. I sat down next to her and asked her if I could help, if she wanted to talk. I'm not saying I thought she was going to shoot herself. It just seemed really bad."

Shea nodded.

"Chloe put her gun in her locker and stopped crying. She said the watch commander had made this big announcement in roll call for people to stop writing on city property. The lieutenant didn't mention her by name, but everyone knew it was about her. He like, completely made it worse. It totally looked like she complained."

Krista took a sip of her drink and continued, "I felt so bad for her. I mean probation's hard enough as it is, let alone someone writing about you. She just couldn't bring herself to put on her uniform that morning. So, we just start talking about different things at Rampart. And we had a lot of same experiences with the same training officers and sergeants. I was kind of surprised because until then I'd never really talked to any other women there."

"I know what you mean; sometimes it's easier to make friends with the guys than the women."

"I know! Exactly. Women aren't very friendly. Unless they're gay."

"Ha. Even if they're gay. I think women just get…territorial about their watch, unit or whatever. Like it's a club or something, 'I got in, but you can't,'" Shea said.

"I know. I worked in retail before I came on the job and the girls always gossiped, but they supported each other, too…you know? It isn't like that here. Anyway, so after the lieutenant had said that, Chloe's training officer chewed her out. He accused her of bringing this on herself and that it reflected poorly on him…that he couldn't control her." Krista screwed up her eyebrows, nearly bringing them together above her nose.

"Did she think he was the one writing on the wall?"

"She didn't know. She had a few enemies, but lots of cute guys were after her, too. I think that's also what made probation hard for her. She looked like a model. Anyway, I get this stupid idea that we should start our own 'Rampart Gazette.' And she loved the idea. We got a couple pens and went to the last stall in the bathroom." Krista smiled. "I went first and I wrote that the assistant watch commander was an asshole. Chloe wrote about her training officer. And that's it. I came back two days later and I go to the bathroom to see if our comments are still up there, and I'm like shocked! The whole wall is filled. I mean the *whole wall*. It took 15 minutes to read. It was like every woman in the station had shit to say. There were poems; there was stuff about a lieutenant that was harassing someone."

"The women just hemorrhaged all their anger on the wall."

"Exactly, exactly like that. So this was a secret for about two weeks, then somehow the lieutenant who was giving unwanted shoulder rubs—which, by the way, I thought I was the only one who was the victim of his creepy claws—anyway, he wanted to take a look at this wall. I guess he got escorted into the bathroom and then demanded that the broom wash it all off."

"Of course."

"Well, then in every roll call they warned everyone about defacing city property again and how disrespectful the women were to desecrate this bathroom because it had just been added onto the building. And he even brings the broom into it, that fat black lady. He talked about how she had to spend an hour washing the wall. Well, that's an hour more than I ever saw that janitor ever work."

"I remember her. At least you guys had a locker room. We used to have to change in a converted public bathroom."

"Yeah, I heard about that. So what really pissed us off was that the men's bathroom was not washed off. They continued to write on the wall. We were really pissed, but who do you complain to? What do you say? 'We want to deface city property? Like the

guys get to?'"

"You guys probably scared the shit out of the men," Shea

said.

"Anyway, we all made probation. I wheeled to Southeast,

Chloe and Ann went to Valley, and then I put a transfer to come here

too, but it took almost a year. By then, Chloe was separated from her

husband and she was dating this gorgeous guy on morning watch,

Jake Cameron."

"Sounds familiar."

"He went to Metro in August." Metropolitan Division, the

elite unit that groomed men for SWAT.

"Tall guy? Blond? Drove a big blue truck?"

"Yeah, blue eyes, great body. Everyone was in love with

him. Chloe was just crazy about him and bragged to everyone that

they were dating. She thought they were going to get married. She

wasn't divorced yet. Personally I think she left him for Jake.

Anyway, Hector Gomez, he works the gang unit--"

"I know him, nice guy," Shea said.

"Yes, he's a sweetheart, anyway he felt sorry for Chloe. He

took her aside. He said that Jake was making a fool of her. That Jake would have *guys* pick a girl—the *guys on the watch*, his little pack—and then he would guarantee he could, not only get the girl in bed, he could get her to do the kinkiest shit they'd suggest and he'd have the girl believing they would get married."

"Did he take pictures of her?"

"Of course. Well, she didn't want to believe Hector, but then he described a picture in Jake's locker of Chloe and Chloe knew it was true. That was part of their fun, they'd say to Jake, 'ok get a picture of her with a cucumber between her tits'...he would and show it to them the next day...maybe they even bet on it, I don't know. Then Hector told her about pictures of other girls and she was devastated."

"I can imagine."

"Chloe felt like a laughing stock...again. So she decided to turn the tables on Jake. Chloe took a picture of him. I'm sure you saw it. He's lying on his stomach on a bed, and he's naked."

Shea nodded. She remembered on the back it said he liked to have a finger in his anus when he was getting oral sex or words to that effect.

"Then, well, she kind of went wild and she slept with different guys from that little pack and detailed stuff about them."

"Wow."

"Yeah, I think she was being self-destructive, but she was pissed. She didn't trust *any* guy."

"Did any of these guys know about this?"

"No. I don't think so."

"What was her plan? What was she going to do with all of the pictures?"

"We used to talk about that. She said she'd like to take all of them and dump them in roll call one day or pin them on the wall or something."

"Do you think, Krista, that there's any chance someone could have hurt Chloe to prevent her from exposing these pictures?"

"Ann and I've talked about that over and over again. I honestly don't think any of these guys knew about it. She just slept with them like a few times and moved on. Maybe some of them thought it was kinky that she could get them to pose. I don't see them telling each other they posed in a feather boa."

"Didn't she care about her reputation?"

"I think she felt powerful." Krista looked at Shea. "She felt in control."

"At the Christmas party, did you see her talk to any of the guys who she had taken pictures of?"

"Oh, yeah, of course. I mean, we were talking to everyone. There wasn't any tension or anything," Krista said.

"Was she involved in any drugs or owe anyone money?"

"No. She drank a lot. No drugs, ever. Not even when she was younger. She was fine with money. She was living with her ex for free and just banking her paychecks."

"What do you think happened to her?"

"I don't know." Krista sighed. "She could take care of herself. I mean, I just can't picture someone getting the drop on her. She didn't have her gun with her at the party, but I can't picture her just walking off into the bushes with a killer."

"What about the shooting she was in?"

"The OIS?"

"Did she ever talk about it?"

"Yeah, she was pissed at all the second-guessing going on. She was so mad at herself for not getting a shot off," Krista said.

"She was tired of all the interviews. She never saw the suspect. She was sick of being accused of writing down the wrong plate. She hated Ornelas. She said he wasn't a partner, just a guy she was stuck working with."

"What was her mood like at the party?"

"She was in a great mood. We all got ready at Ann's house. She was really excited because she heard there was an opening in the gang unit."

"And when she got there…how was her mood?"

"We were just having a lot of fun together. We were all in the bar and then she excused herself to go to the bathroom. Ann and I went back to the dinner and…that's the last time I saw her." Krista's eyes started to water.

"Do you know if she used the bathroom inside the restaurant, or outside?" Shea said.

"Ah, I don't know. I saw her leave the bar, but I can't honestly say she used any bathroom."

"Which bathroom did you use that night?"

"The one inside. I didn't know there was one outside."

"Okay." Shea took a sip of her latte. "Do not, and I repeat *do not* talk to anyone about our interview, other than Ann. And do not let one man know about those pictures, got it?"

"Yes, Detective. Can I say that you're really nice…I was a little intimidated by you and I didn't know how nice you were."

"Well, ah thank you," Shea said. She dug in her pocket for her car key.

"It's just that you seem so…self-assured, I guess. We're all a little afraid of you."

"Ha. Well, don't be."

"No, that sounded bad, but we admire you. We think it's cool there's a woman in homicide."

"I think it's cool, too. Okay, Krista, you have my phone number. Go home and get some sleep."

"I will. We got a deuce at EOW and he wouldn't do a breathalyzer…it was just a big headache," Krista said. "We're heading back to the station, I'm thinking we're gonna get off on time and wham-o here comes a drunk in a Corolla blowing a red light two blocks from the station."

Shea and Krista disposed of their drinks, said their good-byes and as soon as Krista rounded the corner toward her car, Shea bolted across Ventura Blvd. She dug the change from the coffee purchase out of her pocket and shoved a couple quarters into the payphone. Andrew answered on the first ring.

"Hey. I was beginning to think you weren't going to call me back," he said. Shea let his smooth voice wash over her.

"I was working, doing an interview. What's up?"

"I'm on my way out to 77th Division. They had an OIS. It seems like we keep missing each other lately."

"Yes, that's exactly how it seems," Shea said. She thought of Chloe and the dried rose in her locker. How did a woman get to that point?

Shea had never even had a drink with a married man before she met Andrew. Before she came on the police department, her image of a mistress was a woman in a penthouse apartment, who got expensive gifts from her jet-setting lover. It must have been from too many teenage summers reading *Cosmo* by the apartment swimming pool.

When she got on the job, she quickly realized infidelity was just around every corner at the LAPD. In Rampart Division, they actually had two Christmas parties. The Divisional party was the one the men brought their wives to. The "Detective Christmas Party" was where men brought their girlfriends.

Shea's own slide down the slippery moral slope was a slow one. She dated a few civilian men until she couldn't stand to answer any more questions about her gun and if she'd ever shot anyone. She dated single cops who drank too much and moved too fast.

Flirting with Andrew Thorpe was more an exercise than a pursuit, however at the Casting Office, a bar known to be frequented by off-duty cops and members of the movie industry's teamster union, an opportunity to drink enough alcohol to bring the flirtation to a more dangerous level presented itself.

The party was a celebration for four popular rookie officers getting off probation and with the rookies picking up the bar tab, the place was packed. Shea was chaperoning another woman from her sex crimes unit who had her eye on a newly transferred sergeant. Shea figured she'd have a beer, hold her friend's hand until the sergeant made an appearance and she could leave.

Shea drank two beers while her friend stared at the barroom door and Shea struck up a conversation with one of celebrating rookies. He was a clean-cut, energetic 22-year-old, with a Marine's build and an earnest desire to be a good cop. He had caught a rapist for her and she had written him a commendation. While the officer was thanking her for second time and drunkenly calling her ma'am, she looked over his shoulder and saw Andrew walk in. He was wearing a dark suit with a power-red tie. It occurred to her she had only seen him in uniform.

"Oh, cool! Lieutenant Thorpe came, awesome!" The young officer seemed as excited as Shea felt. "I guess he had a captain's oral today and he still came, cool!"

"Really?" Shea took a long swig from her beer bottle and watched Lieutenant Thorpe smile and shake hands with the rookies. How was it that a kid, who could count the time he had on the job in hours, could know such details about the man she mentally stalked?

"He told us in roll call. Man, I hope they promote him; he's awesome. Did you know he worked SWAT, ma'am?"

"Yeah, I heard something about that."

"Did you know he was shot? We had the reenactment of his shooting when I was in the academy. Him and his partner were on a traffic stop and when they got the suspects out, one started shooting at them. He was shot in the leg and in the shoulder, but he returned fire from underneath his police car…"

"Yeah, we studied that one when I was in the academy too. He shot all four suspects…but I didn't know it was Thorpe."

"Yeah. And did you know that one of the suspects, the one who didn't die, did his sentence, got released, and morning watch cops arrested him for possession of PCP. When Lieutenant Thorpe did the booking approval, he said, 'I know this guy. He tried to kill me.' He just got up from his desk and stood in front of the holding tank and stared at the guy. I was there; it was awesome. He just looked at him, all Clint Eastwood-like."

"When was this?"

"Just last DP."

Shea had not heard about this, either. This was just the beginning of her feeling like everyone knew Andrew Thorpe better than she did.

"Wow."

"Yeah, he's the real deal. You know, he talks to you like you're a person."

"Well, that should be a basic requirement of communication for all humans." Shea drained her beer.

"It should." The officer became serious. "I get that I gotta sit in the front row in roll call because I'm a boot, and I gotta carry everything and I gotta earn everything, but the Lieutenant always treated me like a man. And he took time to teach us stuff…like you did, ma'am." A smile broke across his serious face.

"You better go say hi to him." Shea motioned the bartender over to her.

"I will. It was nice talking to you, ma'am and thanks again for writing the commendation."

"Good luck to you," she said, but he was already off the barstool and moving through the crowd to see the most popular boy in school.

Shea thanked the bartender who brought her another beer and thanked him again when he told her she didn't look like a cop. She thought about what the rookie officer said. He was right; when Andrew Thorpe looked at you, you did feel like you were the only person in the world. The more she thought about it, the sillier she felt. If he could have a male officer so enamored with him, all of this attraction she felt was probably one-sided. She was just one of his groupies.

The evening progressed and someone put vintage Prince on the jukebox. A handsome officer invited her onto the tiny dance floor. She did not know him well, but had heard he used to play professional basketball. Shea followed him onto the floor and they quickly fell into a rhythm appropriate for "Erotic City."

Shea felt her dancing partner's hand on her lower back, but he was really just the vehicle for her to lose herself in the music. When the song was over she thanked him and declined another dance. Shea moved her long hair off of her sweaty neck as she walked off the dance floor. When she hopped back on her barstool, Andrew Thorpe squeezed in next to her.

"I'd buy you a drink, but the drinks are free tonight."

"It's the thought that counts and I'm not done with this one yet." She reached for her beer.

"You dance well."

"Thanks."

"Provocatively."

"Ah, thanks again," She said, feeling her cheeks burn.

"It made my night."

"You had a captain's oral today?"

It was his turn to be embarrassed. When the upwardly-mobile were called on slumming with the riff-raff, they embarrassed easily.

"Yeah," Andrew said. "I doubt they'll promote me."

"Yeah, 'cause they haven't yet, right?" Shea said.

"Well, they never promote you on your first stab at captain."

"I see. So, this was just a lark?"

"Okay, you got me. I'll own it. I'm attempting to promote." Andrew smiled at her for a long time. She thought about the rookie's impression of Andrew and decided not to warm to him too quickly. *He talks to you like you're a person!*

"So, when you're a captain, will you still come to the 'getting off probation' parties?"

"Sure, the key is…" he lowered his voice and picked up a half empty beer bottle. "You carry around the first beer you're handed all night long."

"But what about witnessing misconduct? When you hang out with a bunch of drunken cops you might see some debauchery."

"Really? Will it look like what I saw on the dance floor?" He leaned towards her a little.

"Would you turn me in for that?" She steeled herself to look into his brown eyes, but he was looking at her lips. She felt her stomach flip.

"Hey, this doesn't look good for a married man to be talking to the best-looking detective in the city!" A booming voice shook them both. A large hand fell on the lieutenant's back. The man behind the voice was a sergeant who worked at Hollywood Division for more than two decades.

"Jim, just because you're on a diet, it doesn't mean you can't look at the menu," Andrew said with a laugh, then moved a few inches away from Shea.

"Well, I've got to get home. You kids be good." The sergeant clapped Andrew on the back again and walked away.

"You're on a diet, but you can still look at the menu?"

Andrew shrugged and smiled at her.

"I have an opinion…I think the only reason anyone looks at the menu is because they're hungry." Shea drank down the last of her beer and put it on the bar. "So, are you?"

"Am I what?"

"Are you hungry, Lieutenant Thorpe?" She hadn't taken a breath in several seconds.

"I am, Detective Reed. I'm real hungry." He looked her in the eyes. "I think we should continue this discussion somewhere else."

"Ahhh…." A tornado ripped through Shea's mind. She was comfortable flirting her ass off with him, she liked drawing him in, but six months of effort suddenly was paying off too fast for her.

"I'm going to drive down Barham to the Coco's, you know which one I'm talking about? I'll meet you in the parking lot and we can have a cup of coffee."

Shea took a deep breath and racked her brain for something clever to say.

"Oh, were you only playing?" Andrew smiled at her. "I have an opinion about that; it's a lot like your opinion on menus."

"Coffee?"

"Sure. Coffee."

"Okay, give me a few minutes…I came here with another detective. I'll see you there." Shea spun off the barstool.

Shea got to her car as quickly as possible. When she got in, she checked to see if her armpits smelled and rooted through her purse for perfume. After a couple squirts of White Musk, she checked her eyes in the rearview mirror. She ran her fingers under her eyes to get rid of the smudges and found a breath mint in her glove box. On the drive down the street to Coco's, she kept the window halfway down to dry off her sweaty neck. She felt awake and alive.

When she pulled in next to his car, he got out right away and opened her car door for her. As she was getting out of the car, he was attempting to put his arm through his suit jacket, but he dropped the jacket on the ground instead and ran his arms around her back. She was so surprised she swallowed what was left of her breath mint. He didn't kiss her at first; he wrapped his arms around her and ran his nose along her neck. Then he moved her away from the open door and shut it with a free hand. He pushed her against her car. She felt the slow pressure of him pushing his groin into her. Shea could feel his arousal and her own.

"You *are* hungry," she said.

"For you. I'm hungry for you," he whispered on her lips, but he still hadn't kissed her.

"Are you sure you want to do this?" She looked at him.

"Are you sure you want to?" He pulled away just a little.

"Oh I do."

"Then here we go," he said and kissed her deeply.

Chapter 8

Shea stood at the public phone across from the Starbucks with the receiver away from her ear, hoping the germs wouldn't leap onto her face. She listened while Andrew told her he loved her, he missed her, he wanted to see her. He promised to come to her house first thing Sunday morning…no matter what.

After she hung up with Andrew, she called Walter Smith and briefed him on her interview with Krista Tanner.

"So the pictures in Chloe's locker were a reaction to a calumny of sorts?" Walter said.

"I suppose," Shea said, knowing she'd have to look up 'calumny' when she got home.

After finishing up with Walter, she hung up the phone and looked at her watch. It was a day off, her only obligation for the rest of the weekend was to wait around for Andrew on Sunday morning. She decided to brave the malls and finish her Christmas shopping. By the time she was done, it was evening and she headed home with a tie and cufflinks the price of a down payment on a car for Andrew and a Baja Fresh salad for dinner.

Shea watched the late night news and learned that Chloe's

husband's distrust for the LAPD had increased since his interview appeared in the *LA Times.* He had hired a lawyer.

She fell asleep to a rerun of Cheers that followed the news. When the phone rang, she rolled over and looked at her digital clock, two in the morning. She groaned as she picked up the phone.

"Good morning. We got one." She recognized Curt's voice.

"What is it?" Shea turned down the sound on the TV with a remote.

"Looks like a car-to-car drive-by. You've got one dead at the hospital. One wit, he drove his buddy to Holy Cross. Nobody in custody," Curt said.

"Oh boy. I'll see you at the station." Shea hung up and rolled out of bed. She pushed the start button on her coffee maker and turned on the hot water in her shower. She turned the volume back up on the television and she got down to the business of getting ready to go to work in the middle of the night. She estimated she'd be back before Andrew got there. No witnesses, no suspects, it shouldn't take long.

Shea stood in the middle of the intersection with Jack. They had met in the parking structure behind the station and jumped into their assigned police Crown Victoria. She looked out across the intersection at handful of 9mm casings resting under little paper FI tents in the street and that was it. Half a trunk-load of yellow police tape wrapped around the light standards blocked off the street from traffic and a half-a-dozen uniformed officers were standing around the back of a police car eating donuts and drinking coffee. It must be a slow night.

"Didn't I say I hoped I wouldn't see you this weekend?" Jack crouched down and directed his flashlight beam at the gutter.

"Yeah. Yeah. A little overtime money will be nice at Christmas, huh?"

"Uh-huh. Well, you want to go to the hospital and I'll do the crime scene?"

"Are you sure?" Shea said.

"It isn't going to take both of us to process six casings. When I finish I'll get a black and white to take me back to the station."

"Okay then. We've got the surviving witness at the station, how 'bout I meet you back there when we're done? I'll go take a look at the car at the emergency room and talk to the families.

Maybe we'll all be done with this by dawn's early light." Shea stuck her freezing hands into the pockets of her trench coat. She had meant to take her gloves, but left them on top of the TV.

"You got big plans for tomorrow morning? Going to church?" Jack stood up and shoved the flashlight in his back pocket.

"Let's just say I need to get home before eight," Shea said. "The photographer is en route; Curt called him. How was the dinner for your brother?"

"Nothing like dinner with a buncha heroes." Jack bounced on the balls of his feet and blew into his cupped hands.

"Everyone loves a fireman."

"So I'm told. Okay, let's bust through this. I need to get home at a reasonable hour, too. Sam's fun meter is pegged with all of our call-outs lately. She claims I'm a ghost and the only way she knows I've been home is to count remaining beer bottles in the frig. I'll page you when I'm done processing the scene."

"Okay."

Shea drove to Holy Cross Hospital. Outside the emergency room entrance, a haphazardly parked lowered Impala told the story of a panicked drive to get help. The passenger door hung open and there was a smear of blood across the panel. Someone had strung crime scene tape around the car and a young officer stood with a clipboard nearby. When she approached him, he quickly got out his pen and wrote her name on his crime scene log.

"Were you the first unit here?" Shea asked him. He must be right out of the academy, she thought. She didn't recognize him, but he looked like he was a freshman in high school.

"No ma'am, we relieved the p.m. watch unit, but I got their information."

"Where's your partner?"

"He's inside talking to the security guard, ma'am," the young officer said.

"Okay, has anyone touched the car?"

"No, I started an impound, but I haven't looked inside or anything."

"Okay, good. Even though this is the victim's car, it still needs to be fingerprinted."

Shea pushed through the back doors of the emergency waiting room. A security guard was talking to a uniformed police officer; beyond them a Hispanic family getting news from a doctor.

Shea watched two older women holding each other and crying. Two teenage girls, in costume-like heavy make-up, sat on plastic chairs looking up at the doctor. Three young men, heavily tattooed and menacing-looking, were hovering nearby. One was holding a baby. Shea approached the security guard and officer. She gently touched the officer's arm and he stepped away from the guard.

"Dan, right?"

"Yeah." He seemed pleased she remembered his first name and she wished she could do that more often, but patrol officers came and went out of the division.

"That's the family?"

"Yeah, I think the docs were gonna try to keep the victim on life support, harvest organs, you know. But he flat-lined." That didn't surprise her. Shooting victims made excellent donors. Young and cut down in the prime of their lives, they usually had healthy organs, unless they were damaged by the bullets or drugs.

The officer handed her his index-sized field identification cards containing all of the family's vital information.

"Okay, I'm going to go talk to them, come with me. You speak Spanish, right?" Shea said. Dan nodded and followed her over to the family.

As they walked up, the family turned their attention to her. Shea's trench coat belt was undone and they could see her gun belt and badge. One of the older women crumbled onto a plastic chair next to the bookend teenage girls.

The doctor quickly explained to Shea that he just told the family the sad news about the victim. They had tried their best, but the victim had died.

"I'm sorry. Are you Eduardo's mother?" Shea she bent in front of the woman. She had glanced at her notes for the victim's name to make sure she was correct. "I'm Detective Reed."

The woman nodded. Her family gathered closed in around her.

"He had his birthday yesterday," the younger of the two teenage girls said. She took the baby from one of the men.

"How old was he?" Shea asked.

"He's eighteen. He was going into *The Marines*."

"Are you his sister?" Shea patted the older woman's hand one more time and stood up.

"I'm his girlfriend. This's our son, little Eddie." She kissed the baby's forehead. She looked fifteen.

"I'm so sorry," Shea said gently. She looked at the baby for a long time. "He's beautiful. How many months?"

"Six." The girl kissed him again and the baby squirmed against her.

"What's your name?"

"I already tol' him." She nodded towards the uniformed officer. "Yolanda Ortiz."

"I need to find who did this to Eddie's dad," Shea said.

"Yeah."

"He'll want to know." Shea nodded towards the baby. She wished she could move the girl away from the three hard cases surrounding her. One of them said something to Yolanda in Spanish. She said something back, just as tersely as she had addressed Shea.

Shea knew none of these people would say much in front of each other, so Shea stuck to the basics. Eduardo's mother told her that her son wasn't in a gang, that he was a good boy on his way to the Marine Corps. She knew the boy who drove to the hospital and he was a good boy too. The three amigos hovered and lingered and were of no assistance beyond providing their names.

Shea was able to slip her business card into Eddie Jr.'s blanket, while giving Yolanda a steady gaze. Later, she would end up explaining to Yolanda that the California's Victim's Assistance Program required *cooperation* by the victim's family in order to pay out. It was likely Yolanda or Eduardo's mother knew a great deal about the program already. Word travelled fast in a community where victims of violent crime were as common as the security bars on windows.

Dan followed her outside to the vehicle, translating what he heard the three men telling Yolanda. It was what she expected…don't talk to the police. She went about the work of processing the car. She noticed two casings on the front passenger floorboard. So, this meant a gun was fired from inside this vehicle as well, Shea thought. She looked at the printout of the time the call came out and the time they arrived at the hospital. Whoever drove Eduardo to the hospital probably dumped the gun beforehand.

Shea went back in the hospital and called the station to speak with Curt from the security guard's desk. Curt picked it up on the first ring.

"Talk to me," Curt said. "Are you still at the hospital?"

"I am. It's looking like our victim car might also be a suspect car. I found two small-caliber casings."

"Nice. No gun?"

"Nope."

"You're partner just got done talking to the wit…hold on."

Shea waited and listened to Curt and Jack talking; finally Jack came to the phone.

"Frozen yet?" She could hear the smile in Jack's voice.

"Ah, yes. Apparently you finished the crime scene in record time. You're already back at the station?"

"Yes. And I'm warm, I might add. I interviewed the driver."

"What did he have to say?" Shea sat down on a wobbly wooden chair.

"This little asshole here says that, let's see…let me look at my notes…" Jack rustled some papers. "Okay, Eduardo – your guy, was driving. They're coming from drinking beer at Hansen Dam. They're stopped for a red light at the intersection and a blue car, nothing further, pulls up on the driver side and starts shooting. My guy says Eduardo's gets shot in the neck. My guy jumps out of the car, runs around to the driver's side and pushes Eduardo over and drives to Holy Cross."

As Jack talked, Shea looked through the field identification cards for the witness statements from the hospital.

"What's your guy's name?" Shea said. "It doesn't look like anyone sees them drive up to the hospital. Your guy just runs in and yells that his friend is shot…the security guard sees a guy lying in the front seat."

"Antonio Garcia."

"I'm pretty sure Antonio dumped the gun before they got to the hospital and maybe they dropped off a friend, too. I've got two casings in the front passenger seat, so that would put the gun in the passenger's hand at the time the blue car pulls up, right?"

"Yeah. I did a gunshot residue test on him," Jack said.

"Is he still there?"

"Yeah. He doesn't have any warrants, we gotta kick him. He's waiting on a ride from his mom."

"What did he say when you did his hands?" Shea asked, but she could guess the answer.

"The usual GSR disclaimer, why was I doing the test, he didn't shoot a gun, no one in the car shot. I can tell him you got the blue car pulled over and someone ID'd him."

"No, no, don't tell him that because the blue car is probably a lie and then there goes your pucker factor."

"Pucker factor, very lady-like," Jack said.

"Okay, you don't want to lose *the heightened anxiety you have produced by conducting the test*. Just tell him that the guy at the hospital...ah, Eduardo, can talk and he said, 'I'm not the one who had the gun.'"

"Okay, I gotta get him before he walks out the front door. Oh, by the way, the gang unit is off tonight."

"Great, what gang are our victims?" Shea said.

"He's denying gang affiliation, but he rolls with Westside Players. I found an FI on him."

"Okay, I'll call you later."

Shea went back outside and directed the duties of the fingerprint specialist and the photographer.

She checked her watch and it was almost four in the morning. She still had to take a Polaroid picture of the dead kid, get a positive identification from his family and collect the casings from inside the car. She figured by the time she finished all of that and completed her reports back at the station, she might get home before Andrew arrived. Maybe he'd bring coffee and they could just crawl under the covers. She was so caught up in her thoughts about Andrew she barely heard the call come out over the radio for a unit to respond to Northridge Hospital for a gunshot-wound victim.

"Do you think that could be related to this call, Detective?" the young officer asked her. Shea pulled on plastic gloves and collected the casings.

"Well, it sure took them a long time to get to the hospital if it is." Shea had a sinking feeling that this was going to go from a long night's worth of work, to a long day's worth of work. Her fingers were freezing and she had to pee.

After the victim's car was impounded, Shea jumped in her police car and sped back to the station. When she burst through the back door she was struck how quiet the place was in off hours. Sitting underneath a dangling snowflake, Curt was at his desk talking on the telephone. The records office, the detective squad room, and the watch commander's office were dolled up with sparkling Christmas wreaths and garlands like a second-grade classrooms.

Curt hung up and gave her the coroner's case number.

Jack came out of the tape room and Shea held her frozen hand to his cheek.

"Hey, you picked hospital over crime scene. I can't help that it was the fastest crimes scene I've ever processed," Jack said.

"How'd go with Antonio?"

"I brought him back in the room and told him I had one more question for him. He looked surprised." Jack dropped an audio tape on his desk and leaned against the partition. Shards of glittery tinsel stuck to the back of his shirt. "I told him that I got a call from my partner at the hospital and that Eduardo, was able to talk. Antonio says, 'What did he say?' and I told him that I didn't have all the information…but all I knew was this guy Eduardo said he didn't have the gun. Antonio then let out a classic, 'sheeeeet.' Or something to that effect."

"And he confessed."

"No. Here's the GSR." Jack tossed the package containing the results of the gunshot residue test on her desk. "I did float a mention of self-defense and he needed to tell us up front, etcetera, etcetera. Nada."

Shea flopped down in her chair and pulled her orange evidence envelopes containing the casings out of her black leather bag. She added them to the items that needed to be booked into property.

"Who knows how old these casings are in our victim's car. No independent witnesses. It could have happened how Antonio said," Shea said.

"Yeah, it was that murder fairy again," Jack said. "This time in a phantom blue car. But, when I made a run at him, Antonio added a little. He said that the driver—the shooter—had a spider web tattoo on his neck."

"Oh good, *now* we can catch him. A Hispanic gang member in a blue car with a spider web tat on his neck. That should be easy. How many of those guys could there be?"

"Do you want some coffee, partner?"

"I could use a cup." She handed him her stained cup. "Cream and sugar."

"I think I know that," Jack said. "Boots?"

"No, if you kids don't need me I'm going home," Curt said. "You just have reports left, right?"

"Yeah, but a call came out at Northridge Hospital, a gunshot wound…" Shea trailed off.

"Might be from a shooting in West Valley," Curt said.

"No call came out like that. It was for a unit to respond to the hospital. So it might be our blue car guys."

"Let me call over there and see what they have." Curt swung around in his swivel chair and looked up the hospital phone number from a list taped on his partition.

Jack brought Shea her coffee and sat down at his desk. He took a sip from his cup and made a face. "Eh, I thought it might have been sitting there for awhile. Who do Westside Players have a beef with?"

"Aren't they aligned with Latin Times?"

"I thought they're just taggers…but maybe I'm getting them confused with Player Crew," Jack said. "You got a Polaroid of the dead guy?"

Shea looked through her leather notebook. She pulled the photos from deep in the folder's flap and handed them to Jack.

"I'm going to down the hall to records and run Eduardo and see what kind rap sheet he had." Shea grabbed her paper work and coffee and headed for records.

Although computers were on every detective's desk, the installation wasn't complete and they were nothing more than large paperweights until the contractors completed the job. LAPD technology was at least a decade behind private industry in every regard.

Shea was sitting at the computer, in the Santa's Village that passed for the records department, running her victim for criminal records, tickets, vehicles, and police reports. Shea enjoyed this part of the investigation. A guy could get a ticket in a car and that one simple entry could produce a number of people to interview. He could've been listed as a witness in a crime, and that would lead to more associates. When Shea started weaving through the information on the computer, she fell into a zone much like when she was dancing. Everything faded away around her, including the insipid Christmas music, the records clerk gabbing at the copy machine with a bored jailer, and the FAX machine spitting out paper. She was suddenly popped her out of her concentration by Jack smacking his hand on the top of her computer and she nearly jumped out of her chair.

"The guy at the hospital is gonna be ours. He's shot in the hand. He says he was shot by a guy in a white Impala. That's the car, right?" Jack said. He was bouncing on his toes again, but not to keep warm.

"Yeah, he's cooperating?" Shea was incredulous.

"I don't think so. This came from hospital personnel, not the police. Let's go, let's go."

"Okay, hang on." Shea completed her task on the computer and printed out the results.

"They want to release him. They're just stalling for us, so come on, amiga!"

"Okay!" Shea grabbed the computer printouts and followed him down the hall.

No other time of day sucked the life out of a tired police officer than the break-of-dawn. With white light squeezing through the horizon, every blink hurt. Shea had forgotten to bring her sunglasses again, thinking of course she wouldn't need them. Fortunately, Jack was driving. A second wind had snapped him up and he was chatting away about the case.

Shea leaned her head against the window and watched the strip malls and gas stations whiz by. She wished she could tell Jack about her interview with Krista Tanner. It helped her to find a trail by bouncing theories back and forth with her partner. But, she didn't have a partner in Chloe's murder case, unless she counted Walter Smith.

As they pulled into the hospital parking lot, Jack hit the brakes abruptly, causing Shea to brace herself against the dashboard.

"What's the tattoo?" Jack asked sharply.

"What?" Shea looked down at her notes. "A spider web on the neck."

"That's him." Jack pointed across her lap to a bald Hispanic kid standing outside the emergency entrance smoking a cigarette with a bandaged hand and talking to an obese woman wrapped in a blanket. "Let's see if he books."

He did. As soon as Jack parked the car, the kid took one look at them and dropped his cigarette. He ran into the parking structure with Shea and Jack chasing after him. For a moment Shea thought about going back for the car, but she knew she couldn't separate from her partner.

The suspect ran through the first story of the parking structure and over a small wall into a residential neighborhood. Jack was right on his heels; Shea—who was wearing low heels—kicked them off, but was still several yards behind her partner.

She keyed her radio and put out a broadcast of their foot pursuit. She tried to grab enough oxygen to get the words out clearly, but the radio telephone operator asked her to repeat her broadcast. Shea repeated her request for backup and picked up her pace as she saw Jack dart between two houses after the suspect. She ran through a narrow passageway, the stucco from both houses ripped at her coat. Her lungs were bursting and her heart was pounding in her ears so loudly she could barely hear the sirens in the distance.

The RTO was on the air asking her for their location. She was running through a backyard, avoiding a dog on a chain, just close enough to see her partner's last location before he disappeared behind a trash bin. Shea tried to steady her radio over her mouth and breathlessly told the RTO they were now in the alley south of Mulberry Street and they were pursuing the suspect eastbound. The RTO told her the air unit was en route with a two-minute ETA.

Shea saw the suspect at the end of the alley going up and

over a wall, with Jack right on his heels. She knew she was going to lose sight of Jack again and felt a surge of adrenalin. She hit the wall with one panty-hosed foot and threw her other leg on the top of the cinderblock wall. The wall cut into her hands and slacks. She jumped over to the other side and saw Jack grab the suspect by his tattooed neck and tackle him to the ground in a sea of ice plant groundcover. Shea reached around for her cuffs on the back of her belt while grabbing the suspect's free arm. Jack brought the suspect's other arm around and Shea locked the handcuffs on him.

The three of them lay for a moment in a heaving sandwich of bodies. No one could breathe. Shea rolled off the suspect first and Jack searched him for weapons. Shea sat up and keyed her radio, "Code four. Suspect in custody." She paused to catch her breath. "Stand by for location."

"Do you know where we're at?" Shea asked Jack. Parts of her clothes and feet were wet and sticky from the broken ice plants.

The LAPD helicopter was overhead and Jack pulled a small flash light out of his coat pocket and flashed it in the air. Shea confirmed with the air unit he saw the light and he directed the patrol officers to their location. Jack rolled the suspect over and Shea saw the tattooed web under his right ear. He was bleeding from a cut over his eye.

"Why'd you run?" Shea said.

"No speaky English."

Jack said something to the suspect in Spanish and the suspect responded in Spanish.

"He speaks English," Jack said. "When I say the word 'rabbit,' hit him as hard as you can with your flashlight."

Jack began questioning the suspect in Spanish, suddenly Shea heard him say, 'rabbit.'

She grabbed her flashlight and drew it back in a swing.

"Fuck! Are you crazy?" the suspect yelled at Shea in English.

"I told you. Now why the fuck did you run?" Jack said.

"I got a warrant," the gang banger spit.

"Bullshit," Jack said. Shea looked over at her partner for the first time and saw that he was bleeding from a cut to his lip.

Shea requested a rescue ambulance to respond to their location, even though they could all just walk back to the hospital.

"Look asshole, I'll make this the worse fucking day of your motherfucking life."

"Yeah? Do whatcha gotta do, man," the suspect said, attempting to sound nonchalant.

Jack balled up his fist and lunged for the suspect. Shea dove across the suspect's torso and grabbed Jack before he could make contact. The nonchalance was gone and the suspect's eyes were big.

"I'm fuckin' cuffed!"

"Jack, Jack!" Shea stood up and got the suspect to his feet. She loosened the cuff on his right hand to accommodate the bandage and guided him through the backyard to the street.

"I got an ambulance coming." Shea said to him. She was going to be the detective who brought him a Coke, asked if he was in pain, and she'd hold his hand. Jack just made himself "bad cop" this morning.

A patrol unit was screeching up to the curb and Shea turned the suspect over to the officers before returning to the backyard to collect her partner. He was bent over, hands on his knees, spitting blood onto the lawn. She walked over and put her hand on his back.

"You okay?"

"Yeah." He spit more blood and asked here where her shoes were.

"I have no idea. Somewhere between the parking lot and here," Shea said.

"He head-butted me when I took him down. I think I've got a loose tooth." Jack straightened up. Shea leaned on his arm and looked at the bottom of her feet. Her pantyhose were ripped and her feet were black.

"He'll be our shooter."

"I sure hope so." Shea said. "This was a lot of effort for a traffic warrant."

Chapter 9

Shea didn't get home until 11:30 PM Sunday night. Jack and Shea, ripped, torn and tired, interrogated Mario "Spider" Velacruz for several hours. He admitted to driving the car and to being shot at, but not to returning fire. Jack prepared three photographic line-ups with the Impala's occupants in them, but Mario refused to even look at the pictures. Jack put Velacruz's picture in a photo-line up, and he and Shea tracked down Antonio Garcia at his mother's house, brought him in and he reluctantly identified Mario Velacruz as the person who shot at him and his friend. That was enough to book Velacruz for murder. Once they finished with Velacruz, Jack and Shea were interviewed by a patrol sergeant who was assigned to conduct a Use-of-Force investigation on the incident. From interrogator to interviewee, Shea impatiently answered endless questions about every decision she and Jack made as they pursued the suspect.

It wasn't until Shea found a bouquet of flowers leaning against her door that she remembered her morning date with Andrew. She picked up the flowers and brought them inside. After finding a plastic tumbler, she shoved the flowers in the glass and left the whole romantic gesture in the sink. She yanked off her dirty clothes, crawled under the covers and fell asleep.

Shea woke up the next morning with her mind already formulating a to-do list. She and Jack had a follow-up report to write. They had until Tuesday morning to get the case to the district attorney and they still had to a lot of investigative work to do. At least one of them would have to go to the autopsy and they had to book all of the evidence.

Shea stood in the shower, letting the hot water run down her face. She was embarrassingly sore from her sprint, her feet hurt, and she had two mean bruises on her leg from going over the wall.

She was rinsing her hair when she heard a knock on her door. By the time she wiped the shampoo out of her eyes and turned off the water, there was a series of more insistent knocks. As she wrapped a towel around her torso, she kicked around the dirty clothes on the floor to uncover her gun belt. Shea peeked out of the curtain and was relieved to see Andrew Thorpe, in a navy suit, pink and grass-green striped tie, holding a cardboard tray with coffee cups. She threw open the door.

"Oh, now this is a greeting." He walked in and set the tray down.

"I'm so sorry about yesterday--"

"You got a murder, I know." He kissed her lips, her neck, and shoulders.

"Andrew, I have--"

"Get to work, I know. Fortunately for you I'm going to come fast."

Andrew removed her hands from her towel. The towel fell on her pile of dirty clothes and she was grateful she had been able to shave her legs before he burst through the door. Andrew stepped back and looked at her body appreciatively. She felt a surge of self-consciousness. He kept looking at her as he untied his tie.

"Let me help." Shea reached for his shirt buttons. Andrew carefully draped his clothes over the back of a chair and pulled her naked body to his. The feel of his skin from shoulders to toes pressed against hers was overwhelmingly good. He sat down on the edge of her bed and firmly pulled her legs to straddle him. As she lowered herself on to him, she watched his eyes close as she began to move.

When Shea arrived at the station less than an hour later, her unit was already at their desks. Her hair was still damp and piled on the back of her head. She dropped her bag on her desk and looked over at Jack. His lip was swollen and purple. He was gingerly trying to drink his coffee.

"Oh. My. God."

"I know. I've got an appointment with my dentist at four this afternoon." Jack pulled his lip down and showed her his loose tooth.

"So, was it like Jack described? A lion bringing down a wildebeest?" Vaughn said.

"Exactly, that's how he screwed up his mouth, by taking down the suspect with his teeth," Shea said.

"At least I didn't have to take off my high heels before engaging in police work."

"You were wearing heels?" Vaughn laughed. "I'm picturing Angie Dickenson…big hoop earrings – "

"You didn't break a nail going over that wall did you?" Curt reached over her cubicle and held up her hand. Her nails were shorter then her male counterparts.

"Okay, cavemen. Are you done?" Shea flipped through the pink messages on her desk, pointedly ignoring the men. The post on

Eduardo Lopez was scheduled for 10:00. She passed the message over to Jack.

"Which would you rather do? Autopsy or the reports?" Jack asked her.

"I can do the autopsy. I've got to drop off my interview at Parker Center."

"Would you mind doing the post on my guy from Wednesday while you're there?" Vaughn said. She had forgotten about his homeless murder victim from earlier in the week.

"Is he being done this morning?"

"Yeah, if you're stopping at the *Building*, can you pick up my crime scene photos?" Vaughn said.

"Yeah, write down the DR number and the C-number for me." Shea stood up and grabbed her bag. She waited for Vaughn to look up the reference numbers for the report and the photographs.

"Can you bring us back lunch?" Curt chimed in.

"No, this is the extent of my being the homicide handmaiden," Shea said. She took the note with the numbers from Vaughn. "What's your guy's name, Vaughn?"

"John Doe 39," Vaughn said. Vaughn's homeless man was

the 39th unidentified body found in LA County for 1996.

After a Monday morning grind of traffic, Shea pulled in the back parking lot of the Coroner's office and took note of the other police cars. It must have been a deadly weekend in LA County. Shea grabbed her notebook and headed across the parking lot to observe two autopsies with the indifference of a seasoned homicide detective. But that attitude was still fairly new. Shea remembered how shocked she had been at the first autopsy she viewed.

She pictured it would be like an episode of the TV show *Quincy*. The body would be covered in a sheet—with the exception of the area being worked on—there would be classical music playing, and the observers would be behind glass, watching dispassionately as if it was a mere dissection in biology class.

She remembered the assault to her senses when she walked down the hall, not even to the rooms where they did the posts, but in the hallway. Bodies were lined up on gurneys, some naked, some still dressed. When she had followed Vaughn into one of the autopsy rooms, she was shocked to see bodies being flopped and tugged like sides of beef as the workers placed them on the tables.

A small woman had the ghoulish job of sawing the skulls open and removing the brains. Shea remembered focusing on the tile on the floor, the clock, on the wheels on the gurneys…anything but the way the bodies were being cut and dissected. Vaughn introduced her to everyone, explained the importance of having the doctor place rods through the bullet path, and showed her how to copy the pertinent facts off the doctor's notes as he worked. He gently pushed her back when the doctor cut open the intestines. The smell still almost laid her out. And he did *not* suggest spaghetti afterwards.

In the eighteen months following that first trip, she had attended 25 autopsies. She ended up on nearly every murdered victim's post, even if it wasn't her case. Shea worked an area of the city where the violence was very accommodating for that learning curve. She viewed autopsies of mostly young men, but also children, old people, the grotesquely overweight, and one pregnant woman. She shared the morbid sense of humor of a dead man with a t-shaped coroner incision tattooed on his torso. Another victim had a toe-tag tattooed on his big toe.

This morning when she walked in and signed her name to the log, she barely noticed the smell of human decay over the smell of antiseptic products. The odor was chemical, but not clean. She breezed down the hallway to a small closet-sized room where detectives put on paper aprons, masks, booties, and gloves.

Two detectives from Hollenbeck were getting dressed in their paper gowns when she arrived. One fellow was so large that the paper gown was already ripping at his shoulders. They looked at her as she walked in and then past her for her partner. She smiled at them as if to assure them that she had permission to be out unattended.

After she slipped into her own paper-made biohazard outfit, she took her notebook and went down to the largest autopsy room. She passed the "VIP" room and wondered if that was where they did the post for Chloe Diaz. Even in death there was preferential treatment for people who fell into a special category. But Eduardo Lopez wouldn't be in the VIP room. She found Lopez lying nude next to eight other men who met with untimely deaths over the weekend. Five out of the eight were male Hispanics, all under twenty-five, all were canvases for numerous tattoos and all were shot, two black men, one extremely thin and one who appeared to have been stabbed numerous times, and the last victim was

Vaughn's homeless man.

The Dr. Findley nodded as she placed her business card on his notes. Lopez had a single gunshot wound to the left side of his neck. The bullet was still lodged in his spine and he gently recovered a mangled .380 bullet.

"It may have been deflected off the car, prior to entering the neck?" Dr. Findley wiped the bullet with a tissue and placed it on top of a small evidence envelope. He had a slight accent, Shea wanted to guess South African, but she hadn't asked.

"There was an indentation at the top of the driver's side door. I wasn't sure if it was from a bullet or some other damage...I need to go through the car in the daylight." Shea jotted down a reminder in her notebook.

"Hey, my partner says you're from Valley Division."

She turned and the heavy-set detective from Hollenbeck was standing right behind her. His victim was a couple bodies away from hers.

"I am," Shea said.

"So, what's the deal with the officer from your division? Any leads on that?" As he spoke, the paper mask sucked into his mouth, leaving a wet outline.

"RHD's handling it. I haven't heard if they have any leads."

"Crazy, man. Did you know her?"

"No," Shea said. He stood next to her for a few more beats, but when it was clear she was not going to expound on that, he muttered a "take care" and shuffled back to his body.

"I did the post on her," Dr. Findley said quietly. "*Did* you know her?"

"Yes."

"I thought so."

"I'm helping on some interviews," Shea said.

"Then you know about my findings?" Dr. Findley asked. Shea looked at Dr. Findley's face behind his plexi-glass mask and tried to read his expression. She had a feeling he wanted to tell her something, but she didn't know how to answer his question.

"I…I'm…in a position of *giving* RHD information, not receiving any," Shea said.

"Well, I sometimes listen to detectives and their theories as I do my work…I have the impression the investigators believe the officer committed suicide." Dr. Findley's blue eyes held hers for a moment.

"Do your findings support that?"

If she hadn't been looking at him she would have missed the very slight head shake as Dr. Findley continued, "I've seen curious things throughout the years. One has to examine the totality of the every situation." Shea was not sure if he was talking about the autopsy or the detective's conversation he overheard.

"I always appreciate your insight, Dr. Findley," Shea said.

"As I do yours, Detective." Dr. Findley nodded at her and turned to wash his hands. The autopsy on Eduardo Lopez was completed.

"Dr. Findley, was there anything about her body? Bruises, defensive wounds?"

"Open for interpretation; however, she had what appeared to be dirt under her nails. Bruises on her knees. Maybe she tumbled. A cut on one knee."

Shea thought about that for a moment. She knew the toxicology report would not be back this soon. There was no point in asking her blood alcohol content.

Shea left Lopez and walked to the opposite end of the room

to see Vaughn's victim. It was hard to guess his age; his body was withered like old wood. An attendant came over and poured bleach on his foot where the maggots were starting to spill out onto the table. Shea leaned over so she could see the hole in which they had tunneled into his leg. His nails were an inch long and dirty; they were intact and there did not appear to be any defense wounds on his hands. In the middle of the man's forehead was a black hole where a bullet entered and ended his life.

Shea stepped away from him because his odor was making her eyes water. A small woman approached the body. She was wearing more protective gear then most doctors. Her voice was muffled as she spoke through her mask. Shea said hello and put her business card on the rolling desk next to the body.

The doctor scraped a little of the wound on his foot with a scalpel. She told Shea that the whole lower leg had atrophied and he probably did not feel the maggots at all. Shea could barely hear her and she understood every other word. She decided to stop asking questions and wait for her written report. Shea stood back and watched the doctor work. John Doe 39 must have had a normal life at some point because his appendix had been removed.

Shea went back to the small supply room and removed all of her protective gear. She washed her hands and rubbed in rose-scented lotion. When she walked out of the back door of the coroner's office, she cut through the landscaped area. It was not much of a shortcut to the parking lot, but it kind of cleansed her senses of the sights and sounds of the coroner's office.

Shea drove to Parker Center next. Any police officer in the United States could be dropped into any major city, be asked to find the police headquarters, and could do it. It would be the ugliest, cheapest-looking building in the city, and Parker Center was no exception. Shea wondered why that was. Her best guess was that the architecture had to match the purpose of the building, and nothing good happened to anyone who ended up at a police station, especially headquarters. And for the hundreds of people who woke up every morning and had to work in these bland, dull, institutionalized buildings, their uninviting nature enhanced the sense that nothing good would happen to them either.

What made matters worse for Parker Center is that it was old and decrepit. The paint was peeling, rats and roaches running rampant after nightfall, and it was overcrowded. Despite the building's ugly exterior and vermin population, this was where the throne was; the chief and his minions all toiled here, miles away from the nearest patrol division.

Shea rode the elevator up to the fourth floor and picked up Vaughn's crime scene photos and then back down to the third floor and identified herself to the secretary at the window of RHD. The secretary directed her to Smith's desk. Shea straightened her backbone and walked through the all male squad room.

Walter had the phone pinned to his ear, but he smiled at her and motioned for her to sit down in the empty desk next to him. Shea opened her notebook and pulled out the statement of Krista Tanner. She pretended to read it, just to avoid looking around her. Walter said good-bye to his caller and turned in his chair to her.

"You didn't have to drive all the way down here for such a quotidian task." Walter took the papers from her.

"I had an autopsy this morning. We caught a murder Saturday night."

"Ah. You *are* busy. Are you getting any sleep?" Walter looked at her like a general practitioner.

"Not since summer. We've had a lot of murders."

"What is this latest one?"

"Gang. Car-to-car. We made an arrest yesterday."

"Excellent. This report includes all of the information regarding the pictures?" Walter looked at her report.

"Everything she told me. How's it looking?" Shea asked.

"Well, right now it's more a matter of elimination. Detective Lancaster and his team are sifting through hundreds of interviews from the restaurant, deciding who to re-interview. But they've eliminated the men in the photos as being responsible for the murder. They went hard on them...every one of them is clean."

"Did you tell the officers about the photos?"

"No, they were told that they were being interviewed because we had information that they had a sexual relationship with the victim. They were mostly cooperative, with a few exceptions. One fellow was returning from his honeymoon...that'll make for an interesting discussion with his new bride."

"Good news, bad news. Good news...I'm cleared of a homicide, bad news...I slept with the victim...yeah they might need some marital counseling," Shea said. "I heard on the news last night that her ex-husband hired a lawyer."

"Yes, I heard the same thing."

"What's his angle?"

"I think a combination of things. He harbors a tremendous resentment against the police department. He blames the department for his divorce. He claims she was harassed, miserable, and it is the LAPD's fault; and her death is the LAPD's fault. Plus, I think he enjoys the attention. I watched him being interviewed by Channel 7 and he's very dramatic."

"What will a lawyer do?"

"In reality? Nothing. Issue statements to the press. Perhaps hire private investigators to open an investigation…maybe sue—for what I don't know…" Walter said.

"And you've ruled him out as a suspect?" Shea asked.

"Yes. Iron clad alibi."

"Well, I need to get back to work." Shea slapped her hands on her knees.

"Thank you for your work this weekend. At least we have that portion of her life explained."

"Yeah." Shea stood up and Walter did as well. He shook her hand and thanked her for coming down. Shea detected that he did not want to speculate anymore about the nature of women, the way he had done in the women's locker room. She got the distinct impression that this investigation was floating past her down the river. Which was fine; she did have her own investigations to handle.

Shea walked over to the Officer Involved Shooting section. She saw Andrew sitting at his desk. She smiled to herself when she saw him wearing the same pink and green tie she had pulled off his neck and the heavily starched white shirt she had unbuttoned. He looked up and surprise registered on his face.

"Hi."

"Hello, Lieutenant Thorpe. I was in the neighborhood..." she shrugged.

"I was in the neighborhood earlier myself." He smiled at her.

"Do you want to have lunch?"

"I would. Philippe's?" He looked at his watch.

"That sounds good. Should I meet you over there?" Shea looked around. His secretary eyes flew back to her computer.

"No, I'll drive. I'll drop you back at your car when we're done." Andrew got up and grabbed his suit jacket from a coat rack behind his desk. "Margie, I'm going to Code-7."

Margie looked up and did a bad job of acting as though she was startled.

"Remember Lieutenant Thorpe, you have a meeting with Deputy Chief Ramsey at 1330 hours."

"Yes, thank you," Andrew said. "Margie, have you met Detective Reed? She works Valley Homicide?"

"Mmm, I think I may have talked to you on the phone?" Margie's penciled in eyebrows raised as she drew her lips into a slim smile.

"Nice to meet you," Shea said. As she followed Andrew out of the office, she felt Margie's eyes on her back.

They didn't talk until they hit the elevator banks. They just missed one with the doors closing as they approached, but the next one opened to them right away. They got on and were alone. Andrew leaned over and quickly stole a kiss.

"You're beautiful…" He kissed her again, but she pulled away from him. "There are no secret cameras in the elevators."

"Believe what you will," Shea said. The elevator stopped on the first floor and they got out and walked to the parking structure. Andrew said hello to many people as they made their way to the car.

Some cast her appreciative looks, or at least curious ones.

"I should've called you, but I had to go to my autopsy and then I dropped off some reports at RHD."

"I'm just glad I can go to lunch with you. We've had some bad luck lately trying to get together," Andrew said as he drove out of the parking lot. He waved to the guard in the booth and drove to the historic Philippe's. It was a favorite for people on their way to Dodger Stadium, workers downtown, and tourists who had heard about the delicious French Dip sandwiches. They got their sandwiches at the counter and found a table, in an empty room upstairs. Andrew sat with his legs touching hers under the table.

"You look tired," Andrew said.

"I feel like I haven't slept in a week. Well, I really haven't." Shea sipped her lemonade. The drinks at Philippe's were served in small juice-sized glasses. She filled him in on the highlights of her latest murder investigation.

"Boots is probably pretty pleased with a clearance, right?

"Yup. Gets the Captain off his back." Shea put her sandwich down. "Hey, I hate to bring this up…but where do you live, Andrew?"

"What do you mean?" Andrew bristled.

"Have you left home? Not that I give much of crap at this point, but last I heard you were moving out."

"I don't want to get into this at lunch, Shea."

"Not at lunch, not when your dick's inside of me…when then?"

"I asked Cathleen for a divorce. I said I would and I did. I haven't moved out like you would like."

"'Like I would like'? What does that even mean?"

"That I'm not sleeping in a hotel room or at my brother's house…"

"Andrew, you're saying you're not separated then?"

"I'm sleeping in my den. We're trying to hash all of this out. For Christ sakes, Shea, it's Christmas. I have three kids. It's a little hard to pack a suitcase and step over the Christmas presents on my way out the door." His face was dark and he dropped his sandwich onto his plate.

"You're the one who told me you're going to get a divorce, *you* told me that. I just assumed that you'd actually reside somewhere else."

"She…" Andrew coughed and then rested his forehead on his hand. "She wants to go to counseling."

Shea tried to wrap her mind around what he was saying, compared to what he had told her for months and months. She was under the impression they hated each other; they never had sex.

"I didn't know how to tell you," Andrew said.

"So you plan on working on your marriage and then swinging by my house for a quickie on the way home from work?"

"I'm not *planning* a goddamned thing. I'm just trying to survive." He hadn't looked her in the eye for several minutes.

"I need a plan. We've been together for two years, Andrew. We're bordering on a really bad cliché. *You told* me you'd get a divorce." Shea was speaking quickly. "You and I agreed that if it got too serious, we would end it. When I tried, do you remember what happened? *You* said you would get a divorce. I didn't ask, I didn't press. You offered."

"I'm not one of your damned suspects, Shea." He finally looked at her and she could see he was angry. "I know what I said. I know what I've done."

"Why can't you be upfront with me? I've spent the last week

thinking that you were separated."

"Because disappointing you is something that…that I hate doing." Andrew's voice trailed off.

"If we never would've starting talking about a future together, this little love affair would've just run its natural dead-end course, and we could've gone on with our lives. But we can't unring a bell. We just have to end this thing…"

"No. I told her that I want a divorce. I agreed to go to counseling--"

Shea pushed away from the table and began to stand up, but Andrew grabbed her arm.

"Listen to me. Listen to me!"

She sank back down on the wooden bench and his hand remained on her arm.

"I'll go to counseling with her. I think it'll help her accept the divorce. But I'm not sleeping in the same bed with her, Shea. I have to do this slowly. I did this to my older kids with my first wife and now I'm doing it to these kids, and I fucking hate myself. Do you understand that? I have a life with those kids. Do you have an ounce of compassion for my situation? I thought she would say fine, let's

get divorced…give me all your money…but she didn't, Shea."
Andrew released her arm.

"Andrew, what if the counseling improves your marriage?"

"Honey… it won't happen."

"I don't know if I can keep doing this." She chewed on the
inside of her cheek. "I started liking the idea of going on a date with
you. In public, to the movies, holding your hand and planning a
future with you."

"We're going to have that," Andrew said. "Give me some
more time. Just a little more time, Shea."

Shea balled up her napkin and tossed it on her plate. "I've got
to get back to the station. Jack and I have a lot of work to do."

"I didn't want this day to turn out this way. We had such a
good morning," Andrew said.

"It's not about ruining a day, Andrew," Shea said sharply.

"I know what it's about." He put on his jacket.

"I don't even know what you're saying," Shea said as she
began to walk out of the room.

He grabbed her arm and swung her around, "I'm saying,
don't leave me, Shea. Don't leave me over this." He held on to both

of her arms.

"Andrew." She looked at him as he kissed her cheek. A public display of affection, blocks from where he worked. It was the second surprise he handed her today.

She parked her car at her station and as she walked across the parking lot, she saw Jack coming out of the property room. He waved to her and waited for her to catch up.

Jack was reading a property report as she approached. When he looked up, his mouth dropped a little. His lower lip was turning purple.

"Are you okay?"

"As far as you know." Shea's stomach felt like a dumpster fire.

"I have a pregnant, moody wife, which qualifies me as an expert witness," Jack said.

"In what? An expert in what?"

"Knowing when something's wrong." Jack shrugged. "We're going to Miller's tonight."

Miller's was a bar at the local municipal golf course. It was not really called Miller's, but that's what the homicide unit called it. The unit went to Miller's when they celebrated an arrest, a conviction, needed to share station gossip, unload a burden or slight.

"I thought you had to go to the dentist," Shea said. "You look like the loser in a prize fight."

"I rescheduled for tomorrow afternoon."

"Your priorities are screwed up." Shea pointed her finger at his chest.

"Did I mention I have a pregnant, moody wife?" Jack said. "I need a beer or three."

Shea laughed at him as they walked into the station. Shea dropped the crime scene photos and autopsy notes on Vaughn's desk and then sat down at hers. The rest of the afternoon was spent tying up the loose ends in order to take the case to the district attorney for filing in the morning. Jack finished typing his report; Shea filled out the witness list and other required paper work for the next day's filing.

A couple of the gang-unit officers stopped by their desks and discussed the car-to-car shooting. Shea listened to their theories and the character's names. "Dopey" was pissed at "Spider" over what happened with "Lil' Toker." It was like the cast of a sick Disney cartoon. The conversation turned to Chloe Diaz, and did anyone have any information on how the investigation was going? Shea looked up from her work and checked to see if either officer was in Chloe's photo collage. Neither was, and they drifted away from the unit without receiving any information about Chloe's murder.

Later that evening, at the bar, Shea was asked the same question by her unit. She said she didn't know anything, but they pressed her. She was down at RHD talking with one of the detectives on the case; she had to have some information.

"I really don't. All I know is they don't think it's a cop," Shea said.

"Well, that's a relief," Vaughn said.

They were sitting at a round table in the back of the bar. It was nearly empty. There were a few golfers sitting at the bar, but other than that they had the place to themselves. The waitress/bartender brought them over a bowl of popcorn and a second round of beers. She let her hand rest on Vaughn's shoulders for a half beat too long. Shea knew the woman was working hard to get his attention.

"I saw her husband on the news last night. What a head case," Jack said.

"Her funeral's tomorrow. Are you guys going?" Vaughn asked.

"Is it at Forest Lawn?"

"Yeah, at 10:00 a.m. whoever wants to go can, obviously…the Lieutenant just wants everyone to car pool if they can," Curt said.

"Maybe after we get our case filed," Shea said.

"To your foot pursuit and subsequent arrest." Curt raised his fresh beer to them and everyone followed. "By the way, your arrestee is alleging police brutality."

"You're kidding, right?" Jack said.

"No. He told Sergeant Bullock that when he was interviewing him on the use of force," Curt said.

"Oh brother." Shea groaned.

"Bullock was miffed at you," Curt said.

"What did I do?"

"He says you embarrassed him in front of his peers."

"Are you kidding me?" Shea was incredulous.

"Oh, he was still pissed this morning. He came up after you left for the coroner's office and asked how we could work with such a ball-buster." Vaughn laughed and knocked her beer bottle with his own.

"Tell me you are joking," Shea said, but Jack shook his head.

"I guess when you prevented him from entering the interrogation room to interview your suspect, you did it in a manner that was perceived as belittling and what did he say--?" Curt asked Vaughn.

"Emasculating."

"Oh, he didn't say that. He wouldn't even have that word in his vocabulary," Shea said.

"That just sounded belittling, didn't it?" Vaughn said.

"Okay, he didn't say that. But he was put out. Was there anyone around when you confronted him?" Curt said.

"First of all, I didn't 'confront' him. I told him the criminal investigation took precedence over his administrative duties," Shea said primly.

"I think that was loose translation for *this is a murder investigation, moron, and your piddling little admin interview takes a backseat,*'" Jack said, raising his eyebrows and his beer bottle.

"Oh good grief."

"Anyway, he had to initiate a personnel complaint because of the alleged misconduct…" Curt said. "Bullock wants to get into Internal Affairs, so he's going to go by the book and the suspect says you called him a racial slur and punched him when he was handcuffed, Jack."

Jack just shook his head and drank his beer. Everyone agreed it was bullshit. They spent the next hour talking about the demise of the police department.

Jack was the first to leave. Vaughn and Curt speculated about Vaughn's chances with the waitress. She was a little heavier and a little older than his usual conquests, but he was bemoaning a recent dry spell. Shea listened, fighting the urge to go tell the waitress about their conversation.

"Are we boring you, Shea?" Curt asked her.

"No, I feel like Jane Goodall observing apes. It's good for me, it reminds me how absolutely depraved is your gender." Shea was on her fourth beer and feeling spunky.

"Well, Detective Reed, I've done a lot of observing of your

gender, too and I'm telling you—your people have flaws as well," Vaughn said.

"Yes, I'm sure you're an expert."

"Thank you! I'm an authority. I remember having sex with women who wore full slips, un-groomed pubic hair and real boobs," Vaughn said. Curt laughed so hard he snorted beer through his nose.

"And did your research end with their genitalia?" Shea asked.

"See, Shea, this is why guys think you are a ball-buster."

"Shea isn't a ball-buster, she's mean to both sexes. She's an equal opportunity ball-buster," Curt said. He was two beers ahead of her and still appeared sober.

"Thank you, I guess," Shea said.

"I'm going to work my magic with our waitress." Vaughn finished his beer.

"Just don't piss her off. We still want to drink here," Shea said.

"I'll keep that in mind." Vaughn bowed to them and sauntered over to the bar.

"She'll be in his hot tub in a matter of minutes." Shea shook her head as she watched the woman smile sweetly at Vaughn.

"That's how I see him kicking the bucket. In a hot tub full of waitresses all named Monique."

"I guess there're worse ways to go. Do you think he ever misses not getting married?"

"I doubt it. He's had some long-term girlfriends. But when it runs its course, no divorce, no infidelity," Curt said.

"Well, maybe not on his part. I think the waitress has a wedding ring on."

"Well, then she won't spend the night, will she?" Curt said.

"I guess not," Shea agreed.

"Are you okay?"

"Yeah." Shea shrugged. "I'm tired."

"Anything you want to talk about?"

"Not without crying and I don't feel like crying," Shea said.

"He's back home?" With Curt's simple question, and Shea felt a wave of emotion well up in her chest. She nodded and rocked back in her chair a little. Curt drank his beer and looked over her shoulder at the television behind the bar. It was enough time for her to quell the tears before she answered.

"I guess that's why I'm a little irritated at your whole

gender." Shea tried to say it lightly.

"It's a good enough reason," Curt said.

"I need to get home."

"You okay to drive?"

"I'm fine, boss. Really." She got up and waved at Vaughn

and the waitress.

Chapter 10

The next day Shea and Jack got to the courthouse early. Court was one of those places where you can tell who belongs there and who is there for the first time. It was one of those special clubs that either you belonged to or you didn't. A high-priced defense attorney, a tired cop or a criminal, they all had admission.

They met with the DDA from the Hardcore Gang Unit. This particular deputy district attorney actually was *hardcore*. He was a former cop, who took a forced retirement for an injury he received on duty. He got his law degree and was hired by the district attorney's office. He was the only DA Shea knew that carried a gun and she was pretty sure he chewed tobacco, but he was so covert that it might just be gum.

After they presented their case and got their "things to get done before the pre-lim" list, they made their way out of the courthouse and headed to Chloe Diaz's funeral. A police officer's funeral was similar to court, either you belonged there or you didn't.

There was no way to capture how mortality hangs in the air, blown out of bag pipes and shot into the air with gun salutes. Shea observed the officers in their dress blues, hat brims pulled down right on top of sunglasses and black elastic bands over the City Hall image on their badges. Outside of the chapel it was a reunion. In a Department of over 8,000 men and women, retirements and funerals were second only to the firing range for running into old friends. Fortunately retirement parties outnumbered funerals.

Chloe Diaz's funeral had more media coverage than usual. As Shea and Jack walked up, they could see skinny reporters with pretty hair sidling up to officers asking them if they knew Chloe Diaz. Later that day, the funeral would run as the lead story on all the local newscasts and solemn anchors would start with, "LAPD buried one of their own today…"

Shea and Jack walked in unmolested. They were wearing their detective garb and were probably considered boring camera shots compared with uniformed officers wiping away tears. They found seats where Shea could see Chloe's ex-husband and other family members. Shea remembered that Chloe's dead father had been a deputy chief. That explained why retired Chief Daryl Gates was comforting her family. He looked trim and tan to Shea, who—like most of the Department—missed him like crazy. His brand of police work endeared him to police officers, but not necessarily the public.

Beyond the seating for the family and brass, Chloe's coffin was on a stage, draped in a flag. Shea scanned the audience for Chloe's lovers. She wanted to find the Jake Cameron, the stud who had kicked Chloe in the heart and then showed the photos to his friends. She'd love to grab him by the back of his crew cut and pound his face onto her casket. She couldn't pick him out of the hundreds of uniformed officers.

Once everyone was seated, the Department Chaplin gave an invocation and the current Chief of Police Willie Williams made his way to the podium. He read from his notes, which were undoubtedly prepared by his staff—a staff that also didn't know Chloe and who had probably rifled through her personnel package and picked out commendations and ratings to talk about. It could not have come across any more impersonal if Willie from Philly had mispronounced her name.

After the Chief, Captain Sanchez took his place at the podium. He was a couple ranks closer to Chloe, and he did seem to actually remember the infectious smile Chloe displayed when he would pass her in the halls. He was followed by Chloe's girlfriend,

Ann Gross. Shea hadn't seen her since the locker room incident. Ann was not wearing her uniform. Strangely, she was wearing a tie dyed t-shirt, Bermuda shorts, and tennis shoes. She adjusted the microphone to accommodate her height and spoke firmly into it.

"I did it, Chloe." Ann glanced at the coffin for a few seconds. "You might think what I'm wearing is disrespectful. Let me explain. See, a year ago Chloe and I went to the funeral of Officer Danny DeMarina." She paused as there was a general rumbling of acknowledgement. DeMarina was shot in the head responding to a radio call in 77th Division. He was 25 years old, married, with a baby on the way.

"We knew Danny. We all played on the same softball team in Rampart. So, we—the team—we came together to our first LAPD funeral. We were early and we sat close to the front. We were all crying. Everyone loved Danny." She waited as a murmur of agreement traveled through the audience. This crazy girl in a tie-dyed tee shirt held everyone's attention more than the Chief of Police had.

"Anyway, a sergeant comes up to us. I guess he worked for Medical Liaison or something. He says we all have to move to the back. They needed our seats for brass. We had to get up and move to the back so a bunch of people Danny never knew could sit down."

Jack and Shea exchanged glances. This officer was going to die a P-2. She would never be promoted to anything in her entire career. The brass she was talking about had both delicate images of themselves and long memories. Also, they were sitting right up front, breathing down on her as she spoke.

"So we were upset about that. We listened to people that didn't know Danny talk about him like they did—kind of like today. Anyway, on the way back to the station, Chloe told me that if one of us dies, the other has to wear a tie-dyed t-shirt and Bermuda shorts to the funeral and has to promise to get up and say the real deal. I never thought it would be me. I never thought I would be here." Ann's voice broke.

Shea watched as high ranking officials conferred. There was a call being made to Behavioral Sciences for the shrink on duty, Shea thought.

"So here's the real deal. Chloe Diaz loved being a cop. She loved it more than her husband. Sorry, Marco. She loved putting the bad guys in jail. She still went back to get a Tommy's Burger once a week after she wheeled out of Rampart, and she loved it with extra onions. She took better care of her uniform and equipment than a Marine would. She wanted to get in the gang unit at Valley in the worst way. Someday she wanted to go to Metro, and then she wanted to be the first woman in SWAT. That was Chloe's dream. Along the way she got hurt. By people she thought were her friends..." Ann looked around the crowd. Shea thought she was probably looking for the same crew cut Shea had been looking for.

"And then at the Christmas party she was hurt for real. I just wanted you all to know what you lost. Now she's pitching to Danny DeMarina and he's hitting one out of the park..." Ann said. "Save a beer for me, guys."

As she pushed away from the podium something happened that Shea had never seen before at a funeral. People leaped from their seats applauding and hooting their approval. Ann was looking down, watching her step, but she glanced up and gave the crowd a teary smile. The clapping went on for a few minutes and Shea watched the chiefs looking straight ahead, ignoring it, or conferring with one and other.

"Are we going to be witnesses to a bloody coup?" Jack

leaned over to Shea.

"Can you believe it?" She said over the applause.

There was a small group of people at the edge of the stage, probably trying to figure out who would pull the short straw and go to the podium next. It turned out to be the Deputy Chief in charge of the bureau. Chief Kelly asked for everyone to please be seated. He went on to say how touched he was by Officer Gross's commitment to her friend and then white-washed everything she said, by saying something inane about emotions being raw at a time like this. He introduced a black officer, who sang at nearly every funeral, and rushed off-stage. The officer sang a sorrowful rendition of "Amazing Grace" and the boat seemed righted again for the rest of the pomp and circumstance of the day.

Shea and Jack walked back to their car and Shea pointed to a man in a suit with a white dressing over his ear.

"That's her partner who was shot," Shea said.

"I heard he was coming back light-duty on the desk next DP."

"I wonder if Vaughn'll ever find out who shot him."

"He doesn't have any leads." Jack unlocked the door and got

in the driver's side.

"Hey, if I die, you don't have to wear Bermuda shorts," Shea said as she got in.

"Oh good, because that's not a pact I want to have with you or anyone else."

"Just make everyone I ever slept with stands up and says something about me."

"Will there be enough time, or will this be a month-long ceremony?"

"Ha ha," Shea said. But she did think about Andrew in uniform, standing in the back, with a black band around his badge, pretending not to know her very well.

Chapter 11

Shea and Jack spent Christmas day listening to a 57 year old man justify shooting his ex-wife in front of their teenage son. Shea volunteered to book him and write the reports so Jack could get home to his family. She didn't exchange gifts with Andrew until three days after Christmas. He gave her a string of pink pearls and a cellular telephone.

The New Year was ushered in with the usual violence, intended and otherwise. Drunks shooting into the sky sent bullets cascading through walls and skin. Shea's unit handled two murders that night. The investigations took them well into 1997.

The rest of the winter was not memorable for the investigations, but what appeared to be the lack of investigation into Chloe Diaz's death. A rumor was circulating through the ranks that RHD detectives thought it was a suicide and that someone took the gun.

Walter Smith was on vacation. Shea's messages to the lead detective went unreturned. She and Jack were working fourteen-hour days; both were in court on preliminary hearings. After court ended for the day, they'd meet back at the station and work on their murder investigations. It was this kind of schedule that led to frustrated wives, missed workout routines, and a lot of money for the amount of overtime they worked.

On a drive into work one morning, Shea noticed that the Jacaranda trees all over the San Fernando Valley were blooming. Their lavender-colored flowers were a beautiful contrast against the graffiti-stained walls. Shea's sister had returned and this served as a reminder she really needed to find her own place to live. She decided that the house she bought would have to have a Jacaranda tree in the front yard. She was sitting at a traffic light, a block from the station, thinking about her imaginary yard when she glanced to her right. She recognized Ann Gross behind the wheel of a squad car.

Ann's hair was cut short and dyed a burgundy color. Shea figured she was not over her rebel yell from the funeral. Ann was talking aggressively and waving her right hand. Shea leaned over to see who the passenger was. She was surprised to see the bandaged ear of Chloe's former partner. He was looking straight ahead. Shea wondered why he was still wearing a bandage. Then she remembered someone saying he needed to wear it while they reconstructed the outer ear. She didn't think he was back to full duty, but still assigned to the desk. The light turned green and Ann Gross sped off in the direction of the station. Sometimes desk officers went to lunch with full-duty officers, but it was 7:00 a.m. Shea filed the encounter away and drove to work through the swirling Jacaranda blossoms.

When she got to work, there was a message on her desk. Jack had called. Samantha was in labor. She held up the pink slip to Curt.

"Yeah, I just hung up on him. She's only three centimeters dilated, whatever the hell that means," Curt said.

"It means the cervix--" Vaughn started to tell him.

"I know, I know! Enough female talk."

"Funny that he doesn't mind *female* talk if he's talking about breasts," Shea said under her breath to Vaughn.

"Cervixes seem to bother him," Vaughn said in a stage whisper.

"Anyway, we're going to be down a man in the unit for while because he's going to take family bonding leave--"

"Whatever the hell that is," Vaughn finished for him.

"Okay, chuckleheads…we are up to our asses in alligators here. Will one of you please go solve a homicide?" Curt said.

"How long is he going to be off?" Shea said.

"Maybe a month. He's not sure. I guess it depends on if Sam's mom's going to stay with them and help with the older kid," Curt said.

"Can we get a body on loan to the unit, Boots?" Vaughn asked. "I've been without an assigned partner for months now. This is ridiculous. We can barely manage with one-and-a-half teams, let alone now with just one team. Seriously, get us a body on loan, at least."

"I tried. No-can-do. So you two are what's left of the Mod Squad." Curt pulled reports out of his in-box.

"I get to be Linc," Shea said.

"You're Julie," Vaughn said.

"I hate being the girl."

Shea decided to take a look up at the front desk to see if Officer Ornelas was back at work. The front desk in nearly every patrol division was manned by the sick, lame, lazy and/or punished. If an officer was injured, or a malcontent or hot head who needed to cool off, they would ride the pine. With phones ringing non-stop and the walk-in traffic ranging from a simple police report to a person turning in a found WWII grenade, the desk was tedious and dangerous.

Shea saw a line of people to the door and only two officers, both on phones and with impatient citizens standing in front of them. One man had numerous crumpled and dirty pieces of paper spread out in front of the officer like playing cards. Shea assumed it was some kind of auto dispute. The papers were registrations, hand-written bills of sale, and some DMV paperwork. She felt for the officer trying to figure out that mess.

The officer sitting next to him was at least eight months pregnant. The young woman was in uniform, but no bulletproof vest would fit her and her baby, so she wasn't wearing one. Shea knew if the officer had a gun on, which she probably didn't, it was only a two-inch revolver in an ankle holster. The likelihood of her being able to reach the gun perched on a stool and with 30 pounds of belly between her hand and that gun, was not good. It would take a woman getting shot before they did anything about the policy requiring something as absurd as a maternity uniform. Shea knew it wasn't a priority. A pregnant woman in uniform was the biggest reminder of the notion that women didn't belong in law enforcement.

When the pregnant officer hung up the phone, Shea leaned in and asked where the officer was who had his ear shot off.

"Ornelas? He should be back in the report-writing room," the officer said, picking up the already-ringing phone she had just put down.

Shea maneuvered her way through the watch commander's office and back to the officer's report-writing room. Ornelas was the only one in the room, his head down, working on a traffic report. Shea reached above his head to a shelf and pulled down a property report.

"Excuse me," she said. He looked up at her and scooted his chair in to allow more room for her to pass.

"You're Officer Ornelas, right?"

"Yes, ma'am," he said.

"When did you come back to work?"

"Two weeks ago."

"Will you be able to come back full-duty?"

"Yes. The bullet damaged my outer ear, but my hearing is

back to normal," he said. He shifted in his seat when she pulled out the chair next to him and sat down.

"How are you holding up with what happened to Diaz?"

"Okay, I guess. We weren't that close. We just worked together one DP."

"Do you have any opinion on what happened to her?"

His cheeks colored immediately.

"Did Ann tell you to talk to me?" He looked down at his hit-and-run report.

"No. I haven't talked to her. Why?"

"She's on my case all the time," he muttered.

"I'm a peer counselor. Want to talk about it?"

"A peer counselor? Don't you help people with alcohol problems and domestic violence?"

"Among other things." Shea smiled. "I'm an official, non-gossiping person people can talk to at work."

"Did you have to go to special training for that?"

"I did. A three-day school."

"Do people seek you out a lot?"

"Not like you would think. Sometimes I'll be talking to a

person at a crime scene and it's clear they've got something on their mind, so we'll just talk right there. If someone needs serious help though, I recommend them to Behavioral Sciences to see a psychologist."

"I had to see a shrink after the shooting. It was mandatory."

"They gotta make it mandatory, otherwise no one would go. Sometimes it helps to get a different perspective on things, that's all. What's going on with you?" Shea hoped she had warmed him up enough to talk to her.

"Nothing. Chloe's friends are the problem."

"Why's that?"

Officer Ornelas looked around covertly. "It's like they are on their own little investigation to find out what happened to her."

"What does that have to do with you?"

"Nothing. I haven't even been interviewed by RHD. I'm not even on *their* radar. I don't know why these girls think I can help."

"Because of the shooting?" Shea offered.

"I guess."

"How do they think you can help?"

"Do you *really* want to know why?" He looked her in the eye for the first time.

"Sure."

"Because Chloe told them I read the plate wrong. She typed it on the MDT and it came back 'record-not-on-file,'" Ornelas said.

"I'd heard that's why there're no leads…because of the wrong plate being given to Communications."

"But here's a lesser-known fact: I lit the car up before we could get the right plate. Chloe told me not to and I said it wasn't that big of deal. It was 1500 hours, almost EOW, and it was just a 21243," he said, naming the vehicle code for running a red light.

"Is that what happened, or what Chloe told them?"

"Both. I got the plate wrong. I lit him up too soon. It was close to end of watch…I just wanted to get a mover, because my recap sucked for that DP. And I got shot because of it," he said sourly.

"Is this a secret?"

"It isn't common knowledge. I told the OIS investigator, but I wasn't going to get up in roll call and admit it," Ornelas said. "I never intended for Chloe to take the blame. I mean people get plates wrong all the time. But because she didn't shoot back, I guess people just…"

"Assumed she screwed up the whole thing?" Shea finished
for him.

"I guess, but I wasn't here to correct anything. I was in the
hospital!"

"So, maybe I'm missing something, but do Chloe's friends
want you to admit this publicly to defend her memory or because it
will help find who killed her?"

"I don't know. I heard RHD thinks it was a suicide."

"I've heard that too. Do you remember any detail of that
plate?"

"Now? No, of course not. I just remember that fucking—I'm
sorry—arm coming out of the driver window with a gun." He
dropped his pen. "I couldn't believe it was happening to *me*."

"I can imagine."

"*No one* really understands until it happens to them."

"When you read off the license plate, did you notice if the
tabs were expired?"

Ornelas thought about that for a minute. "No one ever asked
me that. They *were* expired because I remember thinking the

registration was up over a month, and we'd probably have to impound it." Ornelas chewed on this revelation for a moment before continuing, "I looked at the tabs when I got out of the car."

"See, you remember more than you think." Shea smiled and prodded gently, "How many heads did you see in the car?"

"Uh, I was asked that and I know it was only one. I know everyone says it was a carload because it sounds really fucking— shit, I'm sorry—dramatic, but it wasn't. It was one guy. That was also why I didn't think it was a big deal about getting the plate wrong."

"Makes sense. Was the guy a gangster?"

"I thought so."

"Tell me why."

"The car for one thing. It was a lowered Buick with that metallic-burgundy paint. I could see he was wearing a wife beater and he had a shaved head."

"Any tattoos on his neck?"

Ornelas thought about for a minute.

"No…I don't think so."

"How much of his neck and back could you see? Sometimes,

you know, they lower the seat and all you can see is the top of their head?"

"I know what you mean. I could see to about here." He put his hand on her upper back. "He might've been tall."

"And fat or thin, muscular?" Shea asked.

"Thin, a thin neck and boney shoulders," Ornelas said.

"Okay, so everything is pretty routine and normal and then tell me what comes next."

An officer came in to pick up a report. Ornelas waited until the officer left before he started talking. "I saw the gun and an instant after I saw it, he was shooting. And I fuckin' hesitated for a second because I was shocked. I pulled out my gun, but I was already falling from being shot, my round went up into a tree."

"Picture the gun…okay…now I want you to picture the hand and arm attached to it."

"Okay."

"Right hand or left?"

"Definitely right, because he had to lean out…that's where I saw a tattoo! I knew I saw one! It's on his upper right arm, almost to the shoulder…but I've got no idea what it was because I just saw a little bit and then I was on the ground."

"Very good. What's your first name?"

"Sean. S-e-a-n, not S-h-a-w-n."

"Sean Ornelas?"

"Mom's Irish and my dad's Mexican," he said.

"Sean, one of the guys in my unit is working on this case. I'm going to tell him what you remember, okay?"

"Detective Powers? He's cool." Ornelas nodded. "But what does that have to do with Chloe?"

"Probably nothing, but this asshole shot your ear off, and we're gonna find him."

"I never saw his face," he said glumly. "Detective Powers wanted to know if I could identify him down the road."

"No, you never saw his face, but look at what you did remember. Now we know we're looking for a tall, skinny guy, with a tattoo on his upper right arm." Shea gently rested her left hand on his arm. "You did good."

"Thanks."

"Well, I'll let you get back to your report. As for whether you should fall on the sword in roll call…I think no matter what you do, there'll always be guys on the job who'll second-guess everything. But I think if someone can learn from a mistake I made, then there's a benefit to the mistake."

"Okay. Have a good day, Detective."

"You too, Sean."

Shea went back to the squad room and directly to the cabinet where the homicide unit kept the murder books. She opened it up and found the Ornelas/Diaz attempted murder binder.

"What are you doing?" Vaughn said when he saw her grab his book.

"Do you mind if I look through this?" Shea held up notebook. "I just talked to Ornelas and he remembered a few things."

"Like what?" Vaughn pushed back from his desk and folded his arms.

"The tabs were expired. The suspect was skinny, maybe tall, with a tattoo on his right shoulder."

"What did you do, hypnotize him?"

"No, haven't you heard? I'm a witch and I put a spell on him." Shea held the book like a tray of food. "Can I look through the book?"

"Yeah, but write up a supplemental on the statement he gave you today."

"I will." Shea headed to the empty roll-call room. She didn't want to be disturbed at her desk, and she didn't want Vaughn leaning over her shoulder.

Shea opened the binder and went first to Vaughn's summary report. After reading that, she flipped through to the section containing all of the vehicle leads. Vaughn had played with every combination of the numbers and letters for the plate the officers saw, but nothing came back to a Buick. Shea assumed it was "cold-plated," meaning the plate had been removed from a different car and placed on the Buick. Vaughn must have assumed the Buick was stolen, because he had pages of computer printouts of stolen GM vehicles.

Shea flipped to the officers' statements. She read Chloe Diaz's statement. Chloe described the incident as a "routine traffic stop." Shea bristled at the word "routine," there was no such thing as routine in police work, the word set the stage for not expecting anything unusual, and that's when an officer might let down his or her guard. Chloe described hearing the gunshot and watching her partner fall to the ground. Shea could imagine Chloe's despair and frustration when she had to put out over the air such a brief description of the car.

Shea finished reading Chloe's statement and flipped through the binder to the crime-scene photos. There weren't that many because there wasn't much of a crime scene. A close up of the puddle of blood where Ornelas had fallen and a stark photo of the police car, the passenger's door open. Shea pictured Chloe stepping out onto the boulevard and suddenly hearing gunshots.

There was a photo of Ornelas in the hospital, his ear gone and blood everywhere. Shea thought that would play well in front of a jury. It was difficult to get a filing from a district attorney for assaults on police officers, let alone getting a jury to convict. Juries felt it was expected in a police officer's line of work that they would be spit on, punched or even shot. It was important to show the jury the officer as a flesh-and-blood person, hurt and damaged.

Shea found a picture of Chloe in an interrogation room. She had removed her uniform shirt and vest, but her t-shirt still had blood on it. She had a diet Pepsi in front of her, and her hands were in her lap. She looked tired, and there was a smear of blood on her temple.

Surviving the shooting would never absolve Chloe from the mistakes made at the incident. She hadn't returned fire and she had no information about the suspect or his license plate. This all seemed to show on Chloe's face as she stared into the camera lens.

Shea closed the blue binder and sat back in her seat in the empty roll-call room. She tapped the cover of the book with her pen and tried to clear her head. Vaughn had covered every base when it came to that car. Learning that the plate had an expired registration didn't make much of a difference. Vaughn had circulated flyers throughout the city for the car. Shea got up and looked at the bulletin board in the roll-call room. She wanted to see if the flyer was still posted. She looked through the wanted posters and the stack of flyers affixed to the wall and she found it, buried. Burgundy Buicks were probably not on anyone's mind anymore.

As she let the wanted posters flip out of her hands, she noticed the top poster was about a robbery and shooting that had occurred in Foothill Division. It was just a run-of-the-mill flyer, with a grainy photo from a surveillance camera that depicted a man in a ski mask pointing a gun at a store clerk. Shea couldn't even tell what race the man was. The flyer was useless, but it was just another thing the investigators could cross off their "list" of things they had done to further their investigation. Shea looked at it again and then grabbed Vaughn's book, running back to the squad room. Vaughn was on the phone when she arrived at his desk.

She waited impatiently while he finished his phone call.

"What?" Vaughn said as he hung up.

"I got a question." She sat down in Jack's cubicle in front of Vaughn's desk.

"Shoot, stick."

"Did you ever go through all of the crimes in the division and neighboring divisions that took place prior to the shooting?"

"I remember doing a search for anything with a Buick, but there was nothing."

"You searched through just the car?"

"Yeah, I guess so."

"Well, I was just thinking, you know how they always say that you might be pulling someone over for a broken taillight, but the suspect thinks you're pulling him over because he robbed a bank?" Shea said.

Vaughn raised his eyebrows at her and answered sarcastically, "No, Shea, I have never had such sophisticated training."

"Stop it. I'm just wondering if this guy might've done a robbery or something prior to the shooting." Shea smacked his arm.

"Yeah, I looked into that, and I can tell you there wasn't a damn thing going on in the whole Valley prior to that call. No bank robberies, nothing."

"Nothing that stood out."

"Nothing with a Buick," Vaughn said.

"Do you mind if I have Communications Division pull all the calls for a 48-hour period for the Valley?"

"The whole San Fernando Valley? Knock yourself out," Vaughn said.

"Hey, I have an announcement." Curt hung up the phone. "Jack just called. Sam had the baby about an hour ago. Mother and daughter are fine."

"Another girl!" Shea laughed. "All of those firemen in his family must just be shitting. All the grandkids so far are girls. So much for third-generation LAFD."

"They might be fire-women someday," Curt said.

"Firefighters; I think the term is 'firefighters,' boss."

"I think the term is 'bull dykes,'" Vaughn said. Shea slugged him again.

Shea picked up a stuffed giraffe at the hospital gift shop and proceeded to the maternity ward. As she arrived on the correct floor, she could tell where Samantha's room was because of the loud men in front of the door. She recognized Jack's father and two brothers laughing with a nurse. They weren't in uniform, but each wore a t-shirt reflecting some LAFD event – a motorcycle ride, a water-ski event, and a charity football game named "Guns-and-Hoses." When Shea walked up to them, their circle opened to accommodate her.

"Here's our favorite lady detective," Jack's father boomed. Shea smiled and shook their hands.

Shea looked past the three timbers into the hospital room. "Can I go in?"

"Yeah, sure you can."

Shea moved past Jack's brothers and father and went into the room. Samantha was holding her new daughter and Jack was looking at the both with an expression Shea had never seen on his face. She guessed that might be what utter love looked like. Jack jumped up and gave Shea a quick hug before closing the door behind her.

"They're just so loud," Samantha whispered to Shea as she sat down. Jack took the giraffe and placed in next to a big bouquet of pink roses. "Thank you, Shea."

"How are you?" Shea looked at the tiny bundle in pink. This baby better get used to her loud grandpa and uncles right away.

"I'm okay. She was a little easier than her sister."

"What's her name?"

"Jack! You never told your partner the baby's name?" Samantha said. Jack shrugged and sat back down in his chair on the other side of the bed.

"He probably did, but--" Shea started to defend him.

"Makena Marie. We had our honeymoon in Hawaii, and I always thought that was a pretty name and a pretty place."

"You stayed in Makena?"

"No, Kaanapali, but we couldn't name her that could we?" Samantha giggled. She gently handed the baby to Shea. "You can hold her."

"No, no…" Shea protested as the baby was arriving in her arms.

"Oh my God, this is as ridiculous as a ballerina holding a football." Jack laughed. Shea gave him a dirty look and attempted to adjust the baby to a position she had seen other women hold babies.

"Now can't you see having one of your own?" Samantha stroked her baby's head.

"I'd like to *see* a husband first," Shea said. Makena had little rosebud lips and the tiniest nose Shea had ever seen.

"You won't break her, you know," Jack said.

"Right. Hey, I talked to Ornelas today," Shea said.

"Who?"

"Sean Ornelas. The officer who got his ear shot off. He remembered a little more about the car and the suspect. Did you know he was the one who got the plate wrong and not Chloe?"

"Really?"

"Oh, you two aren't going to talk murder right over me and my new baby, are you?" Samantha said. Shea put the tiny baby back in her mother's arms. "Go. Go talk guns and blood somewhere else." Samantha shooed them away with the back of her hand.

"No, sweetie…we're not--"

"No really, go on. I'm going to nurse anyway," Samantha said. Shea leaned down and kissed Samantha's forehead.

"Congratulations, she's beautiful."

"Thanks, Shea. Go talk to Jack. He's going stir crazy." Samantha squeezed Shea's hand and they left the room.

Jack's brothers and father met them at the elevator and they rode down to the lobby.

"The only thing I know for sure is, I'm going to have a lot of grandchildren," Chief Rainier said.

"Why is that?" Shea asked.

"I know they aren't going to stop until we get some boys." He towered over Shea and his forearms looked like logs.

"Well, speaking as a member of the 'undesirable sex,' I guess I'm just glad we don't live in China or I would've been drowned in a river," Shea said.

"Oh, she is a pisser." Jack's older brother nudged him. "Who wears the pants in your partnership—oh wait, you both do." He wrapped a bear arm around Shea's shoulders as the elevator doors opened.

"We're just teasing, Shea. We like girls, too," Jack's younger brother said with a smile. They were like circus dogs, jumping over each other's backs and smiling for the audience. After they gave Jack hearty pats on the back, they went to the parking lot to find their oversized pick-up trucks.

"They're exhausting," Shea said, sitting down on a block wall.

"Tell me about it. I lived with those maniacs." He sat down next to her and offered her a cigar.

"No, thank you, I'm trying to cut down." They sat swinging their legs on the wall. "Is your Dad serious? All you guys having girls…"

"I don't know. He loves his granddaughters. He's a helluva lot nicer to them than he'd be to grandsons…that's for sure."

"Are you disappointed?"

"Not at all. If she turns out anything like her sister Kaylee, I'm blessed," Jack said. "But my Dad's wrong about one thing. No more kids for us. I'm going to get a vasectomy now."

"You're kidding."

"No. Two was all we wanted," Jack said.

"That's so final."

"Okay, now tell me about what you're working on and why," Jack said.

Shea told him about her day and about ordering all of the reports from Communications Division. A car pulled up in the red zone and the driver stayed in the car with the windows down as his passenger ran inside the hospital. On the radio blasted *More Than a Feeling*.

"I love this song," Jack said.

"Yeah? What does it remind you of?"

"Oh. Summer of 1977. My Nova. Lee Ann Sondermeyer in the backseat." Jack closed his eyes.

"What grade would that be?"

"I'd be going into 11th grade." He opened his eyes. "Jeez, the birth of my second child and I'm thinking about Lee Ann Sondermeyer."

"Fleeting youth."

"True." Jack smiled, his dimples folding back to his ears.

"Was she a cheerleader?"

"Homecoming queen. Auburn hair and green eyes."

"She dyed her hair. No one has auburn hair. Clairol made it up."

"No, she did, it was natural."

"You'd believe anything." Shea rolled her eyes.

"Anyway, this song was playing on my radio –"

"Don't you mean eight-track tape player?"

"That's my older brother's car. *I* had a cassette player. Anyway, it was playing when we did it for the first time."

"'*Did it?*'" Shea laughed at him. "What are you, fourteen?"

"Do you want to hear my story or not?"

"Oh, gee, more than anything," Shea said.

"Well, we had been making out for an hour and then this song came on, and I thought, I'm going to get laid for the first time to this song and I pulled her down on the seat and she let me."

"Did you make it through the whole song?"

"Oh yeah and into the next song." The passenger ran back out of the hospital and hopped in the car; the car and the song drove away.

"And just like that, 1977 is over," Shea said.

"You have no sensitivity at all."

227

"Do you ever think why things were so intense when you were a teenager and now, it's like…ah never mind."

"Watch it Jack, you're coming dangerously close to revealing something about yourself," Shea chided gently and kicked her leg into his.

"I tell you a lot."

"Maybe to you, you do."

"What do you want to know?" Jack turned to look at her. Shea thought her partner's eyes seemed to always be held in a squint, as if the morning sun had caught him by surprise.

"I want to know something," Shea said. "I want to know why you dropped out of UCLA and became a cop."

"That's your burning question?"

"That or what happened with the red-headed homecoming queen. Take your pick," Shea said.

"Auburn. And she went with me to UCLA. So maybe sometime I'll answer both questions at the same time. We'll save it for the next time we're stuck on an airplane going to do an extradition."

"Is it true you aren't coming back to work for a month?"

"A month? Did Boots say that? No, I'm only going to take a week off. But I told him to call me if we picked up a homicide," Jack said.

"I'm going to use this time without a partner to investigate the OIS with Ornelas and Chloe."

"Don't forget to get to get the discovery on *Macias* to the DA by Wednesday, and get the subpoenas served on the *Johnson* case before Friday," Jack said.

"When you're done playing 'stay-at-home daddy,' all the crappy work will be done." She gave him a quick hug. "Congratulations on your baby, Jack."

She drove back to the San Fernando Valley thinking about the way Jack looked at his wife when she was holding their baby. She wondered if she would experience that type of adoration. There was something so sweet, yet so overwhelming about the scene. It made her think of gilded cages and satin-lined handcuffs. She didn't realize it but she had unknowingly floored the gas pedal.

Chapter 12

When Shea arrived home, she pulled into the driveway next to an unfamiliar car. Shannon came out of her front door and stopped Shea before she could make it down the walkway to her apartment.

"Company?" Shea nodded toward the brand new Cadillac. Shea assumed it was one of Shannon's music industry friends.

"For both of us," Shannon said. Shea stopped and eyed her sister. Shannon was wearing a red silk robe with a giant dragon embroidered on the back. It was what she threw on over just about anything. Today it was hiding frayed jeans and Van Halen t-shirt.

"Who?"

"William Shea," Shannon said.

"What's *he* doing here?"

"He was in the neighborhood and thought he'd stop by and see his goddaughters," Shannon said.

"You're his goddaughter, not me."

"Well, you're his namesake."

"Good grief, has he been drinking?"

"No, he just got here. Come in and say hi." Shannon grabbed her sister's arm. Shea pulled away as if they were on a playground.

"He heard your car pull up. He'll just go down to your place. At least here you can make an excuse and leave if you want to."

Shea sighed and followed her sister into the house.

William Shea was sitting on one of Shannon's over-stuffed couches, his legs spread wide apart and his long arms were draped across the back of the couch. He pushed himself up and walked across the room to greet Shea. Shea noticed he had the same overly groomed graying goatee and the same ridiculous rat's tail tied in leather down his neck. He looked like a cross between a greasy porn-actor and a greasy civil-rights attorney. William Shea was the latter.

"Shea, you look lovely." He kissed her hand, leaving a damp stamp that she wanted to wipe off.

"William. What brings you here?"

"I have a client in Encino. I decided to take the Canyon over and then it occurred to me how long it's been since I've seen Liam's girls."

"Shea, would you like some iced tea?" Shannon asked, slipping into the kitchen.

"No, I really can't stay."

"Hot date?" William reclined back on the couch. Shea

ignored him and followed her sister into the kitchen. Shannon handed Shea a glass of ice tea and mouthed, "Be nice."

"So who's your client, William? Another victim of LAPD brutality?" Shea said, staring at her sister. Shannon shook her head and pushed past Shea into the living room.

"She didn't mean that." Shannon handed their father's oldest friend a glass of tea.

"Yes she did. Right, Shea?" William sipped his tea.

"Actually, I didn't mean it. I don't care who your client is." Shea stood in the doorway of the kitchen.

"I was really hoping we could put aside our differences. Just because we serve different masters, doesn't mean we can't be friends."

"Is that what's preventing our becoming friends? Occupation?" Shea looked at him pointedly.

"I remember you as a curious little girl, sitting at the table watching your dad and I play bridge and talk politics." William turned his nose in the air like he just caught a whiff of homemade chocolate chip cookies.

"And I remember you passed out on our couch. I remember

dumping ashtrays and empty vodka bottles while you two slept it off," Shea said.

"A curious *and* responsible little girl," William said.

A few years ago William had feigned interest in her department's policy on the use of force. At the time, Shea was convinced that he genuinely wanted to understand. She retrieved for him all of directives and even notes she had taken in classes since the academy. She sat with him and explained the policy to him in detail. For one evening, he had stopped calling her the Gestapo and seemed to genuinely respect her line-of-work. He asked her if he could take the paperwork home, so he could really read through it and she agreed.

A few months later she heard her own words come through in his opening statement at a civil trial of an officer accused of excessive force. William had twisted her meaning and intent, but she recognized the content.

No one on the police department knew of her connection to William Shea, but every officer knew William Shea. He made a living and achieved a degree of local fame by suing the City of Los Angeles for outrageous amounts of money for brutality, discrimination, and one case of sexual harassment.

He was a regular guest on LA news programs, analyzing televised vehicle pursuits, pontificating about the new Chief of Police Willie Williams (while taking credit for running out Daryl Gates) and all the while alluding to the fact he had a mole on the LAPD. Shea would rather have a family member on death row then admit to knowing William Shea. His smug expression was burned into the minds of every police officer. He was their personal boogeyman.

"I think your rebellion from your father's ideals and, of course, mine, have damaged our relationship more than anything, Shea."

"You used me."

"I did no such thing. You knew what I did for a living when we sat down and discussed your Department's policy. Your ego just let you believe that you'd convert me."

"Thanks for the lesson."

"You're welcome, Shea," William said. "I always thought you were going to be a lawyer; you would've made a good one."

"She probably would've ended up a prosecutor," Shannon

said companionably.

Shannon was either choosing to ignore the tension in the room, or she believed Shea and William were making up.

"How are things with your new chief?"

"Are you kidding me? What would make you ever think I'd discuss the LAPD with you again?"

"I was just making conversation. Shannon, how are things going in the entertainment biz?"

Shea listened to Shannon drone on about leaving her personal assistant position to produce a record for this new band and how she was up for the challenge. Shannon always liked William. He had let Shannon borrow his car when she was just fifteen, which apparently earned him her undying loyalty. That was back when William taught alongside their father at the junior college and was driving a Vega instead of a Cadillac.

"I need to get going." Shea put her glass down on the kitchen counter.

"Oh, Shea. We haven't had a chance to catch up at all." William pushed out his lower lip in a pout. "I don't suppose you'd tell me anything about the murdered cop from your division?"

"Why would I, and why do you ask?"

"We might be on the same side on this one." William's mouth was twisted in a smug little smile.

"It would be impossible for us to be on the same side of anything." Shea stalled. She wanted to storm out, but her curiosity was piqued.

"Are you still a homicide detective? A woman?"

"Are you still a back-stabbing attorney?" Shea shot back.

"Shea!" Shannon said.

"It's okay, Shannon. Shea hasn't worked through all her issues. Someday she'll understand that it wasn't me who used her, but her own department who uses her every day. Your loyalty is admirable, but childish. Someday you will see that for yourself. You're just a serf working for the *Man*, Shea."

"Grow up, William. You've never filled me in on how the world works without law enforcement." She decided it was time to leave before she let his hook sink in her lip.

"Well, for a person who likes to make it known she's on the side of the angels, you don't seem interested in yet another colossal cover-up by the Building." His words grated like sand. He loved to talk like an insider. Police officers were the only people who called Parker Center the "Building," and repeat criminal offenders called it the "Glass House."

"After we all got together at one of our secret meetings to plant all of the evidence in the OJ case, we were bored and decided to kill a female police officer."

"My colleague and his client are not getting any answers from the investigators."

"It is an ongoing investigation, William. It doesn't matter if you're the mom of a gangbanger or the president, investigators can't discuss the details of their investigations. That doesn't mean there's a conspiracy afoot."

"Well, based on what I've been told, I smell a cover-up 'afoot.'" William took a slow sip of his iced tea.

"So, you thought you would drop by here and what? Feed me some truth serum and I would spill the secrets? Go back and tell Chloe's husband and his lawyer that you don't have the mole you think you do." Shea walked out the front door with William's voice trailing after her.

"Shea, if this is another LAPD cover-up, you know it'll be

above the fold in the Times."

Shea shook her head, his insider lingo wasn't reserved for police department, it stretched to reporters as well.

"How did you know my colleague was the husband's lawyer?" William called after her. Shea ignored him and continued walking down the stone steps to her apartment. She had a feeling he would follow her, so she changed course. She ran back to her car and drove away as William appeared on her sister's porch.

When she reached Sunset Blvd, she pulled into a gas station and rooted through her bag to find her day planner. She found Walter Smith's home phone number and dialed. Walter picked up on the second ring.

"Detective Smith, Shea Reed from Valley Homicide."

"Hello Shea. What can I do for you?"

"Can you tell me if the rumors are true? Are they thinking it was a suicide?"

"The Chloe Diaz case? Is there something going on?"

"I'm sorry for calling you at home." Shea realized he was anticipating some sort of urgency if he was being called at home.

"No, that's okay. I was just wondering what prompted your

call."

"You said to let you know what was being said at the division. This rumor is rampant."

"Okay…" Walter said.

"I--I…you know, I'm sorry for bothering you."

"You could have called me any time with this, so there must be something urgent. Please don't apologize for calling me, just tell me what happened or what is on your mind?"

"Oh…" Shea was regretting calling him. "I just heard that the ex-husband and his lawyer believe there is a cover-up."

"At the station, you heard this?"

"No, that's more complicated. I was just wondering if there was anything you could tell me."

"It's being investigated as a homicide. There are some indications that this was a suicide, including the statement you obtained from Krista Tanner. She saw Chloe holding her gun and looking despondent in Rampart. The investigators are considering every possibility. It is disconcerting that this is a rumor…not a very confidential investigation." He was speaking slowly. Shea suspected he was choosing his words carefully.

"Okay, first of all, Krista did not say she thought Chloe was going to kill herself that day. And I was at the crime scene, Detective Smith. There was no gun. She shot herself and then someone took the gun?" Shea looked out her windshield at a prostitute lingering on the corner.

"The theory would be someone wanted to make it appear not to be suicide."

"To what end?"

"Protecting the dead person's reputation, or their own. They didn't or couldn't stop it...or they caused it."

"I've never heard of such a thing."

"Have you ever worked an investigation in which something *wasn't* versus what it *was*?" Walter asked.

"I'm not following you."

"If no motives, no suspects, and a dead end...maybe it is not a murder. And that's when you have to think outside the box," Walter said.

"I've had murders where I couldn't find a motive or a suspect, but that just means I haven't turned over the right rock yet. It doesn't mean the people killed themselves."

"But you have to consider everything. The longer you work homicides, the more experience you'll have, and the more acumen. You'll see all kinds of things that don't quite add up," Walter said. "In this case, there is no cover up. That is ludicrous; no one has anything to gain…"

"I don't think my resistance to the idea of suicide has anything to do with a lack of experience, it just doesn't make sense. Common sense or otherwise," Shea said.

"Do you remember how Chloe's friends wanted to protect her reputation by removing the photos from her locker?"

"Of course."

"Do you remember learning about her poor judgment with men? What I am saying is if you think about what occurred from that angle, you might be able to see the possibility of a suicide."

"Okay. But, pass along to whoever cares that the attorney and ex-husband think whatever is going on is a cover-up." Shea was done talking in circles with Walter.

"Have you talked to the husband?"

"No, of course not. Look, I just wanted to check with you," Shea said. "I'll let you go."

"Hold on a second, don't hang up. I apologize for not being able to answer your questions directly. I did a victim profile and I have shared my opinions with the I/O's, but it's not my case."

Shea waited; he was trying to tell her something. Maybe he needed some prompting and she thought carefully about what she should say next.

"I understand that a profile isn't evidence, but it does show a victim's state of mind."

"If I were to go into your house, would I see items that would indicate your state of mind?" Walter asked.

Shea thought about that. Just her bathroom alone would indicate her state of mind. Dirty underwear on the floor of the bathroom; the bathroom trashcan needed to be emptied. A *People* magazine next to the toilet and her toothpaste cap was long gone. It was clear that she didn't expect a man sleeping over and it proved she was a slob, she surmised.

"Yes."

"I'll only say to you that there is no cover-up. The detectives assigned to this case are knowledgeable and hard-working. If there is something you have uncovered, you really need to share it with them or with me, whichever you prefer."

"Honestly, I'm just hearing rumors. But I did look over the OIS investigation and there are a couple of clues I'm going to look into."

"Clues to the OIS or the murder?"

"The OIS. I appreciate you taking the time to talk to me," Shea said, preparing to hang up.

"I firmly believe in a fresh set of eyes looking over an investigation. Just don't commit *career* suicide by not sharing what you have found with the investigators."

"I wouldn't do that, and I haven't even found anything out that would be of any value."

"Stay in touch, Shea," Walter Smith said. He sounded warm to her, like an uncle who was fond of a fractious niece.

Shea hung up her cell phone and tossed it in the bucket seat. She leaned her head against the headrest and tried to figure out what she was going to do next. She didn't want to drive home; William Shea was probably still there.

She checked her backseat and confirmed that her workout bag was intact and decided to drive up to the academy for a run. It was getting dark, but if she confined her run to the track on the academy grounds and not the surrounding Elysian Park, she'd be safe.

Shea drove through Hollywood on Sunset Blvd, watching the landscape change from misguided tourists on the hunt for a lost society of movie stars to Central American flavor as she continued east into Rampart. She headed north on Alvarado and then onto the little side streets of the hilly Chavez Ravine section of Los Angeles.

With no Dodger game tonight she was able to make it to the academy parking lot without waiting in an endless line of cars or driving in the oncoming lane of traffic. Shea walked through the empty parking lot and up the short steep hill to the women's locker room and changed her clothes. The academy staff and recruits had gone home and the usual cacophony of drill instructors shouting and gun fire at the range was done for the day.

Shea breathed in the smells of evening in Elysian Park. With thousands of eucalyptus trees, the menthol smell didn't just linger in her nose, it permeated her sinuses. As she ran around the field, the aroma of damp dirt and grass brought back memories of hundreds of push-ups, her nose inches away from the ground. She was home.

She pushed herself to sprint the straights of the track, her lungs and legs burning. Ghosts of herself and every other recruit practiced with their batons, sung cadence, and wrestled each other to the wet ground. It was on this field Shea found a since of belonging she never had before. The more rigorous the training, the harder the challenge, the more she more she leaned into it, like bucking a head wind.

After tearing through her last lap she leaned over, hands on her knees trying to catch her breath. Out of the corner of her eye, she noticed a thin man leaning against the chain link fence. Shea strained her eyes to see him in the dark. His hair was too long to be part of the academy staff. He could be an undercover cop or something more sinister. She stood up and took a moment to stretch her quads by pulling her ankle up to her rear end while she assessed him. Ripped jeans, a beat-up leather jacket and Van tennis shoes were an odd combination for a crook.

"You have good form," he said. Shadows hid most of his face, but she walked toward him, keeping an eye on his hands shoved in his pockets. He stood at the opening of the fence leading to locker rooms

"Uh huh." She stalled a moment, putting her hands on her hips and willed herself to calm her breathing.

"I'm not a stalker," he said. "I can tell you're sizing me up." He opened his leather jacket to reveal a badge that caught the light of an overhead street lamp.

"Well, you fit the profile," Shea said. She had no intention of standing around talking to this guy and kept her pace as she approached him.

"I was up in the lounge. Promotional party…" he continued talking. He threw a thumb over his shoulder, referring to the bar above the restaurant and next to the bonus range.

"Congratulations."

"Oh, not for me. My boss made lieutenant." He gave a quick glance towards the bar. "He's an insufferable prick, so I'm sure he'll go far."

Shea chuckled as she approached him. His face was smooth and tan, cheeks gaunt enough to pass for an addict and so handsome she stopped in her tracks. She suddenly felt self-conscious about her hair piled up in a hideous scrunchie and she was sure her mascara was running.

"Where do you work?"

"Internal Affairs." He let a beat pass then laughed. "No, of course not. Narcotics."

"I probably could've guessed that."

"They call my look 'heroin chic,' I'm told," he said. "I used to run five miles a day. Now I probably couldn't run 10 minutes. That's why I was standing out here watching you. Well, that and I'm trying to clear my head before I drive home."

"I was trying to clear my head, too."

"Running does that. I used to be a road guard in the academy."

"Me too," Shea said. Road guards ran with their batons, ahead of rest of the class, to block traffic and then sprint back to join the group on road runs.

"What class were you in?" He pulled a shaggy mess of long blonde hair from his face.

"9-84. How about you?"

"9-94. Wow, I didn't think – "

"I was that old?" Shea said.

"Exactly." He laughed and shrugged. "Somehow that's a

compliment."

"Oh really?"

"Can I buy you a beer?" he asked. "Come on, we're meant to meet. Both road guards, both in September academies. It's Kismet."

"Hmm, I don't think I could refrain from making age jokes. Like right now, I want to ask you if it's past your bedtime."

He surprised her by reaching out to grab her left hand. "You're not married; you can stay out past your bedtime, too."

"What's your name?"

"If I answer correctly, will you let me buy you a beer?" He let her pull her hand from his.

"Oh, you are amusing. Look, I appreciate the offer. We old gals flatter easily. But I'm not going up to the lounge with a bunch of narco guys that I don't know."

"I can see your point. Let me walk you to the locker room." He pushed himself off of the fence and they walked down the hill. She had no intention of having a beer with a stranger, but why had he given up so easily? Maybe she was too old.

"Chad Hanson," he said.

Shea placed her 999 key in the door. She turned and looked

at him. He was only about an inch taller than her and twenty pounds lighter. More reasons for her to feel self-conscious, she thought.

"Shea Reed." She offered her hand. His hand closed in around hers and he held it firmly for a moment.

"Nice to meet you. Can I buy you a Gatorade?"

Shea drew in a deep breath before making a decision against her better judgment.

"If you can wait for me to shower."

Chad stepped away from the building and looked up at the narrow rectangular windows near the door. "Are those the showers?"

"Ah, yes."

"Okay." He leaned against the wall under the window. "I'll wait here."

"You're going to listen to me shower?"

"Won't this make an interesting story for our grandchildren?" He squatted down and began to speak to imaginary child, "and then grandma took off all of her clothes and got into a hot, steamy shower. Grandpa –"

"Okay, okay, I'll see you in a few minutes."

Shea went inside the locker room and sat down next to her

workout bag. She felt the pulse of her carotid artery. It was pounding and not from the run. She hadn't planned on showering at the academy and she had no idea what she would change into. She brought her wrinkled heap of work clothes to her nose and tossed the sour smelling garments back on the floor. She rooted through her duffle bag and found a clean pair of shorts and an old sweatshirt that would have to do. The offer was Gatorade, not wine at the Four Seasons.

She grabbed her travel bag of shampoo and soap and padded to the showers. She knew Chad Hanson couldn't see in through the window, it was about ten feet from the ground. Standing on cold tiles and turning on even colder water, she felt exposed and certainly not alone. She jumped in as soon as it was warm enough to tolerate and quickly shampooed her hair. She thought about him sitting outside as she ran the bar soap across the back of her neck and it slipped out of her hands and skidded across the tiles.

Shea used the hand dryer on the wall to blow her hair nearly dry. She searched through her purse for some make-up, but only found an old tube of a beige-colored lipstick. She slipped into the clean cotton running shorts and soft navy blue sweatshirt. She pulled on her tennis shoes, without socks, and went out the door.

"You're fast," Chad said.

"Okay, listen." She held up her hand in a stop motion. "I'm not wearing makeup, these are the only clean clothes I have, and I haven't brushed my teeth."

"Oh, well, then it's off." He reached over and swiped a bit of soap off of her neck.

"Thank goodness." She tossed her bag over her shoulder and started towards the parking lot.

"Do you want to get a burrito instead of a Gatorade?"

"I do," she said. "If I don't have to get out of the car."

"Right," Chad said. He stopped next to a black El Camino. "My car."

"We're going in your car?" Shea stopped.

"Well, we could go in separate cars. You could follow me to the taco stand. You could wait in the car while I go in and get your order and bring it to you."

"You're going to tell the grandchildren I was weird aren't you?" She tossed her bag into the bed of his El Camino. "Is this a '69?"

"1969 Super Sport." He unlocked her door. "You like old cars?"

"Yes. I have a 1965 Mustang," Shea said.

"Very cool."

"Were you even alive in 1969?" She got in.

"No. I wasn't. But that doesn't mean I don't appreciate things that are older than me." He shut the door on her and she laughed again. She rubbed her temples. What was she doing here? He got in and drove out of Elysian Park into Rampart Division. He pulled into a taco stand near the Shortstop, a cop bar.

"Have you eaten here?" Chad asked.

"Sure. I worked Rampart."

"Okay then, you know what you want?"

"Carne asada burrito and a Diet Coke." She didn't even pretend to reach for her wallet.

"I'll be right back," he said.

Shea watched him get in line. She couldn't wait to tell this story to Jack. He always accused her of not being spontaneous, of always wanting to be in charge. She was definitely being spontaneous tonight and she wasn't in charge, either. Chad returned to the car with their food.

"This's gonna taste so good. I don't eat much. When you're trying to buy dope, it helps if you look like a dope addict." He turned in the seat to face her. Their windows were rolled down; the sounds of the north end of Rampart floated through the car, Ranchero music blared from a nearby car stereo, a baby crying in a stroller while a couple argued, a fire engine siren in the distance. Shea grabbed her Diet Coke from the dashboard and took a long drink.

"Do you like being a UC?" she asked.

"Sometimes. It's kinda cool. Like acting in a play." He handed her a thick burrito.

"It never appealed much to me. What *don't* you like?"

"I hate the fact that I look like a speed-freak off-duty, too. I walk through a store and security follows me." He unwrapped the foil and took a bite of his burrito.

"How long have you been doing this?"

"Too long. I got picked right out of the academy to go into the school buy-bust program, and then I transferred to the adult side. Do you know I was in patrol for just six months and I've been on the job almost three years?" He made three years sound like a long time.

"Are you going to stay in Narco or go to patrol?"

"I don't have enough time on the job to take the detective exam. So I don't know. What do you do?"

"I'm a homicide detective at Valley Division." She bit into her burrito, savoring the sharp tang of fresh cilantro.

"Cool. Do you like doing that?"

"I do. It's hard work. I never watch the clock."

"Did you always want to be a cop?"

"No."

"Me neither. I was an art major. I always wonder about the people who say they always knew they wanted to be a cop. You know the type, the 'Admin of Justice' geeks." Chad took another big bite of his burrito, it was disappearing quickly.

Shea chewed her food and thought about some geeks she knew. She looked up at Chad and almost choked. A black man in a hooded jacket reached through the open window with a pocketknife aimed an eighth of an inch from the side of Chad's throat. Shea dropped her burrito in her lap and reached for her purse on the floorboard. Wedged in a side pocket was her back-up gun. Chad saw the expression on her face or felt the knife, she didn't know which.

He slowly turned back towards his steering wheel.

"Hey motherfucker, don't fucking move, don't move!" The man was giving commands in one long breath. Shea's right hand was sifting through her bag trying to reach her gun, but she stopped when she saw Chad's lift his right index finger from the seat, subtly instructing her not to move. Shea froze.

"Okay, man, no worries," Chad said. His voice was as cool as if he was talking to Shea.

"Give me your motherfuckin' wallet, now." With a hood obscuring nearly all of his face, Shea could only see his mouth was lined with dried white saliva like a rabid dog.

"Okay, okay." Chad leaned up against the steering wheel and reached around with his right arm to get his wallet out of his back pocket. Shea itched to grab her gun and end this dance, but could see by the tilt of Chad's head, the tip of the knife was making contact with his neck. If she wasn't quick enough, the robber would shove the blade into Chad's throat.

In a split second, Chad knocked the knife away with his left hand, grabbed the man by the jacket, and pulled him halfway through the window. With his right hand, he yanked a 9mm from his belt and pressed it hard into the man's forehead.

"How about you give me your motherfuckin' wallet, asshole!" Chad demanded.

"What the –"

"Now!"

The robber's chest was pressed against the door frame as Chad held him in an iron grip. The robber awkwardly moved his free arm behind him to his back pocket, pulled out a worn wallet and delicately flipped it onto the front seat with long, yellowed fingernails. Shea's eyes burned from his sweaty alcohol-soaked stench. Chad released the robber and pushed open the car door. Shea snatched her two-inch revolver out of her purse and flew out of the car. The suspect fell back on his butt, scrambling away from them. In one gymnastic twist of motion, he propelled himself back up and tore off across the parking lot to the busy street. Shea started after him when Chad grabbed her by the tail of her sweatshirt.

"Hold up, hold up," he said. "You may be dressed for the pursuit, but not for the fight."

Shea stopped and tucked her gun in her waistband before anyone noticed.

"Besides, we have his wallet. Someone else'll get him." Chad walked her back to the car. "He was just a junkie, anyhow."

"Are you crazy?" She was pacing next to him. "You almost got robbed! Killed! How're you so calm?"

"Oh, I've had this happen before. Trust me, when you look like me and my dirt bag partner, we're always getting hit up." Chad grinned. He reached inside the car and pulled out the wallet. "Javeen Jones. What kind of name is Javeen?"

"This has happened to you before? Like this? A knife to your throat?" Shea stop pacing and crossed her arms.

"Sure. In fact, we made so much money off of one asshole we went to the racetrack and put it all on a long shot," he said. Shea just stared at him and he started laughing. "No, Shea. I'm kidding about that part."

"You are crazy."

"But when you're Code 5 in a dope neighborhood, sitting there, shit happens." Chad reached under the seat of his car and pulled out his police radio. "I'm gonna get a black-and-white out here."

"Hold on," Shea said. "Before you call anyone, you do

understand this was a   'use-of- force' incident, so a sergeant's going to investigate and your boss is going to be called out."

"So what are you saying?"

"I'm saying we need to talk about how you disarmed him by *robbing* him. That's not an approved technique." What was she doing in Rampart at ten o'clock at night with a crazy undercover cop?

"So we need to get our stories straight? What are we, Bonnie and Clyde?"

"I don't know what your discipline record looks like or how many use-of-force investigations you've been in, but you can't possibly think this's going to be a quick little report. How much have you had to drink? When they talk to your friends, your boss even, back at the lounge, how many beers will they say you've had? Do you see how this could look… ah… reckless, to say the least?"

"When I tell our grandkids how grandma saved my career…"

"Do not joke with me, Chad Hanson, don't make me regret trying to help your sorry ass," Shea said.

"Okay." He took another look at Javeen Jones driver's license.

"Look, I'm not saying we shouldn't report this. I'm just saying we need to eliminate the part where you robbed the robber," Shea said. "We say he 'dropped his wallet in the scuffle.' That's all we change. And somewhere you identify yourself as a police officer."

"Right. I can do that." He held up his radio. "Ready?"

"Yup," Shea said.

Chapter 13

Three hours later, Shea and Chad were driving back to the academy.

"This has been an interesting evening," Chad said.

"To say the least."

"So you knew the sergeant, huh?"

"Sergeant Lange? Yeah, he's been at Rampart for a hundred years," Shea said.

"He asked me if we were dating," Chad said. That didn't surprise her. Lange was always looking for gossip. It would be all over the Department that she was half-dressed in the middle of the night, in Rampart Division, with a scruffy young cop.

"And you said..."

"I told him I didn't think it was any of his fucking business," Chad said. Shea didn't believe him at first, but then she remembered he just robbed a robber, so it was entirely possible.

"But I said it in a nice way." He smiled at her. "I swear it's like high school."

"You would know; you were there not too long ago."

"True," Chad said. He made an abrupt turn heading on a road

leading away from the academy and up a steep hill known to every officer as "Cardiac." He pulled into a turnout overlooking downtown Los Angeles. She knew every inch of Cardiac; she had run it more times than she cared to remember. And now she was parked here. What a turn of events for a woman who had just wanted to go for a simple run a few hours ago.

"I just didn't want to talk in the parking lot," he said. "We didn't get a chance to talk at all tonight."

"No, we didn't. Listen, Chad…I'm sort of involved with someone." She turned to face him. He tilted his head.

"Is that like being a little pregnant?"

"I guess." The LA skyline glittered just over the outlines of the eucalyptus, palm, pine trees, and Dodger Stadium. She took the view for granted on most runs up Cardiac, but tonight she let the city's beauty linger on her mind.

"Do you have a boyfriend?"

"Now, *that* does sound like high school." Shea gave a shallow laugh.

"Wait, are you just not into me or do you have someone else?"

"I don't even know you," Shea said. "How could I say whether I was 'into you' or not?"

"My sister says a woman knows as soon as she looks at a guy how far she will go," Chad said with a smile that said many women went very far with him.

"Well, that's probably true," Shea said. "But I'm involved with someone."

"Is he your boyfriend?"

"What is with you and this 'boyfriend' business?"

"Are you in the CIA? Is he? Why is this so hard to answer?"

"He's married," Shea said. "But he –"

"Okay, okay," Chad said. He held up his hands. "I get it. You just don't strike me as the mistress type."

"I'm not a mistress."

"Semantics."

"I'm not a mistress," Shea repeated. "I don't even know why I told you this. I should've just said I'm in a relationship—with my 'boyfriend.'"

"I'm not judging. I hope it didn't sound that way," he said.

"Oh, don't be sorry. You're entitled to judge. Look at your

first impression of me. I tell you to lie to your boss and I'm having an affair with a married man. That'll be something to tell the grandkids," Shea said.

"You were protecting me by suggesting we not be completely honest with how I disarmed the guy. That's experience talking, not morality. As for the affair, well you must be in love; and man, people compromise all kinds of principles when they want someone," Chad said.

"Did you learn that on MTV?" Shea asked. He laughed and touched her knee with one of his long fingers.

"An *After School Special*," he said. She reached for his hand.

They were quiet for a moment, looking at the city they had sworn to protect. She drew a deep breath before she started talking again.

"When you work homicide, you're constantly exposed to the rotten things humans do to each other. It's the same with working sex crimes, but worse. I guess your own morals can get a little dubious. I mean, an affair's certainly not in the same league as the coward who lets his brother take the rap for a murder he committed. Or the wife who sleeps with her husband, knowing she's going to poison him. When you work in a barnyard, you're get mud on your shoes," she said.

"You have completely lost me. Is the affair because you love him or because you work on a farm?" Chad said and she laughed again.

She looked at his eyes and studied them in the dark. Greenish blue, with yellow bursts spraying out from the pupils, they reminded her of sunshine and water.

"I've laughed more tonight then I have in ages."

"You've got a serious job, a serious relationship, and I watched you run—you take yourself pretty seriously, too." Chad brushed her hair over her shoulder and Shea tried to think of something to say, but her mind went blank. Chad leaned in and kissed her lightly on the lips.

His hands were on her cheeks and then he slipped them down to her neck. She hadn't responded, but she didn't resist either. She closed her eyes. If she was going to do this with a stranger, she might as well do it right. Shea pulled Chad's head to her and kissed him hard on the lips.

Shea ran her hand through his hair, it took her back to high school boys wearing pukka shell necklaces, smelling like pot and tasting like beer. These days she was used to crisp haircuts or crew cuts. She gripped his silky hair as he opened his mouth to hers. His tongue met hers, leaving her breathing hard and causing the windows to steam up.

Chad slid his hand in the back of her shorts waistband, and she remembered she had forgone underwear because she didn't have a clean pair in her bag. He removed her gun from the front of her shorts and put it on the floorboard. In one quick movement he deftly lifted her up by the small of the back and pulled her underneath him. Her tennis-shoed feet were wedged between the backseat and the window. Chad lowered himself between her legs and she could feel his soft jeans rubbing against her bare legs.

"Oh, Chad we can't do this. What if we get robbed again and we're naked?"

"I'm not taking any clothes off," he whispered.

"I don't want a one-night stand. And I definitely don't want one in a car."

"We're not having a one-night stand." He kissed her neck and her hips rolled up to meet his. She ran her hand over his hips to his erection and she gasped a little. Long, like his fingers. She held him tightly and he returned her gasp.

"We're not going all the way…" Shea cautioned. His fingers were slipping into the leg of her shorts.

"Third base." Chad licked her ear as he slipped his fingers inside of her.

A white beam of light illuminated the cab of the El Camino and Chad withdrew his wet hand as Shea scrambled to sit up, pulling down her shirt. Without looking out the rear window, she knew they had been lit up by Northeast Division patrol officers.

"You've got to be fucking kidding me!" Chad rolled down his window and searched for his badge. It had fallen to the floorboard. Shea grabbed it and handed it to him as they heard the driver officer open his patrol car door. Chad held his badge out of the window.

"Whoa. Sorry, buddy—Code 4," the driver officer said. He got back in the car and drove away. Shea and Chad sat in stunned silence for a minute and then they both started to laugh.

"I have to go home Chad," she said. "A robbery and a heavy make-out session busted up by the po-lice; it's time to call it a night."

Chad started the engine and headed back down the hill.

"Why did I think we wouldn't be bothered here? It's like making out on an ant hill." Chad grabbed her hand and held it all the way back to her car.

"Thank you for an interesting evening," Shea said.

"Can I call you?"

"My situation...I just can't think about dating..."

"Let me worry about that part. Can I get you to commit to pursuing a friendship?" Chad asked. He popped open his glove box and took out a pen, "Come on, Bonnie...give Clyde your number."

Shea laughed. She gave him the number at her desk.

"Really? Valley Dicks? I coulda looked that one up on my own."

"It's a start, Clyde."

As she reached for her car door, he jumped out and ran around the car and took her car keys from her hand and unlocked her car door. After he completed his gentlemanly duties he pulled her to him and hugged her tightly. She buried her head in his neck.

"I don't even know you, and you almost got killed in front of me."

"I know."

"And I don't even know you but I almost had sex with you."

"No, we wouldn't've had sex, not in a car. But I can't wait to have sex with you, Shea."

"Friends—just friends." Shea pulled away.

"Exactly." He kissed her. "Thank you for saving my ass tonight. My only regret is that now I won't be able to brag about my reverse robbery with Javeen."

"Only I will know what a crazy idiot you are," Shea said with a smile. "I have to go home."

The next morning she came into work grinning like the Cheshire cat. She decided to devote her morning to the photocopying another murder book for the district attorney and defense attorney. It was a tedious job, pulling each property report, interview, and miscellaneous scrap of paper out of the binder and feeding it into the copy machine. But it was the right task for a daydreamer. As she placed pieces of paper under the lid of the machine she thought of Chad's lean body in between her legs.

"Do you mind if I get in here? I just need to make one copy."

Shea wondered how long the sex crimes detective had been standing next to her.

"Oh, yeah." Shea moved her book and papers off the copy machine to accommodate the older woman.

"How are things going?"

"Real good. How about you?"

"Fine. I just got a seventy-five year sentence on a rapist."

"Good for you. I had a murder that was pled down to voluntary manslaughter; the guy'll be out in less than seven years. Isn't it ridiculous?" Shea wandered away from the woman, who was making more than one copy.

She went through the homicide unit's mail slot and found a gray intradepartmental envelope addressed to her, unraveling the thin cord securing the envelope she found the computer printout from Communications Division of all the radio calls in a 48-hour period before the Ornelas OIS.

"It's all yours," the woman called over to Shea. Shea barely acknowledged her and returned to the copy machine. As she made her copies she picked through the printout for calls that caught her interest—violent crimes where the suspect description was a Hispanic male.

Curt interrupted her to tell her that she had a call. She grabbed all of her papers and notebook and hustled back to her desk. She cradled her phone between her shoulder and her ear as she tried to straighten out her piles of papers.

"Detective Reed."

"It's me." *Me* was Andrew Thorpe.

"Hi," Shea said. "Listen, I'm in the middle of something. Can we talk later?"

"That was why I was calling. Can I take you to dinner tonight?" Andrew said.

"Yes, where?"

"Well, I was hoping you'd say Domino's pizza at your house." He chuckled. She didn't respond. "Okay, how about I pick you up at your house at six and I surprise you?"

"Sounds good. I have to go." Shea hung up the phone.

Shea spent the rest of the day researching the radio calls until she narrowed it down to two calls that occurred prior to the shooting: a robbery in West Valley that occurred an hour before the shooting, and a rape that happened the day before in Foothill Division. Each case described a suspect as a thin, male Hispanic, possibly a gang member.

She talked to a robbery detective in West Valley and found out they had made an arrest in that case. She drew a line through that one.

The rape was reported on the morning of the shooting, but it occurred the night before. The suspect description matched what Ornelas described and Shea knew sex offenders could be counted on to defy logic. Shea called up to Foothill Division and waited on hold for a sex detective to come to the phone. After six minutes on hold, she hung up and dialed again. This time the phone rang continuously. Shea hung up in frustration and tried a different phone number for general detectives, but again no answer.

Shea got up from her desk and walked across the squad room to the sex unit, where she found the female detective she had talked to at the copy machine.

"Do you have a phone number for sex detectives at Foothill? No one's picking up on their main number and when I did get through, I just sat on hold," Shea said. The woman flipped through her rolodex and wrote down a number on a pink message note for Shea.

"Good luck. They're real busy over there."

Shea thanked her and went back to her desk and tried again. This time a hurried voice barked out a salutation and a name.

"I'm sorry, I didn't catch your name," Shea said.

"Ellingsworth," the woman said.

"I'm Shea Reed. I'm working homicide at--"

"Good for you, how can I help you?" The woman said. "I'm really busy."

"I can appreciate that, I'm busy too. I'm calling about a rape you folks had back in October of last year, it occurred on--"

"Do you have a DR number?"

"No, I just have a print-out of calls from communications, let me see if there's a PR in the comments here…" Shea said.

"I can't do a hand search for you right now, I have a victim sitting in an interview room, I have an arrestee in a holding tank and it's just me and my boss today," Ellingsworth said.

"Do you think I could drive over and look myself?"

"Sure. I probably won't be here, but my boss will be,"

Ellingsworth said. "He can direct you to the cabinet where we keep our old books."

"Thanks," Shea said, but the line went dead.

Shea drove to Foothill Division. It took her over an hour to locate the PIR, Preliminary Incident Report. The rape was assigned to the busy Detective Ellingsworth, who was nowhere to be found. Shea sat at an empty desk to read the report and Ellingsworth's notes.

The victim was an eighth grade teacher, abducted in the parking lot of the junior high after coaching a basketball game. The report listed two suspects. The suspects directed her to drive her car, at gunpoint, to the nearest ATM, where they forced her to withdraw three hundred dollars.

The suspects forced her to drive into the bowels of the Hansen Dam basin, where they took turns raping and sodomizing her. One suspect was described as tall and thin, about twenty years old, with a shaved head. There was no mention of tattoos. The second suspect was described as younger, with a tattoo on his right knuckles of the word "fuck." The tall suspect was armed. He made the victim place the barrel in her mouth and pretend to suck on it.

The suspects stole the victim's car and purse and left her in the basin. It took her several hours to find her way out. She finally flagged down a car and the Good Samaritan drove her to the hospital. It was not clear why the report was not made until the following day. Shea looked over the medical reports briefly. The woman had suffered numerous tears to her vagina and anus, and several soft tissue injuries to her face and arms.

Detective Ellingsworth showed the victim numerous photos of sex offenders and gang members, but the victim hadn't identified anyone. Ellingsworth carefully documented all of her work on the case in daily entries in her investigation log. The suspect had used the ATM card the next day at 10:00 a.m. at a bank just blocks away from where the OIS occurred.

Shea excitedly searched through the documents until she found the ATM surveillance photos Detective Ellingsworth had ordered. They were grainy, but enlarged and enhanced as possible. Shea saw the tall thin suspect, in a white undershirt, the kind that Officer Ornelas referred to as a "wife-beater." He had a blurry tattoo on his upper right arm and he was bald.

Shea fell back in the chair. She had found the suspect. He

shot at the police because he had just used the victim's ATM card and probably had the victim's purse sitting next to him in the car.

A female detective hurried down the aisle of crowded desks and dumped a bag of clothing on the desk across from where Shea was sitting. The woman's suit was mismatched, the blazer was a dark navy, but her pants were black.

"You must be who I talked to on the phone," the woman said. "I'm sorry I was rude. I'm Ellingsworth."

"Shea Reed. I was just looking through this case." Shea showed her the initial report.

"Oh yeah. I never solved that one."

"It's never too late," Shea said. She wanted to add there was no expiration dates on solving crimes.

"It's too late when you have a thousand more and no help," Detective Ellingsworth said.

"Well, this guy--" Shea held up a picture of the ATM surveillance photo, "I think he shot an officer's ear off in my division just a few minutes after he used your victim's ATM card."

"You're kidding me. I never heard anything about the cases being related."

"I just figured it out two minutes ago," Shea said.

"Oh crap. Now you're going to take a hard look at my investigation. Let me just say in advance, I haven't had a partner for seven months and I can barely keep my head above water here." Detective Ellingsworth looked miserable.

"I've been there. I worked sex in Hollywood," Shea said.

Detective Ellingsworth smiled a tight smile for the first time. Her lipstick had worn off, leaving only a faint red outline on the edges.

"Do you remember anything about this case?"

Detective Ellingsworth took her notes and looked them over. "Let's see, the suspects weren't in the database because I had the fluids analyzed and submitted. They were definitely gangsters…let's see…"

"You know what I'm thinking? He used an ATM in my division the next day. He might have been from a gang there. I noticed you showed the victim gang photos from Foothill gangs."

"Yeah, I did. I should've showed her pictures from your division, too. That's a good point."

"Wait, listen – I'm not critiquing your work, I promise. I'm trying to see where we can go next. Does a burgundy Buick mean anything to you?"

"No, from the OIS right? No. There were no wits to her abduction. They had to have driven to the school or walked. If they walked then they're local guys."

"Did you have any similars?"

"A fourteen-year-old was kidnapped a month later from the south end of the division. They put a hood on her head and she couldn't ID anyone, ever," Detective Ellingsworth said with a familiar sigh. "I think it might be the same guys though. Just because of the order of the sex acts. She thought they were Hispanic."

"I'm going back to my division and check with my sex people. Maybe they hit there too and we can piece something together," Shea said. "Can I make copies of a few things?"

"Sure." Detective Ellingsworth handed the papers back to Shea. "That OIS is the one where the female officer was murdered at your Christmas party, right?"

"Yes," Shea said. "Where's the copy machine?"

"We just got a new one, you're in luck. The last one was broken more than it ran."

Detective Ellingsworth led her to a very modern machine that looked like it could launch a rocket. She could lay 25 rounds down-range in the ten ring of a target, but FAX machines and copy machines baffled her.

"Push this button here. I gotta go book those clothes. Stay in touch," Detective Ellingsworth said.

As soon as Shea returned to the station, she grabbed Vaughn at the coffee machine and dragged him back to his desk.

"What? What?"

Shea plopped down copies of the surveillance photos on his desk and told him about her leads. She reminded him of Sean Ornelas' description and the location of the bank.

"Holy shit," Vaughn whispered. Usually he was subdued about any good work Shea did. He didn't want her to get a big head. There was no chance of that in this unit. The insults and sarcasm outweighed the compliments two-to-one.

"Shea, this is gonna be the guy!"

"I know. The bad news is I don't have him identified." She sat down at her desk and rifled through her messages.

"He shot Ornelas because he had just used the ATM with the

victim's card."

"And probably had her purse with him. And he's a crazy fucker. Wait until you read the rape PIR. I'm going to see if our sex unit had any similars. Maybe we have something with some clues on it," Shea said.

"He looks like a gangster-hype."

"Yeah. Now you've got a photo to show your snitches. You might be able to get this ID'd sooner than you think."

"This is a shitty picture, but I'll give it a try," Vaughn said. Curt came out of the lieutenant's office and lingered at Vaughn's desk. Vaughn and Shea filled him in on her investigation.

"That's promising," Curt said.

"Hey, I want credit if I solve this attempt 187," Shea said. As soon as the words left her mouth she knew she set herself up.

"Okay, when you're done solving someone else's OIS, do you think you can solve a murder while you're at it?" Now *that* attitude she recognized. "When Jack's away you just run amok."

Vaughn took the picture and headed out to talk to his informants. Shea went across the squad room to check with the sex detectives, but discovered everyone had gone home. She looked up at the clock, it was already after five. She realized she needed to get home if she was going to be there when Andrew arrived. She went back to her desk and told Curt that she was end-of-watch.

Andrew's car was in the driveway and he was leaning against the driver's door talking to her sister. Shannon arms were crossed and she was nodding enthusiastically. Shannon and Andrew had met before, but since his visits were usually in the middle of the night, on his way home from a call-out, their paths rarely crossed.

"Hi, I'm sorry I'm late. The traffic was horrible on the Canyon coming home." Shea was ready to interrupt whatever they were talking about.

"I didn't know William Shea was your godfather." Andrew looked at her as if she had a warrant for her arrest.

"Well, he's not *my* godfather." Shea gave her sister a dirty look.

"Namesake," Shannon said. "He's actually my godfather. She's his namesake."

"How in the world does *that* come up in conversation, Shannon?"

"Because William just left here. He and Dad came over and we all went to lunch today," Shannon said.

"You met them?" She turned to Andrew.

"No. I was driving in when they were pulling out. Of course I recognized William Shea," he said.

"Dad was hoping you'd be home," Shannon said.

"I need to change." Shea brushed past her sister and hustled toward the stone steps that led down to her apartment.

"Where are you guys going?" Shannon asked Andrew.

"I thought I'd surprise your sister with a fancy dinner. Would you like to join us?" Andrew said.

"Oh, no. Big lunch and lots of wine." Shannon was giggly and unstable on her feet. Andrew caught up with Shea at her apartment.

"It's a mess." Shea unlocked her door. Her bed was unmade. The clothes from last night were in a pile on the floor. As she scooped them up and tossed them in the hamper, she remembered for the first time in several hours her crazy night at the police academy.

"Hey, how come you never told me about William Shea?" Andrew moved a stack of novels from her only chair, a wingback she found at a secondhand store in Hollywood. He sat down and watched as she tidying up.

"Why would I?"

"It's a funny thing to keep to yourself. He's notorious."

Shea ignored him and pulled the covers up on her bed and arranged the pillows.

"Is he as big an asshole as he seems?" Andrew asked.

"Yes."

"He's best friends with your dad?"

"Yes."

"Well, that must make family dinners interesting."

"We don't have family dinners." Shea sat down on her bed.

"Did you see that press conference when he held up the picture of his client in a little league uniform, the asshole who killed the Southeast officer, and then he said –"

"Yes, Andrew, I know. This is exactly why I don't talk about it."

"I'm sorry," Andrew said. "It must be hard."

"What should I change into?"

"You look beautiful exactly the way you are. Are you

hungry?"

"I'm starving." She couldn't remember when she last ate. Andrew got up and moved over to her bed. He put his arm around her.

"Let's go, okay?" Shea jumped up.

Shea knew Andrew wouldn't want to waste what little time they had together driving somewhere for a meal. Before she knew it they were at sitting across from each other in a dimly lit restaurant.

"God, I still can't get over that you never told me about William Shea." Andrew shook his head as if he was pondering a great mystery. He opened his menu, maddening Shea by continuing the contemplative head shaking.

"And I can't get over you still being married, so we're even," Shea said.

"Ow, touché."

The waitress approached and he ordered an expensive bottle of merlot.

"The seafood's incredible."

"You've been here? Don't tell me you're taking me to a romantic restaurant you went to with your wife." Shea shut her menu.

"I've been here. And it was with Cathleen and two other couples. And all I could think about was that I wanted to take you here. I know you love lobster and that's what I ordered, and that's *why* I ordered it."

Shea stared at him. She pictured him with his arm around his wife, chatting with the other couples in one of the large booths they had passed on their way to their table. Shea wanted to believe that Andrew and Cathleen were miserable, their only shared activity being the counseling that was supposed to not be working. But here was another nugget of Andrew's life—socializing with other couples. It didn't sound like a couple on the brink of divorce.

The waitress returned with the wine and asked if they were ready to order. Shea ordered steak.

"You're going to be sorry you didn't order the lobster," Andrew said. He ordered lobster for himself. After the waitress left, he told Shea that he would switch with her if she changed her mind.

"How's the counseling going?"

"Shea." Andrew put an elbow on the table and rubbed his eye. "Let's not do this tonight."

"Do what? Let's not talk?"

"Let's not fight," Andrew said tiredly.

"I'm not fighting. We haven't discussed this topic since Christmas. That's almost five months since the last update on your life."

"Yes," Andrew said.

"So, how's the plan working? Have you convinced her that you've tried everything and nothing's working, so you'll have to divorce?" Shea took a long drink of her merlot. It was delicate and almost evaporated in her mouth.

"She's getting the message, but she's insistent on working on it and she's trying…" Andrew said. He made it sound like she was studying for an exam.

"What if I dated someone else?" Shea balanced the ridiculously large goblet with her fingertips.

"Where's this coming from?" Andrew asked. "Are you trying to get back at me?"

"Well, this waiting for you is bordering on ridiculous." She enjoyed watching Andrew's look of confusion.

"Is there someone in particular?" Andrew said. The waitress

brought their salads and they sat silently as the waitress peppered their lettuce.

"I think I'll keep that information to myself for right now," Shea said.

"I can't tell you what to do, can I?" Andrew said casually. His surprise had worn off and he was back to not revealing his hand.

"That's what I was thinking."

"I'll just tell you that I love you, Shea." Andrew took a sip of his wine. "I'm doing the best I can to get out of my marriage. I'm not purposely screwing with you."

"I'm not purposely screwing with you," Shea said.

"Yes, you are. You're pissed and I don't blame you. But I wish you wouldn't have a revenge fuck with someone just to get back at me." His brown eyes were on fire, but his face was expressionless.

"Have you had sex with your wife in the last five months?" Shea watched him intently, waiting for a reveal somewhere on his face. He fumbled with his fork and finally put it down.

"What has gotten into you?" Andrew said.

"You're stalling."

"If I say yes, you'll use it to justify fucking someone else."

"And if you say no, you'll be lying." Shea drank her wine.

"What do you want me to say?" Andrew picked his fork back up. "Fuck whoever you want and we'll call it even." He was angry.

"Date. I never said fuck."

"Fine. Date. The next dinner we have, I'll ask you if you're fucking the guy you're dating."

They ate in silence for several minutes; the only sound at their table was of forks hitting the plates. Shea took a long drink of her wine before speaking.

"I just think this thing between us…it's run its course."

"I don't think it has."

After the meal they waited outside for the valet to get Andrew's car. He pulled her to him, his arm tight around her waist. She rested her head on his shoulder, waiting for him to say something, but he remained silent.

Chapter 14

Shea got to work early the next morning and went directly to the sex crimes unit. She asked the supervisor if he knew about any cases related to the Foothill rapes. He was tying his tie as he listened to her describe the incidents.

"What does this have to do with murders?"

"We might have a suspect in common," Shea said.

"I'll look through our books and get back to you," he said.

"Ah, if you're busy, I can do it," Shea offered.

"No, I've got nothing better to do then help out homicide." He said it with a smile, but Shea could hear the sarcasm in his voice. Shea thanked him and went to her desk. She had arrived before the rest of her unit. She was rereading Ellingsworth's follow up report when her phone rang.

"Hey, you're there early." She was pretty sure of the voice, but not enough to say his name.

"Early bird, worms...you've heard the story."

"It's just the opposite for dope. They're all late birds." Now she was sure it was Chad Hanson.

"So, are you just getting off work then?"

"Not too long ago. I caught a nap in the cot room; I've got downtown court this morning," he said.

"That makes for a long day," Shea said. Why was she nervous?

"So, by waiting a day to call you, have I proven I'm not a desperate stalker?"

"I just sat by my phone all day like a sophomore hoping to get asked to the prom," Shea said.

"I don't believe you. You were out there busting murderers and dodging death," Chad said. "I picture you like Heather Locklear on T.J. Hooker."

"Did your babysitter used to let you stay up late to watch that show?"

"Actually, she did. My favorite part was when Heather throws her baton at the fleeing suspect in the opening credits."

"You're very peculiar."

"Do you want to come over to my house this weekend?"

"This weekend? How about narrowing down to a day?" Shea flipped through her desk calendar to the weekend. She wasn't on call.

"How about you come over on Saturday morning and if you're having a good time you stay until Sunday?"

"I thought we're going to go slow and get to know each other—be friends and all of that stuff," Shea said.

"Look at all we packed into a few hours. We're a lot further down the road then most people."

"Where do you live?"

"Venice. I'm right on the beach. My roommate's going to be out of town this weekend."

"I'm going to say yes, but --"

"No pressure, I promise. Or leave your overnight bag in the trunk of your car. We can just kick back and get to know each other. And I won't even kiss you. Unless you ask me to, okay?"

"Give me your address." Shea pulled a pen from an old coffee mug on her desk. He gave her the address and directions.

"I'll see you on Saturday morning?"

Shea wondered why he hadn't invited her for Friday night…probably had a date.

"Yes, I'll be there," she said and hung up. She couldn't find her way back to her paperwork after the phone call. She felt silly and giddy, and she couldn't remember when she last felt that way. This spontaneity stuff was hard to get used to.

"Earth to Shea." Vaughn waved his hand in front of her face.

"Good morning. Anything from your informants last night?"

"My main guy says he thinks he's seen the suspect before. He thinks he's a Roland Street Loco."

"They haven't been active for months," Shea said.

"I know. I was going to talk to the gang officers this morning. They weren't working last night and of course their trailer is locked. Super security. But I've got court this morning, so it'll have to wait." Vaughn was going through his briefcase as he talked to Shea.

"I can do it."

"Aren't you the eager beaver?" He handed her back the Ornelas OIS notebook.

"All I have to do today is serve some subpoenas and drop some discovery off at the DA's office," Shea said.

"I can drop that off for you. Which DA?"

"Mitzer," Shea said.

"You have a murder trial with Mitzer? Good luck, she's a bitch," Vaughn said.

"She likes Jack."

"*Everyone* likes Jack," Vaughn said. He shut his briefcase and put it under his desk

"I know, it's annoying," Shea said. "Did you find out when the gang unit is coming in today?"

"Noon. Or at least that's what the schedule in the lieutenant's office says."

Curt came in the back door carrying his LA Times under his arm and 7-11 extra-large coffee cup in the other hand.

"Good morning troops," Curt said. "Please remember there's a squad meeting this morning at eight."

"I've got court," Vaughn said.

"I've got court," Shea repeated.

"I sincerely don't give a shit. It's mandatory and you people are becoming notorious for your absences. Court doesn't cut it, because everyone knows you don't have to be there until 9:30, and don't tell me you have wits to pick up." Curt dropped his newspaper on his desk.

"Seriously, I do have to pick up two wits." Vaughn turned in his chair to face their boss.

"One day I hope you both promote to D3 and you have to supervise a God-damned homicide unit. A bunch of prima donnas and I have to hear about it constantly." Curt put his briefcase under his desk and sat down in a huff. Shea couldn't tell if he was kidding or not.

"Professional jealousy," Vaughn said.

"Not only do you manage to avoid squad meetings, you managed three times in a row to weasel out of supervisor meetings; why we made you a D2, I'll never know." Curt never chewed out Vaughn. Shea knew she would be next. She picked up her phone and began to dial.

"Don't try to squirm away – you're the worst of them all," Curt said.

"Worst?"

"You could be nicer to your colleagues. How was it worded to me?" He looked up at the ceiling before continuing, "Oh yeah, 'she never bothers to say hello or talk to anyone from another table unless she wants something.'"

"Well. What a delicate group of cops we work with," Shea said.

"Any complaints about Jack?" Vaughn asked.

"None," Curt said.

"Everyone likes Jack," Shea and Vaughn said at the same time.

"I'm glad you two find this amusing. You both are going to the squad meeting. Vaughn, you can leave at 8:30. Keep in mind that your colleagues are under the impression that you folks think you breathe rarified air, get all the overtime, and can get out of meetings."

Shea thought about who might've told him that she wasn't friendly, but it was a long suspect list. She didn't have time to linger over pictures from some detectives' vacation to the Colorado River. She didn't much care who was pregnant, and when birthday cards floated around the squad room she usually signed her name and passed them on—not even looking at who the card was for. Just like the silly decorations for every holiday from Valentine's Day to Thanksgiving; she had little patience for small talk and banal Department gossip.

The detective squad meeting was held in the patrol roll-call room. Like a slow-moving herd of cattle, detectives moseyed down the hall, holding coffee cups and griping about having to attend another meeting. Curt sat up in front with the sex crimes supervisor and the robbery supervisor. Shea found a seat in the back next to a nice guy from the burglary table. Vaughn, anticipating his early departure, leaned against the wall near the door.

The lieutenant directed a sergeant to pass out copies of a list of topics he hoped to cover this morning. Shea looked at her copy. No wonder she always tried to miss these meetings. They were the same topics from the last meeting she attended. Overtime issues, parking issues, upcoming orals for a detective II spot. They watched a mandatory film on the proper disposal of motor oil and the sanctity of storm drains in the City of Los Angeles. When the meeting was over, Shea hurried back to her desk and studied the reports she had gathered.

At noon Shea walked across the parking lot to a long, single-wide trailer that housed the gang and vice units. Like nearly every LAPD station, Valley Division was outdated and too small. The parking lot looked like a carnie camp. Tuff Sheds held bicycles for the Bike squad, and cargo containers housed thousands of police

reports stored in boxes until they made their way downtown.

The inside of the trailer was as bad as the exterior.

Mismatched tables, desks and chairs made up the workspace, and

tin-looking file cabinets lined the walls. The gang officers hadn't

changed into their uniforms yet. They were eating fast-food tacos

and burritos and having a loose meeting. The sergeant stopped

talking when Shea walked in.

"Can we help you, Shea?"

Shea liked Hubert Jackson. She asked him once why he went

by Hubert and not a nickname. He proudly told the story of his

grandfather and namesake, a famous jazz musician who pulled

several patrons out of a burning nightclub in the 1940's. Shea wished

she had a namesake to be proud of.

"I'm looking for some information on the Roland Street

Locos." Shea leaned over one of her favorite officer's shoulders and

swiped one of his nachos.

"Really? They've been quiet. Who has RSL?" Sergeant

Jackson asked. Each gang officer had several gangs he was

responsible for—gathering and filing intelligence, documenting graffiti, keeping car files and interviewing members.

"It's me." Hector Gomez raised his hand and shoved the last bit of burrito into his mouth. Shea remembered Hector was the officer who befriended Chloe, telling her about Jake Cameron taking the obscene pictures.

"I just need to look through your files," Shea said.

Hector had a teddy bear demeanor, but Shea knew he could take care of business. His soft voice and easy mannerisms helped him get information from gang members, but she had seen him break the leg of a suspect who failed to heed his warnings to drop a lead pipe. Hector had served him with a power stroke of his baton and the man's leg turned into a 'Z' as he fell to the ground.

"RSL's are in the last cabinet. I'll be right there." He pointed to the back of the trailer.

Shea walked past their "Valley's Most Wanted" wall of suspects, mostly Hispanic and black. The White supremacist gangs had a foothold further west. She pulled out a file drawer and flipped through gang names until she found the Roland Street Locos. She took the identification cards for the gang and sat down at an empty desk in the back of the room. Hector joined her with his extra-large soda.

"Murder suspect?"

"No, actually the suspect in the Ornelas OIS." Shea opened her folder and pulled out the ATM surveillance photo of the suspect.

"Chloe's shooting?" Hector asked.

"Yup." She spun the photo around the desk to face Hector. He picked it up and studied it.

"Have you ever seen him before?" Shea said.

"You know, Chloe came back here not long after the shooting, wanting to know about Roland Street."

"Why?"

"I'm trying to remember. She really wanted to get in the unit, so she was always trying to do gang intel." Hector looked over Shea's head at the wall, thinking about something.

"We went through all our intel on cars, looking for a Buick, she was always asking about Buicks." He tapped his fingers on the picture. "This guy…is this the only picture you have?"

"I've got a close up of the tattoo, but it's pretty blurry." She handed him a close up of the right arm. "I talked to Ornelas and he remembered a tattoo. And a white wife-beater shirt, skinny, bald.

The guy in the picture was using his rape victim's ATM at the Wells Fargo—just down the street from the OIS—about ten minutes before he's pulled over."

"That's why he shoots at them," Hector said.

"That's what I think happened. There's a second suspect with him on that rape. Hispanic, short, and the letters f-u-c-k on his right knuckles."

"Fuck!" Hector cried. "Jimmy, where's that FI from Saturday night, the guy with 'fuck' on his hand?"

Officer Jimmy Mora hauled his 6'3" frame out of his seat and ambled over to an in-box on the Sergeant Jackson's desk.

"You got something?" Jimmy looked through the paperwork in the in-box. That was the way of cops, when one guy got excited, the other became subdued. Jimmy wasn't going to let on he might be intrigued.

"Maybe." Hector turned back to Shea. "Saturday Jimmy stopped a bunch of wannabee's near Foothill border. Youngsters. One of them had f-u-c-k on his hand."

"That would be--"

"Wait! That's it. Chloe was talking to a girl. She really

wasn't a snitch, but a runaway that Chloe had found, but let her stay with the girl's aunt or something…instead of returning her to her parents…she was working her up as a baby snitch, I think. Chloe said the girl was going to try to find out what she could about the shooting, and I saw Chloe at the gas pumps….when? I think it was a week before the Christmas party. The girl told her she thought it was RSL, but I told Chloe that didn't sound right because they're not active and they're just a bunch of taggers."

"Did you tell Vaughn or did Chloe tell Vaughn?"

"I didn't, I don't know if she did. She was always back here with a theory on it. I mean she was obsessed. She wanted the guy bad and I know she thought it'd look good and help get her in the unit at the same time."

"She was working her own investigation?"

"I think so."

"Okay, I got it." Jimmy was holding several field investigation cards in his hands. The rest of the unit got up and followed him back to Shea and Hector.

"What's going on?" Sergeant Jackson said.

"Well, maybe something good," Shea said. Hector took the

FI's from Jimmy and showed Shea. She read over the description.

"Oh, it's on his left hand," Shea said to Hector.

"The 'fuck' tattoo?" Jimmy looked at his partner, Dan Telles.

"It was on his right hand," Dan said.

"You wrote left," Shea told Jimmy.

"I did? It was definitely the right hand," Jimmy said.

"Okay, I've had to tell this to my four-year-old, when you look at your left hand, the thumb and index finger makes an "L" and that's how you know which is which," Dan said. Jimmy gave Dan a quick flick of his middle finger.

"What gang did they claim?" Shea said.

"They didn't claim any and they didn't have any gang tattoos. They were in Valley Players territory, but it borders RSL and Latin Kings. The "fuck" guy was only fifteen. We thought they were taggers or wannabee's. Nobody had warrants or a rap sheet. We got Polaroid's on them all."

"Do you recognize this guy?" Hector handed Jimmy the picture of the suspect at the ATM and the rest of the officers peered looked over his shoulders to get a look.

"Is this a murder suspect, Shea?" Sergeant Jackson said.

"No, Hubert, he's the guy who shot Ornelas." Shea went on to tell the unit what she had learned and asked them to keep it confidential.

"I don't recognize him." Jimmy handed the picture to Dan.

Shea looked through the other FI's, but none of the young men met the suspect's description. She went back to the first suspect with the tattoo on his right hand.

"Edgar Padilla." She read off the address.

"That's a group home," Sergeant Jackson said.

"I'm going to go talk to him. Hubert, I don't have a partner. Jack's wife just had their baby..." She was interrupted by the guys telling her to wish Jack congratulations. "Do you think I can borrow Hector? Are you busy?"

Hector shook his head but looked up at his boss.

"You can take him. Whatever we can do to help, Shea. It's always bothered me that the shooting just kind of went by the wayside," Sergeant Jackson said.

"Do you want me in uniform?" Hector stood up.

"Do you need another unit, in case this guy rabbits?" Jimmy asked.

"I would prefer to do this as low key as possible, so no uniform, if that's okay with Hubert," Shea said. "If you guys just want to follow us over and lay off, that would be good."

"A vest and a raid jacket, okay?" Hubert asked Shea. "Take Jimmy and Dan with you."

The officers grabbed their vests and their raid jackets, and hurried to their cars. Hector rode with Shea to the group home.

"I'm just pissed at myself that I didn't take Chloe seriously. I should've helped her," Hector gnawed on the side of his finger tip.

"From what I understand you did help her in other ways."

"It was bad. Chloe was a nice girl and Cameron was a pig. He used her." Hector began tapping his knuckles on the door handle.

"It sounds like it."

"It screwed her up big time. She just seemed to not care after that."

"She did care about work. She was looking for the shooter," Shea said.

"Yeah, she was always straight up when it came to work, but you know she wouldn't have gotten into gangs no matter how hard she worked. Hubert said the lieutenant and captain thought she had a promiscuous reputation and that'd be trouble in a unit full of men."

"Well, I guess that could be trouble in a department full of men, too," Shea said. She checked her rearview mirror and noted that Jimmy and Dan were behind them.

"It's funny, because we gotta lot of promiscuous men in my unit. That never seemed to bother anyone."

Shea parked her car a few houses down from the correct address. Jimmy told him over the radio that they'd wait in the alley behind the location.

"I'm not going to make an arrest for rape today, unless the idiot confesses. All I want to do is get a better picture of him, so I can put it in a six-pack and show it to the victim," Shea said, referring to the photo line-up folder with six squares to place pictures in it. "So let's play it by ear, maybe just talk to him about gang stuff."

"Right on." Hector followed Shea to the door.

The front lawn was non-existent. Dirty cars, in all stages of disrepair, were strewn in the driveway and yard. Shea knocked on the steel security door with the small flashlight on her key chain. A large black woman came to the door, but didn't open it for them.

Shea could hear a television droning in the background and the sound of a phone ringing somewhere deep in the house.

"Good afternoon, ma'am. I'm Detective Reed, can we come in?"

"Why?" Shea could barely make out the woman's shape behind the door. This placed them in a huge tactical disadvantage.

"I'd rather discuss this inside your house than out here where your neighbors can see," Shea said, trying to sound pleasant.

"I don't care what my neighbors see."

"What's your name?" Shea opened her notebook and began to write.

"Mary Jones."

"Ms. Jones, I have a cellular telephone." Shea pulled her phone out of her blazer pocket; she held it up for the woman to see. "I have the Department of Children's Services on speed dial. If you don't open this door, I'll make a call and explain that you're denying law enforcement access to your county-supported group home. I'll tell them what I'm observing here, every child will be taken away from you, and every single paycheck that goes with them will also. When you do finally open the door, I'm sure they'll find evidence of neglect, in which case I'll book your ass."

"Mmmhmmm." Mary Jones twisted the key in the lock on her side of the door and pushed the security door open.

Shea and Hector walked into the hot living room. Shea did a quick visual sweep over the room. The house smelled of mildew. It was as if someone had wiped down the whole house with an old, damp washcloth.

Two boys sat on the couch watching a big-screen television. Either the cartoons were mesmerizing, or seeing police officers in their house was nothing unusual, because they didn't look up. The carpet hadn't been vacuumed since it was installed, Shea thought. The house had a familiar stale, spoiled smell that was synonymous with apathy, not poverty.

"Is Edgar Padilla here?" Shea asked.

"Eddie? No, he's at school," Mary Jones said. She crossed her arms. She was wearing a robe on top of another robe.

"Why aren't they in school?" Shea nodded to the boys on the couch.

"They got the flu." Mary twisted her lips in a peeved pout.

"Do you mind if I check around?" Hector spoke for the first

time. He was already moving out of the living room.

"Look all you want. What he do?"

"I'm not sure if he did anything, that's why I want to talk to him. How many children live here?" Shea said.

"It's all boys. I got about six right now."

"*About* six?'" Shea said. "What do you mean, 'about six?'"

"One stay with his grandma most of the time now."

"What school does Edgar go to?"

"Who?" Mary looked more confused than she needed to be.

"Edgar Padilla."

"Eddie," Mary corrected her. "Don't no one call him Edgar."

"Okay." Shea sighed. "What school does Eddie go to?"

"The continuation school…Zero, what's the name of the school Eddie and them go to?" Mary asked one of the boys on the couch. Neither looked up at her, but the boy she called Zero responded, "Clark-Williams."

"His name is Zero?" Shea asked Mary.

"That's what he like to be called." Mary chuckled. Hector returned to the living room and shook his head at Shea.

"I told you he wasn't here. You didn't find him under a bed

or in a hamper, did you?" Mary said to Hector. Hector did not acknowledge her.

"What time does he get out of school?" Shea said.

"Oh, 'bout two, I'd say."

"What's his caseworker's name?" Shea asked. She looked at her watch. It was already 2:30.

"I gotta look for it...hold on." Mary left them and shuffled into the kitchen in worn slippers.

"Send Jimmy and Mario over to Clark-Williams Continuation and see if Edgar is still there," Shea told Hector. Hector nodded and stepped out on the porch to talk on his radio.

Shea walked over to the two boys on the couch. They looked up at her with sleepy eyes.

"Does Eddie come home from school or does he go somewhere else usually?"

"Is he in trouble?" Zero asked.

"No, I don't think so, but I need to talk to him."

Zero nodded, but the other boy lost interest in the conversation and returned his attention to the television.

"Do you know where he goes?" Shea said. The little boy's

pajama bottoms were stained and worn thin.

"Sometimes he goes with his brother to get something to eat," Zero said. Shea stared at the boy. All the information was falling together in her brain so fast she barely could get the next question out.

"Is this his brother?" Shea pulled the ATM photo out of her notebook. Zero looked it over.

"Uh huh."

"Does he live here?"

"He used to, but he don't no more. He don't like Miss Mary." Zero looked past Shea into the kitchen.

"What's his name?" Shea said. Her chest was tight with anticipation.

"Caesar, but he likes to be called Pimp Caesar," Zero said. Shea replaced the photo in her notebook.

"What's *your* real name?" Shea said. She saw his dark skin blush. She could not say for certain his ethnicity, but she guessed a mix of black and Hispanic, maybe Filipino.

"Jason," he said bashfully.

"Why do you call yourself Zero?"

"That's what my Daddy call me," he said wistfully, turning back to the television.

"Jason...Jason." Shea got his attention back. He smiled at her and she saw he was missing his two front teeth. Mary came back in the room and the light behind his smile vanished. He turned back to the television.

"Here's his card." Mary handed a worn business card to Shea.

"Thank you. How long has Eddie lived here?" Shea slipped the business card in pocket.

"Um, 'bout two years, maybe less."

"Is he the oldest boy you have?"

"Right now?" Mary thought about it. "Yes, he's the oldest now. What kind of trouble he in?"

"I don't know. That's why I need to talk to him. Did you let him get that tattoo on his hand?"

"That? Of course not, I don't allow that kind of language to be spoke in this house. He had it when he got here."

"When he was just thirteen?" Shea said. "What were the circumstances he was taken from his home and placed with you?"

"I don't like to know. It's all the same anyway. Nobody wants them." Mary shrugged.

Shea looked quickly over at the boys, but they didn't seem to have heard her. Shea thanked her again and said good-bye to the boys. The one barely waved, but Jason looked up at her and Shea could hardly stand leaving him behind in this awful house. Out on the lawn she grabbed Hector's arm.

"You're not going to believe this," Shea said.

"Are you okay?"

"Oh, that little boy in there just broke my heart," Shea said. "Hector, the little boy says Edgar has an older brother. I showed him the suspect's picture." Shea unlocked her car door. She got in and unlocked Hector's door.

"He identified him as Edgar's older brother, Caesar. Or Pimp Caesar as he likes to be called." Shea put her keys in the ignition and turned to look at Hector. Hector stared at her in stunned silence. She anticipated his next question, "No, he doesn't live there anymore. I didn't ask Miss Mary anything about him. I'm going to call their caseworker."

"Jimmy's going to get us on the air if they can find Edgar."

"Okay, great," Shea said excitedly. "I gotta get back to the station and run up this guy. I have to let Vaughn know."

"I can't believe it."

"I know. It was two brothers who were doing the rapes. The older one teaching the younger one. And all of those cars on the property? He could've got the Buick from there, changed the plate with another car. I need to run Miss Mary up for cars. See what she's got registered to her." Shea was running her to do list off verbally.

"If we don't know where Caesar is, we might not want to jam the brother…he might warn Caesar off," Hector said.

"Good point. Let's do this, ask Jimmy to pull off of Edgar for now," Shea said.

Close. She was getting closer.

Chapter 15

By the time they got back to the station and parked, it was end-of-watch. Detectives streamed out the back door through the parking lot to their personal vehicles. Curt was one of them. Shea called to him and he stopped next to his old mini-van. His children were off in college now; he no longer chauffeured them to soccer games and school, but the bumper stickers were still there, "student of the month" and "super kid" proclamations glued for life. The license plate frame announced to the world that happiness was being married. A simple wedding ring was not enough for Curt's wife; she needed everyone to know he was married to her, even if he was in his car.

"Curt, I've got big news."

"You got a job in the gang unit?" Curt said, nodding to Hector. "What are you doing out with the gang cops?"

Hector was heading back to the gang trailer.

"Oh my God, you aren't going to believe it. I've got the shooter in the OIS identified. He's also the rapist on the Foothill case, and his little brother is, too!"

"Okay, you solved an attempted murder on a cop, and a rape

now?" Curt unlocked the van door and tossed in his brief case. He undid his tie with maddening nonchalance.

"Curt, I know where the little brother lives, but the shooter's still outstanding. I need to get in and run him up on the computer," Shea said.

"Are you going to turn over this info to Foothill sex?" Curt said.

"Well, I'm going to call the detective, of course. She'll need to show pictures of the suspects to the victim."

"Are you closer to an arrest in the sex case or the OIS?"

"Hmmm, the sex case. The sex case makes the OIS case because that puts him in the area of the traffic stop that leads to the shooting," Shea said.

"So you're a little ways off from an arrest," Curt said.

"Yes."

"I don't need to lose you on a lengthy sex investigation. If these suspects are good for one, they might be good for several. If that doesn't lead to the OIS, then you'll be doing a lot of work that doesn't have anything to do with murders. Those sex detectives will toss this in your lap and run, you know that," Curt said.

"I know…" Shea felt deflated.

"You're doing good work," Curt said. "You're solving cases that no one else did…I'm proud of you, but remember to focus at the job at hand, Shea."

"I know what you're saying. I'm getting tangled up in mess of things that don't have anything to do with *my* caseload."

"Sometimes that happens, but you have a tendency to bite off more than you can chew. What do I always tell you, Shea?" Curt tipped her chin up so he could look in her eyes.

"Homicide is a marathon, not a sprint," Shea recited.

"You have more potential than I've seen in a long time, but if you don't learn how to pace yourself, you'll burn out. Did you eat lunch today?"

"No… I was going to after I checked on the I-cards with the gang unit, and this whole thing just broke," Shea said.

"Well, eat something before you do anything else. I've got to get going, but page me if we need to bring in everyone for a search warrant," Curt said.

"Yes, of course. I'm going to get in touch with Foothill sex before they go home and see what I can find on Caesar. Is Vaughn still in court?"

"I haven't seen him, so I assume so," Curt said. "Get some sleep tonight. A calm sea does not make a skilled sailor...but you still need to rest up for the storms."

"Yes, boss." Shea gave him a wave as he got in the van.

She went in the back door of the station and directly to her desk. The gang unit was already sitting in all of the homicide seats. Hector got out of hers as she approached. She plopped down her bag and fell back into her chair.

"I was just filling them in," Hector said.

"This is fantastic, Shea." Sergeant Jackson patted her on the shoulder.

"What do you need us to do?" Jimmy asked.

"Here's the thing, we don't have enough probable cause to arrest either of them for anything just yet. I have show photos to the rape victim. And I'm not sure if I'm going to jump the case or let the sex detective do it."

"Shea, you gotta do it, this'll take too long if you pass it off," Hector said.

"I agree. In the meantime, you can be on the lookout for both of them. If you can, bring Edgar in on some bogus crime, but don't ask him anything about his brother."

"The only thing I'm concerned about, Shea, is an officer safety issue. Caesar already shot one of our police officers; if we don't warn patrol and they pull him over…" Sergeant Jackson said.

"We don't know enough to issue a bulletin yet," Shea said. "I can't have someone rousting him and running him off before we can make a case on him."

"Right," Sergeant Jackson said. "Okay, we're going to leave you to your work, but we're available. Just get us on the air."

"Thank you guys," Shea said. "It's all your intel as usual. We wouldn't be this far along if Jimmy and Dan hadn't got the information. And Hector remembered it."

"Do you need anything right now?" Hector asked.

"I hate to ask, but if you go through a drive-thru, can you get me a burger and a vanilla shake?" Shea pulled her wallet out. Hector wouldn't take her money and told her he'd be right back. Shea got a Diet Coke from the vending machine and dialed Foothill sex. The phone rang several times before Detective Ellingsworth answered.

"Thank God you're still there," Shea said.

"Not for long, is this Detective Reed?"

"Yeah, how did you know?"

"Some gang cop from your division called me and told me to sit at my desk until you called. He said you had my rape suspects identified. Kind of bossy for an officer." Probably Hector, Shea thought with a smile.

"I do have your suspects identified; hopefully, one of them is mine on the OIS."

"What do you need from me?"

"I already got counseled by my boss about not jumping your case; I really need a couple six packs shown to your victim ASAP."

"I'd love to do it, but my daughter's soccer game starts in twenty-five minutes and it's in Palmdale. Why don't you set up an appointment with the victim and show her your photo line-ups. The way I see it, the rapes are just going to lead you to your attempted murder anyway."

"I hope so, I just wanted to check with you before I did anything," Shea said. She pulled out the copy of the rape report and wrote down the contact numbers of the victim.

"That's nice of you, but as you can see, I need all the help I can get. Show the pictures and if you can write up everything you did, I'll take it from there, okay?"

"Terrific. Have a good night, hope your daughter wins."

"Thanks, it'll be the first one I've made in four weeks."

Shea hung up and called the victim's home phone number.

"I'm sorry, I'm confused; you said your name was Detective Reed? I was working with a Detective Ellingsworth." The woman had a tight, tired voice.

Shea quickly tried to explain the situation.

"So, they might have done this where you work as well?"

Shea looked at a note from the sex crimes supervisor; it was attached to three rape reports. The note simply said, "Here are some possibles."

"Yes, ma'am," Shea said. The woman said she could be there in an hour.

Shea got to work on the computer to try to identify Caesar Padilla and find a photograph of him. She let out a silent shout when she saw that he had been arrested in West Valley Division for auto theft last year. The case against him was never prosecuted, but it meant there was a booking photo on file. That was the good news;

the bad news was that photo would be located at West Valley Division, several miles away. During rush hour traffic, it would be quicker to drive to downtown LA than to get across the San Fernando Valley.

She picked up the phone and dialed their homicide unit. She hoped that they hadn't gone home for the day. Luckily, the homicide supervisor, Rick Swanston, was still there. She explained her predicament and he told her he would find the booking photo and send an officer with the photo to her right away. Before hanging up Detective Swanston asked her to tell Boots they needed to go to another Dodger game real soon and that Boots needed to improve his solve rate.

Shea had just a half-an-hour before the victim would arrive. She hoped the officer would get to her in time. While she waited, Shea called the Department of Children's Services and left a message for the caseworker. The likelihood she would get a call back this evening was slim.

She went to work finding similar photos of Edgar Padilla and putting together the photo line-up. Detectives kept shoeboxes of photos based on physical characteristics—white women, Hispanic women, black men with glasses, white men with facial hair. The

category she was looking in, "young, bald male Hispanics," was the

biggest box of all.

Shea was taping photos into the six-pack line-up when a desk

officer brought another uniformed officer back to her desk,

"Detective Reed, this guy's here from West Valley."

The patrol officer brought a small envelope over to her. Shea

thanked him and the officer told her it was okay, he was a U-car and

he was glad not to be taking any burglary reports for a while.

Shea took the picture out of the envelope. An angry young

man stared back at her. He was wearing a Dallas Cowboy uniform

shirt and scowling at the camera. His head was not bald, there was

about a quarter inch of hair on his head. He was thin and he had

large ears. Shea went back to the photo lineup boxes and found five

photos of young men that looked similar to Caesar Padilla. As soon

as she finished with the second six-pack, the same desk officer came

back to her desk.

"You're popular today. There's a woman at the front desk

for you."

"Please send her back," Shea said, running over to the copy

machine to make photocopies of the line-ups. Shea double-checked the woman's name on the rape report.

A tall, thin, athletic-looking woman in her mid-thirties came through the detective squad room door with the desk officer. The desk officer pointed to Shea at the copy machine and went back to the desk.

"Carrie Ingram?" Shea walked over to the woman. The woman nodded and gave her a solid handshake. "I'm Shea Reed. Can I get you some water? Soda?"

"No, thank you." The woman looked around her surroundings.

"I'm going to take you back to an interview room and then I'll be right with you." Shea motioned for the woman to follow her and placed her in one of the interrogation rooms. As soon as she returned to her desk to get her notebook, Hector came in with her hamburger and shake. She grabbed her notebook and photos and went in to talk to the victim.

"I'm going to show you two photo line-ups in a moment," Shea said, sitting down across from her. "I'm going to read you a required admonishment first, and you need to sign that I read it to you."

Shea read the paragraph that explained to the victim or witness that the suspect may or may not appear in these photos and that appearance can be altered, etcetera. Carrie Ingram sat with her hands in her lap and listened to Shea. Afterwards, she took Shea's pen and signed that she understood the admonishment.

"I looked at thousands of pictures before," Carrie said quietly.

"I know, Detective Ellingsworth told me she showed you numerous pictures." She handed her the six-pack with Edgar Padilla in it. She was careful not to touch the line-up, so it did not appear she was pointing to any picture. She had put Edgar's photo in the first row, the last picture, number three. Shea noticed that Carrie's eyes went right to him, and then she looked at all of the pictures. She finally went back to Edgar's picture and stared at it for 15 seconds.

"This guy…" Carrie pointed to Edgar. "He looks like the little one…" She looked up at Shea for confirmation.

"I can't comment on your selection," Shea said. "Please circle the one you think it is and initial inside the circle."

"Number three," Carrie said. She circled and initialed the

photo and handed it back to Shea. Shea pulled out the six-pack with Caesar in it. The anticipation was nerve-wracking. She could work months on a case and it could all boil down to a live line-up or a photo line-up. If the victim or witness could not identify the suspect, it was back to the drawing board.

Shea handed Carrie the second six-pack containing Caesar's picture in the middle bottom row, number five. Carrie looked at each photo. Shea could track her eyes from photo to photo. When she got to Caesar's photo she spent as much time as she did on the others, but there did not appear to be any recognition. She looked at the last photo and then put the six-pack down on the table in front of her. Carrie chewed her lip.

"My assailant was bald, I know he was bald," she muttered.

"Carrie, remember what I told you, appearances change, men have mustaches and then they shave them off, for example," Shea said.

"Number....not number one," Carrie said. "Not number three, not six."

Shea sat quietly.

"I think that it's between two and five," Carrie said.

"Okay, tell me what about those two guys looks familiar to you," Shea said.

"Well, the shape of number two's face is more how I remember it…" Shea looked at number two, he was the most gaunt-looking of all the photos. "But, number five…the eyes, the ears looks just like him. He was thinner and had no hair," Carrie said.

"Carrie, remember that looks can change, people gain and lose weight, grow hair and cut hair. Try to focus on things that can't change. Things like the ears and eyes."

Carrie took a piece of paper and put it over number two's hair. She did the same thing for number five. "It's five. It's number five. The eyes." Carrie looked up at Shea. "Is he in jail?"

"Not yet." Shea gave her the photocopy to circle the suspect's photo and the form to fill out.

"Did they do this to other women?" Carrie asked when she was done writing.

"Maybe."

"Why has it taken so long to find them? My God, this happened last year," Carrie said.

"I know. Sometimes it just doesn't come together quickly."

"If you were able to find them, why couldn't the other detective?"

"Detective Ellingsworth did a lot of work on your case. I just got a lucky break on something I was working on."

"I've been in counseling…I just can't get past this." Carrie shook her head.

"It takes time. The suspects going to jail will help." Shea put the photos back in her notebook.

"I'm not sure it will. I just can't understand why I did not fight back in the parking lot. I just let them in the car, let them rape me…" Carrie hung her head.

"It sounds like they caught you unaware."

"I took karate when I was a kid. I didn't use it. Not once. Not one time. I was just…" Carrie shook her head again. Shea gave up her desire to get out of the room and move on with the case. She told Carrie she would be right back.

She went out and got Carrie a cup of water and a box of Kleenex and listened to her talk without looking at her watch again. Later that evening, she walked Carrie to her car and Carrie hugged her. She thanked her for listening and she thanked her for finding the "animals that did this to me." After Shea watched her drive away, she went back in the station to her desk.

It was almost 6:00 p.m. She wondered if Vaughn had come back from court and left for home without her knowing. She walked over to the sign-in and sign-out sheet and saw that he hadn't returned from court. She paged him and waited for him to call her back as she ate her cold burger. Five minutes later he came in through the back door.

"You rang?" Vaughn asked.

"How'd court go?"

"All right. I had to take two wits home. They were pissed because they sat there all day and neither of them testified. The DA had me on the stand all day. Oh well, tomorrow we'll probably have a tough time finding them. I tried to tell the DA that, but she thought I should go up first." Vaughn tossed his murder book on his desk. "I haven't been on the stand that long for a crime scene in my life."

"I have some news. Your suspect in the OIS is identified." Shea pulled her chair over to Vaughn and told him the story of the day's events ending with the rape victim picking out Caesar's photo.

"Thank God for that gang unit," Vaughn said. "If Jimmy and

Dan hadn't taken that FI…"

"I know," Shea said.

"Okay, where do you want to go next?"

"It's your case."

"It's our case now," Vaughn corrected. "We've got enough to bring them in on the rapes."

"Exactly, but I can't get an address on Caesar yet, and if we get Edgar first, Caesar will rabbit."

"Okay, let me do some work on Caesar." Shea handed him Caesar's rap sheet. Vaughn undid his tie and took off his sports coat.

Vaughn spent the next few hours working on the computer. He would jot down little notes, dates of births, license plate numbers and names, and then he'd go back to the computer and run another program. Shea busied herself with writing her reports for the rape investigation and catching up with the chronological log for the OIS. At 9:00 p.m. her desk phone rang.

"Detective Reed? I didn't think anyone would be there," a man stated. "This is Juan Alba from Department of Children's Services."

"Mr. Alba! Thank you for calling me back," Shea said,

waving her hand at Vaughn. "DCS!"

"I don't have the full file on the Padilla brothers with me, just a cursory one...what do you want to know?"

"First of all, do you have an address for Caesar?"

"The older one?" Juan Alba read off a familiar address.

"He's not there anymore, just Edgar."

"Well, he's supposed to be. He just turned 18, but he was still enrolled in high school. He should be there until June," Juan said. Shea could hear him rustling through papers.

"Do you have any contact addresses?"

"No...not with me now. I really wasn't prepared to talk to you. I thought I would just leave a message on your voicemail...returning your call."

"Can you tell me why they were removed from their home?"

"Because of neglect, physical abuse, and sexual abuse. The sex abuse was on the part of the grandfather. That was their first placement after they were removed from the mother. They were troubled boys."

"I'll say. They're good for a least one violent rape."

"Oh no."

"And Caesar shot a police officer last year."

"Did the officer survive?"

"Yes. He lost an ear."

"Oh my gosh. Well, can I call you back tomorrow? I need to pull all of the reports on these two."

"Yes, tomorrow would be fine. Thank you." Shea hung up.

"Anything?" Vaughn asked.

"Not really. He's going to call back tomorrow."

"I'm at a dead end. Let's call it a night," Vaughn said. She had made such a major breakthrough in the case, she hated that it hadn't ended with people in handcuffs.

Chapter 16

Friday morning Shea woke up with a start. She had a dream about the Christmas party and she woke up trying to remember it. She was spinning on the dance floor of the restaurant, music playing, and she saw Chloe in her dream—she was standing in the doorway in that beautiful black dress. Shea stopped dancing and tried to make her way across the dance floor to Chloe, but Chloe was gone. A long, cool woman in a black dress…that's what the witness had said about her. Shea threw her legs out of bed and sat for a moment thinking about Chloe outside of the restaurant…talking to a bell boy or a valet.

Shea took a quick shower and cursed herself for not picking up her clothes from the dry cleaners. She settled on a black suit that was a half-a-size too small and a white shirt. She pulled her wet hair into a bun, quickly put on her makeup, and ran out of the house. Shea got to work before the rest of her unit, signed in on the sign-in sheet, and signed herself right back out again. She grabbed her car keys and notebook and hustled to her detective vehicle.

The sex crimes supervisor stopped her as she got to the car.

"Did you get the reports I placed on your desk?" he asked.

"Yes, I did. Thank you," she said, unlocking her door.

"So, what do you think? Are they related to the Foothill rape?"

"I didn't get a chance to look at them yet," Shea said. She had the car door open and she was about to step in.

"You were in a pretty big hurry to get them," he said.

"I was. And, unfortunately, I'm in a real hurry now," Shea said.

He made a sweeping motion with his hand.

"Don't let me stop you," he said. She wanted to explain, but she didn't have time.

She drove as quickly as morning traffic would allow to the Odyssey restaurant where the Christmas party was held. She parked her car in the empty lot and pulled on the handle of the large wooden door. It was locked.

She sighed, too early in the morning for the place to be open. She was walking back to the car when a woman pulled up in a small compact car.

"We're not open," the woman told Shea. Shea pulled back her blazer and showed the woman the badge on her belt. The badge was placed right in front of the gun on her hip. The gun was the force behind the badge.

"Okay." The woman gave her look that said 'so what.' She reached in her car and pulled out a shopping bag and her purse.

"You do work here?" Shea asked.

"Sure do." The woman slammed her car door. She was going to give Shea a hard time because a cop must have given her a ticket at some point, took her boyfriend to jail, or took too long to respond to a burglary call at her house.

"I only need a few minutes of your time," Shea said.

"Okay, can I get to my office?" She raised her arched eyebrows and pointed her keys to the restaurant door.

"Of course. What do you do here?" Shea walked with her to the restaurant.

"I'm the assistant manager for special events. I don't know how I can help you."

"I'm sure you can." Shea held the door open for her and followed her to the same office where she had interviewed Krista Tanner the night of the Christmas party.

The woman made a big deal about putting down her

shopping bag, pulling out the contents and placing her purse in a file-cabinet drawer. When she was done with her duties, she was forced to engage Shea.

"All right, what is it you need?"

"I'm Detective Reed, from Valley Homicide--"

"If this is about the murder of that cop, I'm supposed to refer all inquiries to our general manager of operations." She held up her manicured hands in front of her chest.

"What's your name?" Shea opened her notebook.

"Donna Stewart. What's this about?"

"Ms. Stewart, does this man work for you?" Shea handed her a picture of Caesar Padilla. Donna Stewart took the booking photo, looked at it, and handed it back to Shea.

"I couldn't tell you. As I said, I work in special events and I would assume he's part of the busboy crew or whatever."

"Ms. Stewart, this is very important. Can you look through your personnel records and tell me if Caesar Padilla is employed here? And, for the record, he's a rapist."

"But you said you worked homicide." Donna Stewart looked at her skeptically. Shea got out a business card and handed it to her.

"That's where I'm assigned, but I'm currently working a rape investigation."

"Do you have a subpoena?"

"Are you kidding me?" Shea lost her temper. "Get your general manager on the phone, and if that is not part of your job description give me the telephone number and I'll call him or her myself."

"I don't think it's necessary to talk to me in that tone of voice," Donna said.

"Ms. Stewart, I'm looking for a man who made a woman suck on the barrel of his gun. A man who tore up this woman's anus so badly she needed 15 stitches and --"

"Detective, that's really not necessary. I do *not* need to hear this stuff first thing in the morning."

"Of course not, I apologize that it's tough to hear. Maybe you can imagine for a second what it's like for it to actually happen to you. Hell, if this guy is employed here and you don't feel like you can find it in your best interests to help me determine that, he might be working today…are you here alone?" Shea looked around the office for effect. Donna rolled her eyes and grabbed her key chain.

"The personnel records are kept in a different office. What was the name again?"

"Caesar Padilla," Shea said. Donna Stewart left the office and Shea knew she would keep her waiting for a while.

When Donna returned she was holding a manila folder. Shea felt her heart pound.

"There's a Caesar Padilla Gonzalez." Donna handed her the folder. She checked the date of birth and it was not what was listed on Padilla's rap sheet, but the year was correct. She looked at the address and it was the group home address.

"When does he work?" Shea asked.

Donna took the folder. "Okay, Gonzalez…" Donna went to the second page of the file. "Bus boy, hired June 5…he was fired December 23rd last year."

"What?" Shea tried to remember the date of the Christmas party. It was the second week of December, she remembered that.

"He was terminated because he failed to show up for work. Let me see…Ingrid's notes are hard to read. She's our Human Resources gal." Donna looked through the hand-written notes. Shea could see that a paycheck was attached with a paper clip to the second sheet of paper. "He didn't pick up his last paycheck. It was only for $42.50, but still," Donna said.

"Does it say when he stopped showing up for work?" Shea wanted to grab the paperwork out of Donna's hands.

"I'm looking. December 17th."

"Can I make a copy of all of this?" Shea asked. "Does he have a supervisor, someone that would remember him?"

"This was a few months ago. These bus boys are always changing here. I'll make you a copy, but you can't have the original, and I'll need a receipt," Donna said.

"Fine. Thank you," Shea said.

After Shea got the file, she hustled to her car and called Vaughn as soon as she got in.

"Hey, where you at?" Vaughn asked.

"Look at your calendar for last year. When was the Christmas party?"

"Hold on." She hoped he could tell by the tone of her voice, she was not in the mood to joke around. He kept a large desk calendar under the plastic blotter of his desk and didn't toss it out until it got so thick it changed the shape of his desk.

"December 16th," Vaughn said.

"Caesar Padilla was a bus boy at the Odyssey Restaurant. He never showed up for work after the Christmas party."

"What? How did you end up at Odyssey?" Vaughn was trying to catch up.

"I'm not sure what I'm saying yet," Shea said.

Vaughn was the one that taught her to think things through before she made a pronouncement. There was a certain moment of knowing something on some level that you still couldn't quite touch with your conscious mind, but until you worked the parts out, it was better to keep it to yourself. What she *knew* was that Caesar Padilla killed Chloe Diaz. She didn't know anything more than that yet.

"Are you coming back to the station?" Vaughn asked.

"Yeah, right now, but you have court, right?"

"I'm leaving in an hour," Vaughn said. "Shea, if this has to do with Chloe's murder, you know you are going to have to turn everything over to RHD."

"I'll be right there." Shea hung up on Vaughn and pulled out of the parking lot. As she drove, she looked through Padilla's employment record. He listed his guidance counselor from the continuation school as his reference person. And his emergency contact was Mary Jones from the group home. The information was scant. She was no closer to finding him then she was yesterday.

As she drove back to the station, she turned off her police radio and the AM/FM radio as well. In the silence of the car, she tried to clear her head to let her brain catch up with something she seemed to already know. Padilla had killed Chloe.

How was he able to get the jump on her? Did he kill her because she confronted him as the person who shot her partner, or was he acting as a violent rapist and he happened to pick Chloe in some twisted coincidence? But how would Chloe be able to identify Padilla as the person who shot her partner? She never saw him. And if she had him identified by her informant, why wouldn't she share that information with Vaughn or the gang unit? Shea remembered the blood in the bathroom and how it was gone when she returned.

Vaughn was standing outside the back door of the detective squad room, smoking a cigarette. Shea parked in a handicapped spot near Vaughn, instead of looking for a space in the parking lot.

"You're going to get into trouble if the Captain catches you." Vaughn nodded to her car.

"I know, I know." Shea handed him Padilla's employment record. Vaughn dragged on his cigarette as he read through the two pages of information.

"He went by Gonzalez and a different DOB. We can play around with that combination on the computer." Vaughn stepped on his cigarette butt. "How'd you end up at the restaurant?"

"It was a hunch." Shea blushed. "I had a dream about the Christmas party when I was taking a shower this morning. It just occurred to me that he might've worked there."

"You know you gotta call in RHD."

"Vaughn, I don't mean to sound like a conspiracy theorist, but if the I/O's think it's a suicide and I give them this information…they might just bury it. All we have for sure is a rapist. It sure looks like it was him that shot at Ornelas, but how do I connect it to Chloe?"

"Even those guys couldn't ignore this. He bails out of his job the day after the murder? See, that's why you gotta get with RHD, they had to have interviewed this guy that night."

"Yeah, but what if they interviewed him and he had an alibi and then…"

"Okay, you do what you have to do, but don't bring Boots into the loop, because when you get in trouble, and you will, you don't want him in trouble too. Keep going as if you're only investigating my OIS. Show Ornelas the photo line-up, see if he can identify him."

"All I want to do is hand them an investigation that they can't ignore or dismiss. Do you understand what I mean? I *know* this guy killed Chloe."

"I get it, Shea. Keep me posted," Vaughn said. "I gotta get to court."

"Good luck."

"You, too," Vaughn said.

She went inside and was glad to see that Curt was not at his desk. She sat still for a minute and then began to organize her paperwork and her thoughts. She had a number of phone messages: Ellingsworth from Foothill Division wanting to know if her victim had identified the suspects; Dan Alba from DCS, two district attorneys from upcoming trials, and the mother of her last homicide victim. She neatly stacked the pink messages as she tried to figure out whom she should call first.

She turned her attention to the small stack of rape investigations from her sex unit. She needed to go through each of them to see if any were related to Foothill's. It was going to become very complicated, very soon. She wished Jack was back at work. There was no way she could handle this investigation by herself; and as soon as she involved anyone else, it would no longer be hers.

She stared at her phone. All she had to do was pick it up and call RHD. She could take this hot potato and dump it right on their laps. The telephone rang and she jumped in her seat.

"Hey, it's me." She listened with combined disappointment and relief that it was Andrew.

"Hi."

"What're your plans for this weekend?" Andrew said.

She remembered her date with Chad that was set to begin in less than 24 hours.

"I have plans."

"Anything you can break? I gotta drive to San Diego to take care of some family stuff...parents. I thought maybe you would come with me. I don't have to stay with my folks. Have you ever stayed at the Hotel Del Coronado?"

"I'm really busy."

"Right now or this weekend?"

"Both. I think I've identified the shooter on the Ornelas shooting."

"The ear shooting? You're kidding. I'll let my guys know--"

"No! I'm not ready to get a filing, I'm just in the baby stages here," Shea said.

"I can't wait to hear how you did it."

"I've really got to go." Over the loud speaker, she heard her name being called, announcing that she had a call on another line.

"I'll call you later?"

"Yes, yes, I have to go." She hung up and picked up her other line.

"Detective Reed, it's Ellingsworth at Foothill. I called my victim this morning and she told me that she met with you."

"Hi, yeah, I was just going to call you." Shea pulled the pink message slip with Ellingsworth's name on it and threw it in the trash. "She ID'd both guys."

"Yes!" Ellingsworth said. "Okay, you need me to present it?"

"Ah, well…I don't have a location on the older brother. In

fact, I have a message to call his DCS worker…" Shea was stalling.

"Okay, why aren't we hooking these guys up right now? We have enough for a PC arrest, we don't need to get warrants."

"Yeah, I know…but I think the older brother is good for--"

"The OIS, I know, but these guys need to go to jail yesterday. You can work the OIS with them in custody."

"I think…I can't run the risk of running off the older brother by hooking up the younger one. I know he's good for the OIS, but there might be something more."

"Oh God, I hate it when things get mysterious." Ellingsworth sighed. "You do understand my situation, I have two guys identified on a violent rape, and if I don't do everything I can to get them in jail and they rape again, you do see where that puts me?"

"I do. I'm without a partner and this case's growing exponentially and honestly…"

"Stay at your desk. I'm getting in my car and I'll be there in fifteen minutes and we'll figure something out," Ellingsworth said in a motherly fashion.

"Okay." Help was on the way.

Shea called Juan Alba, who was not at his desk, so she left a message. She also called the two district attorneys, but she didn't have time to call the mother of her last homicide victim. Detective Ellingsworth was coming through the front door, talking to some of the old-time detectives in a familiar, friendly manner, not harried and stressed as she did the day Shea met her. Shea gathered up her books and notes and met with Ellingsworth before she could make it to Shea's desk.

"Hey, Jenny. Are you here about those rapes that are related to yours?" The sex crimes supervisor asked as he passed her.

"Oh, hi Bill,"

Shea thought that Ellingsworth did not look like a Jenny.

"I gave all the ones I have to Reed, here. We could use the clearances." The supervisor thumbed to Shea.

"We're going to look it all over. Hi, Shea." Ellingsworth smiled at Shea, but Shea didn't remember telling Ellingsworth her first name.

"Hi, let's go into an interview room."

"So what does this have to do with homicides?" The supervisor asked as he followed them.

"Oh, all the bad guys overlap at some point, Bill."

Ellingsworth laughed and followed Shea into an interview room.

"He is a bonehead," she whispered to Shea as she shut the door.

"This room isn't bugged," Shea said. "The other two are, but this one isn't rigged to tape."

"Good, he's a bonehead," Ellingsworth repeated in a normal voice. "I was a sergeant here for three years. The same grumps are still here."

"You have dual status?" Shea pulled out her notes as Ellingsworth sat down.

"I made detective two years ago. The theory was that I'd just do detectives for a year and then take the lieutenant's exam. But I bombed my oral, so I might be here for awhile," she said.

"Okay, let me tell you what I have…" Shea told Ellingsworth her story. Ellingsworth was probably an outstanding interviewer, Shea thought. Ellingsworth actively listened to Shea, nodding and leaning in.

"So what do you want to do, in a perfect world?" Ellingsworth asked when Shea finished. Shea could have hugged her for not telling her she needed to notify RHD.

"Work on locating Caesar Padilla."

"Okay, how about we do this? It's Friday and there's no one in my unit, so I'll be at your disposal today. I'll work on the follow-up report and putting everything together. I'll go through all of the rapes in your division to see if we have any similars. You keep trying to bed down Caesar Padilla."

"Thank you," Shea said with deep relief.

"But listen, you have no idea what RHD had on Padilla. Let's say…I know you think they think it was a suicide…but let's say that they have Padilla as suspect and they've got SIS following him and we never tell them and go about our investigation…we could really jeopardize their murder investigation and I know you don't want that."

The idea that the elite Special Investigations Section might be following her suspect gave Shea pause. She thought for a moment.

"I know. I want to take this a little bit further. I want to give them so much that they can't ignore it. What if they never interviewed Padilla that night? What if Padilla slipped away after he murdered Chloe? They'd never know about him."

"They had to have had an employee roster for that night."

"I know, but you weren't there. It was mayhem. There were hundreds of interviews. Done by RHD and by us."

"Okay, let's get to work, but by the end of the day…you have to make a call, okay?"

Shea nodded and they went to work.

Jenny Ellingsworth sat down at Jack's desk and worked quietly for hours. She determined that the same suspects were likely good for two rapes in Valley Division. Shea spent the time on the computer running Caesar Padilla with the last name of Gonzalez and his different date of birth. She spoke to Juan Alba, who faxed her all of the information he had on the Padilla brothers.

Their mother was a heroin user and habitually arrested. Their father was murdered and they were sent to live with their paternal grandparents, the grandfather sexually-abused them. Shea moved through the information that led to their demise without emotion. All she was looking for were addresses and names of relatives that Caesar might still be in contact with.

By afternoon, Curt finally appeared. He remembered Ellingsworth from when she was sergeant. After making small talk with her, he turned to Shea and asked to be updated. Shea explained her investigation for the third time that day.

"Are you ready to go ask for a warrant?" Curt asked Ellingsworth.

"I am. If you're ready to review the follow-up report." Ellingsworth handed him her work.

"We have to focus on the job at hand and that's to get a couple of rapists off the street. Priority one," Curt said.

"I agree," Ellingsworth said.

"You *will* call RHD and bring them up to speed. Immediately." Curt looked over his glasses at Shea.

"Yes, boss," Shea said. Ellingsworth gave her look that was a combination of sympathy and "I told you so."

Shea went to her desk and looked up the phone number for Walter Smith. No one answered on Smith's line, so she called the main number and asked to speak with Detective Smith or one of the investigating officers on the Chloe Diaz case. Shea had forgotten their names.

After a few minutes a hurried voice came on the line, "Detective Lancaster."

"Detective Reed, from Valley Homicide. I was sort of working with Walter Smith a little on the Diaz case." She listened to herself choose words that diminished her input.

"What can I do for you?"

"Ah, okay here's the thing."

"Go ahead."

"I think I've got a suspect in her homicide. He's a rapist from Foothill Division. He and his brother raped a woman and then the next day he was using the victim's ATM card at a bank just a few blocks from the OIS, a few minutes before Ornelas and Diaz pulled him over. He probably had the victim's purse in the car with him. Anyway, he worked at the Odyssey restaurant and never showed up for work the day after our Christmas party. I think that Diaz must have recognized him or something..." Shea said.

Lancaster was quiet for a minute and then told her he had to put her on hold and go back to his desk.

"What's his name?" Detective Lancaster asked when he came back on the line.

"Caesar Padilla." Shea gave him all of the information she had on Padilla. "I don't know if you guys interviewed him that night or not."

"And tell me how you have him on a rape?" Shea told him about her investigation in detail. It took several minutes to give him all of the details.

"I take it Foothill wants to make an arrest for rape as soon as they can."

"Yes. The brothers look like they are good for two rapes in my division as well," Shea said.

"And the attempted murder of Ornelas, you're ready to arrest on that?"

"Well, we conceivably could. We have the PC, but I still need to show a photo line-up to Ornelas."

"I thought he couldn't ID?"

"Well, he gave me a few more details than he did the first interview," Shea said.

"Fax me all the information you have on Padilla. I need you to write out a statement on everything you did on this."

"I have. What's your fax number?" Shea asked and wrote down the numbers.

"I'll call you back in about a half-hour. Wait until we talk before you make any arrests," Lancaster said. Shea told him she would and hung up.

Curt and Detective Ellingsworth were looking at her expectantly. Shea gathered up the information and went to the fax machine. As she stood feeding the papers into the fax machine, Detective Ellingsworth joined her.

"It's frustrating to deal with RHD," Ellingsworth said quietly. "But they do have more resources at their fingertips then we do. If they take this whole thing you know they'll have Metro to serve the warrants and all lab requests will go to the front of the line."

"I'm not worried about that. Good for them, and bad guys go to jail. I'm worried about the opposite. That they disregard this and then there's no recourse for me."

"I don't think they will."

"They think Chloe committed suicide," Shea whispered. "That's what they've hung their hats on. This investigation's five months old; they've made no arrests. And they think it's a suicide, which conveniently supports why there's no arrest. If some goofy cop in the Valley finds them a murder suspect, do you really think they're going to embrace that information with open arms?"

"Yes, Shea, I do. This isn't the OJ case; this is a police officer who was murdered. They aren't going to let petty politics, appearances, egos and nonsense get in the way of doing what's right. I'm pretty cynical myself, especially about Rape Specials up there at RHD, but bottom line is we're all on the same side."

"I hope you're right," Shea said, as the last paper went through the fax machine.

"I am." Ellingsworth gave Shea's upper arm a squeeze.

When she got back to her desk, Curt was waiting for her.

"Steve Lancaster called." It was not lost on Shea that Detective Lancaster had called the supervisor back and not her.

"What did he say?"

"Okay, here's what we're going to do. We're going to proceed on the rape investigation as we normally would. When there's an arrest made of either suspect, RHD wants to be notified," Curt said.

"In other words, we do all the work," Shea muttered.

"I reviewed your follow-up. Good work." Curt ignored Shea's comment and handed Ellingsworth's reports back to her. "Get your warrants."

"I'll call Judge Nantroup." Shea pulled her address book out of her bag.

"I think we can give the warrants to the gang unit. They know who they're looking for. If they get both guys, you'll have your search warrant ready to go," Curt said.

"Yeah." Shea sat down at her desk. "I'll write the search warrant then."

After all of the warrants were written, Ellingsworth took them to the judge while Shea met with the gang unit and updated them. Sergeant Jackson assured her they would work on finding the suspects all weekend.

"You have to call me as soon as you get them," Shea said. She handed him her cell number and her pager number.

"We'll pick up Edgar Padilla for sure," Hector Gomez promised her. "I bet he's going to be hanging out with the same knuckleheads we caught him with before."

"We'll find Caesar too," Sergeant Jackson said.

By the time their paperwork was done, it was 9:00 p.m. Ellingsworth was loading up her bag. "Okay, maybe they'll get them this weekend. Hopefully."

"I hope so."

"I've got a bridal shower on Saturday night," Ellingsworth said. "But you can interrogate on the rapes, right?"

"Of course," Shea said.

"Shea, go home. You're going to need your rest." Ellingsworth slung her bag over her shoulder.

"Thanks for all of your help. I couldn't have done--"

"Hey, stop! You found my rapists to begin with, thank you." Ellingsworth said before giving her a wave and heading out the door. Shea sat at her desk for another half-an-hour, too tired to work anymore, but too stubborn to call it a day.

Chapter 17

Shea was in a sound sleep at 7:00 a.m. when her phone rang. She was instantly awake; she knew it was going to be news about the Padilla brothers.

"Hello?" Shea said.

"Goooood morning. It's Chad. I was just making a pot of coffee and hoping my date hadn't forgotten about me."

"I didn't forget about you." Shea yawned.

"You're still asleep, I'm sorry."

"No, I'm awake. I thought we said ten," she said.

"Did we? I thought it was seven."

"Do you want to go for a run?"

"Now?"

"No, when I get there." Shea threw her legs out of bed. "I haven't run since that night at the academy, and I have all kinds of pent-up anger that I need to burn off. And I love running on the beach."

"Didn't I mention that I haven't been running? We're going to start the day off with you kicking my ass?" Chad said.

"You're younger than me; you used to be a road guard…"

"Okay, okay. Running it is."

"What should I bring to wear…are we going out?"

"Just bring comfortable clothes. And any kind of sexy

lingerie you want." She heard him chuckle.

She confirmed the directions to his apartment and hung up.

She changed into her favorite nylon running shorts, sports bra, and

sweatshirt. It would be cooler at the beach. She tossed jeans and a

blouse in her duffle bag. She didn't want to look like she was trying

too hard, but after pulling her long hair back in a ponytail, she put

just enough mascara so her eyes didn't disappear. She double-

checked to make sure she had her pager and her cell phone and then

hopped into her car and drove south on the 405 freeway.

The neighborhood that Chad lived in was typical of Venice, a

combination of low-income apartments interspersed with million-

dollar homes. Venice was in a constant state of redefining itself. Was

it a hippie haven, a laid-back beach community, or an affluent

enclave? Chad's apartment was a non-descript sallow orange box of

a building, but the rent was probably steep due to the proximity to

the beach.

Chad opened the door as she knocked. Wearing a pair of low-slung gray sweatpants and a black Bob Marley t-shirt, he gave her a smile and an appraising glance at her legs.

"This was a good idea. You have great legs," he said, standing back so she could walk in.

The living room was full of mismatched furniture and had a counter-culture feel to it. Maybe it was the giant Buddha statue on the coffee table, or all the houseplants, or the fact there was a fat black cat grooming himself in the window, but it didn't look like a bachelor cop residence.

"The cat belongs to my roommate."

"I see." She put down her bag.

"Do you want some coffee?"

"Maybe after we run."

"I can see I'm not going to talk you out of this running business, am I?"

"I had busy week and I didn't get a chance to run at all."

"Okay, okay, let me get my keys. I can see we aren't going to get anywhere until we get this run out of the way."

They ran on the wet sand next to the surf all the way to the

Santa Monica pier. Chad not only kept pace with her, he ran a little in front of her and was able to talk the whole time. Shea decided he must have been sandbagging about the lack of running. It was still a little foggy and the air filling her lungs felt cold and clean. She listened to him talk; his words fell into a nice rhythm with their strides.

When they got to the pier they slowed to a walk. Shea hadn't been to the pier since she was a teenager. She and her sister used to take the bus to the beach every day during the summer.

"Tell me about your busy week," Chad said. He wasn't winded and Shea was certain he had lied about not being able to run anymore.

She caught her breath and began to tell him about her investigation as they walked along the pier. They shooed a seagull from a bench and watched fishermen drop their lines off the end of the pier. Shea breathed in the fresh, salty air, along with the cinnamon smell of a nearby churro stand. Shea told Chad every detail of her investigation and then the conversation turned to life histories.

Chad was from Minneapolis originally. He came out to

California to apply at the LAPD and the LA County Sheriff's Department. LAPD processed his application quicker.

"How did you decide on all of this?" Shea asked.

"I was tired of the snow. The usual stuff people from the Midwest gripe about. I was in my first year of college and miserable. I got in my car and just drove. I knew I wanted to be a cop or an artist, but I decided I wanted to be a cop or an artist where I could wear short sleeves. I spent the night in Phoenix and I was going to just stop there, but for some reason I kept going until I made it all the way to the coast."

He told her about staying in a hotel in Chinatown while he was in the testing process and eating Chinese food every day for weeks and how the door of his extended-stay hotel was made of plywood with a latch for a lock. He used 150 N. Los Angeles Street, Parker Center, as his place of residence for his address when he got his driver's license; it was the only address he could remember. When he was in the academy he got an apartment in 77th Division, not realizing he was going to be the only white resident for several miles.

"I'd never even been to LA before. The instructors in the

academy made so much fun of me. Called me hayseed. I did find another apartment before the academy was over, though. I couldn't sleep with the helicopters going all night long," Chad said.

While they walked back to his apartment, he held her hand and Shea was jolted by the feeling. She had never held hands in public with Andrew, even when they were out of Los Angeles.

"My mom really dug Venice. I think she'd like to live here," Chad said.

"You're kidding, no way. This place couldn't be more foreign to a housewife from the Midwest," Shea said.

"The Midwestern housewife's my mom's cover. She's really not that. She lived on a cucumber farm. It was a commune in Wisconsin. Then she met my Dad. She reads palms and tarot cards," Chad said.

"You're right, she would fit in here."

"I know. Have you ever used a psychic on any of your murder investigations?" They left the beach and made their way back to his apartment.

"No. Vaughn Powers has a crazy psychic lady that calls him every now and then. I think they used to date. Her name is Cocoa

Capelli."

"Ha. You'd have to be a psychic or a stripper with a name like that," Chad said.

"Yeah. It's funny though, no one's interested in our murders. Not the news, not even psychics. Gang murders and dope murders aren't interesting to anyone except the people involved."

Shea followed him up the stairs to his apartment. She made a mental note that his ass was definitely smaller then hers.

"I suppose so." Chad unlocked his door.

"The obsession with serial murders is ridiculous. They make up only one percent of all the homicides in the whole country."

"I'll make a fresh pot of coffee while you shower." Chad showed her to the bathroom. "The towels were clean. Coffee'll be ready when you're done."

Shea placed her bag on the toilet, stripped off her damp clothes and stepped into the shower. The hot water felt good against her cold skin. Several shampoo bottles were lined up like spectators in the windowsill. The labels boasted apples, peaches, seaweed, and milk. All the food groups, Shea thought.

She knew Chad had long hair, but this seemed like a

woman's domain. A man could shampoo his hair with a bar of soap if he had to. She picked one and while she rinsed her hair she noticed the pink razor in the corner of the tub. Shea picked it up and wondered whose leg it made its path on. It would be ridiculous to think he didn't date, but these were the intimate necessities of a woman who spent the night often…or lived there.

Shea got out of the shower and dried herself off. Chad's out of town "roommate" must be a live-in girlfriend. She opened the cabinet under the sink and confirmed her suspicions with the box of Tampax. Shea shut the cabinet and went about the business of making herself pretty enough to have him regret her stomping out of his apartment.

Chad was in the kitchen, pouring her a cup of coffee. He held up a container of half and half, "Cream?"

"It's not necessary." Shea pulled on her running shoes.

"People are usually pretty committed to what goes in their coffee."

"I don't want any coffee, I'm not staying."

"What?" He put down the creamer and came into the living room. He sat down on the coffee table in front of her. He grabbed her hand before she could reach for her other shoe.

"I couldn't have screwed up if I wasn't even in the room with you. What is it?"

She pulled her hand away, "It's the Tampax in the bathroom. It's the fact that it's obvious you have a live-in girlfriend. Why did you lie to me?"

"Lie to you?" Chad started to laugh, but stopped when he saw her expression.

"Yes, being a girl myself I can tell if one lives here."

"One does. My roommate."

"Yeah, right. Convenient out-of-town roommate." Shea pulled on her other shoe.

"Shea, Shea, hold on. I guess I didn't tell you my roommate was a female. She works West Bureau Traffic." Chad walked back to a different bedroom and told Shea to come with him.

"No, that's okay," Shea said. Chad returned and took her by the hand.

"She's going to kill me."

Chad took her into a very feminine bedroom with a flowered bedspread, ruffled pillows, and women's clothing strewn on the floor. Chad grabbed a picture off her bureau. Two women: one small and blonde, the other tall and gaunt, standing arm and arm in the surf.

"My roommate, Elizabeth, is gay, this is her girlfriend Jody. Jody works Pacific Division." Shea held onto the photo, not wanting to meet Chad's eyes.

"Elizabeth and I worked the juvenile narco buy program. We thought we'd make perfect roommates. I'm supposed to add that 'manly protection' aspect to it, and she's supposed to keep the place clean, based on our conventional stereotypes." He pointed to her messy room. "She doesn't hold up her end of the bargain."

"I thought your roommate was a guy...I assumed..."

"I guess I didn't say, I never think about it really." He took the photo from her and she had to look at him. She shook her head, feeling stupid.

"I like that you were going to go storming out, it shows you kinda like me."

"I kinda like you," Shea admitted. "I feel so stupid. I saw the shampoo bottles..."

"The shampoo bottles? I thought it was the Tampax."

"That sealed the deal. The apricot-mango conditioner got my attention."

"Oh that's mine." He smiled at her and she laughed. "Drink your coffee, I'm going to shower."

Shea glanced around Elizabeth's room and closed the door behind her. She fixed herself a cup of coffee and wandered around his living room. A surfboard leaned on the wall next to the front door and a road bicycle hung from the ceiling. She drifted over to his bookcase and ran her fingertips over the titles, quantum physics, philosophy, and photography. Shea wondered if they were Elizabeth's or Chad's. She pulled a couple magazines off the tops of the books—a month old Playboy and Penthouse.

She sipped her coffee and examined the framed pictures on the bookshelf. She immediately recognized Chad's mother and father, arms around one and other with the backdrop of Universal Studios behind them. His mother was probably in her fifties, long curly hair, and a bright smile like her son's. Shea could picture her on a cucumber farm. His father looked like Robert Redford. The next picture was of a pretty girl on the beach, wind blowing her hair. She was hugging her body in an oversized sweat jacket.

"Before you storm out of here again, that's my sister." Shea turned to see Chad rubbing his wet curls with a towel and wearing a pair of jeans and no shirt. His tanned stomach was concaved and his faded jeans hung loosely on his hips. Shea smelled the apricot hair conditioner from across the room.

"I might have some trust issues." Shea replaced the frame on the shelf. Chad dropped the towel on the counter and pulled out a coffee cup from his cupboard.

"Ya think?" He laughed.

Shea picked up the next picture; it was an academy graduation picture. She recognized Chad, with a crew-cut, standing in between his parents.

"You're close with your family?"

"Yes, as close as you can be when you're a couple time zones away."

Shea replaced the picture and sat down on the couch with Chad.

"You really do use that conditioner," Shea said.

"I told you." He jumped up and went over to his complex stereo equipment. "What are you in the mood for?" She noticed he had a CD player, tape deck, and surprisingly, a turntable.

"You have *records*?"

"Well, it's not like I keep dinosaur bones under the bed." He opened a cabinet, revealing his album collection. Shea left the couch and joined him on the floor. He was looking through his CD collection as she flipped through the albums.

"It's been so long since I heard a record. But you're too young to have records." Shea realized his record collection was as eclectic as his books.

"Some of them are from when I was a kid, but I get a lot of my records from this great store down the street. Some music lends itself to the sound of an LP, like jazz."

"Exactly." Shea pulled out a Miles Davis album and offered it to Chad. Chad nodded and put it on the turntable. As the music poured out over the hisses and pops of the record, Shea smiled at Chad. He tossed her a floor pillow and leaned over on a leopard print pillow himself. He had a silky blond trail of hair from his navel that disappeared into his jeans and it made her breathing short.

"So, you surf?"

"Not well, but I do okay."

"And you bike."

"It's the best way to get around in a beach community. I'm going to enter a race, a hundred mile deal. It might kill me, but I have until September to get ready," Chad said.

"You read palms like your mom?"

"I do, let's see…" he sat back up and took Shea's hand. He stroked her palm with his thumbs and Shea thought maybe he was serious.

"It says you give good head," he said. Shea yanked her hand away and hit him with the back of her hand. "No, that wasn't in your palm. It's 'cause you have small breasts; girls with small breasts think they need more tricks."

"Well, you'll never know if you're right or not." Shea raised her eyebrows.

He laughed with her and tried to take her hand again, but she resisted him. She put her hands underneath her legs. Chad tackled her and tickled her sides until she was forced to remove her hands to fend him off. He pushed her on her back and pinned her hands over her head.

"Okay, I'm going to read your palms if you like it or not," he said. His tanned chest was above her face and it was peeling from a sunburn. His skin smelled clean and fresh and she swallowed hard.

"It says here that you are going to have a long life, let's see…you have trust issues and no, I'm sorry, it's here again…that good head thing." Shea laughed and wrapped her legs around his torso and flipped him over on his back. He was caught off-guard, but he recovered and pulled her back over with him. She found herself half lying on his chest, his hands wrapped tightly around her wrists. They were out of breath and looking into each other's eyes.

"You're strong," he said.

She thought about kissing him, but knew if they started kissing she was going to end up in bed with him this time.

"I'm starving," she said instead.

"We should go have breakfast, or lunch now, huh?" Chad released her wrists and moved out from underneath her. He went into his bedroom and returned wearing a t-shirt and a sweat jacket.

"Did you bring a jacket? It's still kind of cold."

He gave her his sweat jacket and got another sweatshirt from his bedroom. When she put it on, she could smell a combination of the damp odor of living next to the ocean and a masculine deodorant smell. She wrapped herself in it and followed him out the door.

They ate lunch at a funky vegetarian restaurant a few blocks from his house. The mousy waitress recognized him and called him "Chaddy." Shea thought she looked anemic and wanted to feed her a raw steak. After they ate, they ordered Bloody Mary's at a bar overlooking the beach.

Chad pulled her legs up onto his lap and was absent-mindedly stroking her calves as they talked. His eyes really did look like sunshine and water. Chad caught her looking at him and smiled at her.

"What are you thinking?"

"That you are too pretty to be a man," she said, feeling a little drunk.

"Oh no, I'm not sure that's a compliment." He self-consciously pulled his hair behind his ear.

"It is. I think that you're trouble."

"Yeah?"

"Well, when you've been around the block, you know what's coming up around the corner, and I think that you're trouble."

"Oh God. All of this experience you have. Don't judge me

based on your past. It's not fair to me."

"Did I mention I have trust issues?" She laughed dryly.

He leaned into her, over her legs, "Shea, you're involved with a married man. That's like being in charge of the lions at the zoo and not throwing the meat in first."

"I'm not even sure what you said," Shea said. He held up two fingers to the waitress as he finished his Bloody Mary.

"Seriously? Trust isn't even a luxury you can afford with him, right?" Chad asked. Shea felt like she had been driving on a smooth highway and suddenly the pavement was gone.

"No...but I don't think I want to talk about it."

"You nearly had a freakin' meltdown because you thought I had a girlfriend. I get to ask about the married guy."

"Maybe not." She was feeling extremely disloyal to Andrew at that moment.

"Are you with him because he's safe?"

"Safe?"

"He'll never ask for a commitment. I see you as a woman that is a little skittish if she isn't in control," Chad said.

"How can I possibly be in control if I'm involved with a man who is married?"

"You're in total control of your life. He can't ask you to marry him...change everything about your life with a single question." He smiled up at the waitress and she left them with two fresh drinks. An old Blondie song was playing in the bar. It made Shea feel a little melancholy.

They took a detour back to Chad's apartment by strolling on the beach. They walked and talked with linked arms. From time to time, Shea would lean into him, pushing him into the surf. Finally they stopped and found a place on the sand to wait out the sunset. The sky was turning pink and orange at the horizon line.

"Do you still do art...I mean, paint or draw or whatever?"

"A little."

"Do you paint the ocean? Sunsets like this?"

"I did when I first got here. Then I realized I didn't have anything original to say about the ocean, or anything else."

"Can I see some of your work?"

"Like, come up and see my etchings?" Chad laughed. "We'll see."

A homeless man with long, matted hair struggled up the

beach to ask them for change. He was covered in sand and wrapped in a filthy blanket. Chad handed him a couple of dollars.

"What? You thought I was going to rob him like the other night?" Chad looked at her surprised face. "He's my neighbor, so-to-speak."

"That had to be one of craziest nights of my life," Shea said.

"Me, too. I thought it was going to be a boring night at a promotional party and I end up getting robbed and making out with this gorgeous homicide detective." He put his hand on her leg.

"Yeah…that was a surprise, too."

"Man, I haven't made out like that since I was in Minnesota. I wanted you so bad it hurt, literally!" he said, squeezing her leg. Shea felt her pulse catch fire. He looked at her lips and back to her eyes. "You gotta ask me, remember?"

"What?" Shea said thickly.

"That was the deal, I wasn't going to pressure you. I wouldn't kiss you unless you asked me," he whispered onto her parted lips.

Shea just nodded, no words were coming out of her mouth.

He answered with his mouth covering hers. His hands were

on her cheeks and then in her hair.

Kissing was like talking with a new lover. She never stayed up all night talking with Andrew anymore, like they used to. They certainly didn't waste a lot of time kissing either.

"God, your mouth. You kiss good," Chad said.

The sun had sunk into the ocean. All that was left were the blurry watercolors of pink and orange. Chad pulled her up off the sand. They walked back to his apartment without talking too much— both of them anticipating what was going to happen next.

Shea's legs felt weak. She didn't know if it was from the long run in the sand that morning or if it was because of Chad. He held on to her hand possessively. When they got inside his apartment, she went to the bathroom immediately; the Bloody Marys had caught up with her. She was shocked when she saw that she had left her pager and cell phone on the bathroom counter. She checked for messages and she had none. She was never without her pager, ever. When she came back in the living room Chad had taken off his sweatshirt and lit a few candles. He handed her a beer and dropped the needle back on the Miles Davis album.

"I left my pager and cell phone here," Shea said.

"Did they call about your suspects?"

"No, they didn't." She put the phone and pager on the coffee table.

Chad excused himself to the bathroom and Shea kicked off her shoes. Now that the passion had dipped and time had passed since the kiss on the beach, she felt herself growing nervous about what was coming next. She hadn't been with anyone else for so long, and a thousand second-thoughts raced through her mind. She took a long drink of her beer and closed her eyes, listening to the music. She thought maybe Chad had lit some incense, because she smelled a hint of cedar in the air.

She didn't hear him come out of the bathroom, but he was suddenly next to her, arms wrapping around her waist from behind. He kissed her neck and she kept her eyes closed and moved with the music against his pelvis. She turned to face him. She set her beer down on the coffee table and grabbed the top button of his Levis.

"My palm doesn't lie...I do give good head." Shea said before biting his ear lobe.

"I don't doubt it, I've kissed you." He stopped her from unbuttoning his pants. She looked up at him curiously. "But, I don't need any parlor tricks."

"What do you mean?" she asked. Her boldness had never been questioned before.

"I'm not going to be impressed with technique. I want *you*." He put his index finger on her forehead and then on her heart.

"Come on." Chad took her into his bedroom. It was dimly lit room from a Moroccan-looking lantern in the corner. A Mexican blanket with bright stripes was stretched across his bed, which was a couple of mattresses on the floor. Books stacked on the floor and magazines were strewn everywhere. Shea took off her shoes.

"Will you take off your clothes for me?" he whispered.

"If it was a little darker," Shea said. "Or if I was a little drunker."

He lay down on his bed and propped his head up with some colorful pillows and his hands interlocked behind his head.

"For a guy that doesn't want parlor tricks, you do seem like you want a show." She began to unbutton her blouse. She slipped it off her shoulders.

"God, you're beautiful. All of those freckles." That made it easier for her to slide her jeans off. Her rear end was another story.

No matter how much she managed to run, it was too large in her opinion. She stepped out of her jeans and stood in front of him in her white cotton bikini underwear. Chad removed one hand from behind his head and rested it on his groin over his jeans. Shea moved onto the bed.

"Lay on your stomach," Chad said. She lowered herself onto the scratchy blanket. Chad straddled her butt and began to massage her back. Other than a few harsh squeezes of her shoulders, she had never had a man express any interest in that part of her body. Chad's strong fingers worked the tendons in her neck and then moved slowly down her spine.

"Oh, you're coiled up tight," he said. "This is how I know you're not ready to lose yourself yet."

"Chad, I cannot honestly ever see myself losing myself," she said into a pillow that smelled like him.

"Baby, get motivated." Chad stroked her back so long, she felt guilty. She tried to roll over, but his firm hand held her down. "I'm fine, you can't do anything to me or for me, Shea."

He rolled her over, but moved down to her feet, rubbing them firmly. She had aches she wasn't even aware of. His hair fell across his face as he paid attention to his work.

Chad carefully dropped her foot and moved his hands up her thighs. He gently pushed open her legs, just enough so he could sit between them. Moving his hands up to breasts, Shea felt her body rise. His hands kept moving to her neck and touched it as if it were a more sexual part of her body. His right hand crested her jaw bone, and he ran his hand on her lips; she parted them and one of his fingers slipped inside. She swallowed it up to his knuckle and observed his expression change. She knew she had taken his breath away as well.

"You're going to ruin me," he said, his voice cracking and he withdrew his hand. He pulled her underwear off so quickly she had no time to protest. Shea dreaded the thought of him going down on her. She showered so long ago; she had a whole new list of anxieties to draw from. But his mouth didn't touch her. She opened her eyes to check. He was just back on his knees, hands on the inside of her thighs looking at her. He met her eyes.

"You're beautiful." Shea closed her eyes again, willing him not to use the word "pussy" or anything worse. She felt his fingertips gently parting her, the wetness making soft sucking noises as he separated her and his fingers moving deep inside her. Shea felt like she did when she was dancing, so lost that she was no longer self-conscious.

He might have been talking to her, but she groaned again because the combination of fingers and thumbs made it impossible to hear him or answer him. He was breathing hard too, and somehow she was able to find his groin with her right hand. He didn't stop her this time. She felt his penis pressed tightly against his jeans. Shea popped the top two buttons with her one hand, but couldn't get the third.

"Please, Chad."

He withdrew his wet hand from between her legs and raised up on his knees. He unbuttoned his fly and Shea slipped the jeans down his bony hips. Her hands slipped over the head of his penis and she felt he was wet too. He groaned, his head back. Shea held him tightly in her hand.

Shea pulled him down on top of her and they kissed wildly. He moved in between her legs and hesitated just for a second before he slipped inside of her. Maybe it was his size, maybe it was because she was so aroused, but it seemed as though he filled her up like no one ever had before. He didn't move for a second.

"Shit, if you move at all Shea, I'm going to come," he said breathlessly. She couldn't resist. She moved her legs up onto his backside and he bucked into her. He groaned into her neck and she held him tightly until he stopped moving.

"Oh God, I'm sorry," he said. "How embarrassing. But I didn't even think I'd make it inside of you. I almost came about six times today."

"That's a supreme compliment," she said.

"Don't go anywhere." He held her down. "I'll get hard again, I'm fucking you all night long." And he did just that.

She fell into a deep sleep and woke to him calling her name. She was disoriented as she opened her eyes to the dark room. He was holding her pager. She could hear it beeping.

"Shea, hey this thing is going off." She took it from him and looked at the number. It was the station, the gang unit's number.

"Oh no," she groaned, as he handed her his phone.

"I'll make you some coffee."

Hector picked up halfway through the first ring.

"Hey, Hector."

"Hi, sleepyhead. We got Edgar."

"I'm on my way," Shea said. She was sore and tired and warm. She didn't want to get out of Chad's bed. She searched the floor for her clothes. She was dressed when Chad came back in the room. He had a cup of coffee for her in a plastic cup.

"To go."

"That's service."

"Did they arrest your guys?"

"One of them. Not the one I want, but hopefully he'll tell me something about his brother. What time is it?"

"It's 2:30," Chad said. He pulled his jeans on over his white butt.

"You don't have to get up," Shea said.

"I'm walking you to your car." Chad stepped into a pair of old flip-flop sandals, as Shea gathered up her duffle bag. Chad handed her his sweat jacket.

"No, I don't need this."

"Don't argue." Chad hugged her and she dropped the duffle bag and threw her arms around his shoulders. He squeezed her tightly and started to say something but stopped. He released her and opened the front door.

"Let's get you on the road."

It was cold and damp outside. When they reached her car, she hugged him again. He held her, stroking her hair. She kissed him quickly and got in her car. He waited on the sidewalk until she pulled away.

Chapter 18

The gang detail was waiting for her in the homicide unit at the station. Usually when she was called in from home, she came to work in the same business attire she wore during the day. Tonight she was in a pair of tight jeans, a wrinkled blouse, and a man's sweat jacket.

"We tried your house first, Detective Reed," Jimmy Mora said, getting up from her desk.

"Yeah, yeah. You guys found me, that's the point," Shea said. "So what happened?"

"Edgar was hanging out in the usual spot with his homeboys," Hector said. "We just cuffed him up and tossed him in the backseat. He wanted to know why he was being arrested. I told him for rape."

"Dan's sitting with him in the first interrogation room. He's a juvy, so we had to uncuff him."

"Any word about his brother?"

"Nothing yet," Hector said. "Are we doing the search warrant tonight?"

"You guys overtime? Where's your boss?"

"He's in the watch commander's office. But he already said we'll do the warrant. It shouldn't be that big of a deal," Jimmy said.

"Okay, I have to make some calls, but I think we need to get in his room right away and see if we can get any info on the brother," Shea said. They agreed and went to go find their supervisor.

Shea tried Detective Ellingsworth's home number, but there was no answer. She then called the pager number for Detective Lancaster. She wanted to call Walter Smith, but she knew it was Lancaster's case and she'd have to deal with him. She called Curt from a different phone to advise him of what was going on.

"Do you need help?" he asked sleepily.

"I'm just going to interrogate Edgar and book him for the Foothill rape. The gang unit's going over to the group home to look through his room. If he gives up his brother, that's a different story."

"Call in Jack, he wants the overtime. He's coming back on Monday morning anyway."

"I will," Shea said.

"Did you notify RHD?"

"I have a call into Lancaster right now."

"Okay. Good luck." Shea hung up on Curt and called Jack. It was now almost 4:00 a.m. Samantha answered the phone in a whisper. Shea pictured the baby lying between them. Jack came on the line and told her he'd be right in.

Shea's phone rang and she spoke to Detective Lancaster.

"So, it's the younger brother?" he asked.

"Yes."

"Well, call me back if you get any information about the other one, okay?"

Shea assured him she would and hung up. She headed to the interrogation room. Officer Dan Telles met her in the hall.

"Your unit's going to head over to the group home and search his room," Shea told him quietly.

"Okay. He hasn't said much."

Shea opened the interrogation room door and asked Edgar if he wanted a Coke. He had the same sleepy, empty eyes all the foster kids in Miss Mary's group home had. Except his head was shaved, his body a wall of gang graffiti, and he was facing an interrogation on rape.

Shea went back in the hall and asked Mario to set up the tape and monitor the interview from the tape room. Shea got Edgar a Coke and returned to the interrogation room. She dropped a big notebook on the table and sat down across from him. She began by asking him general questions about his name, address, school, tattoos, for several minutes. He answered her questions impatiently. She asked him to name his close relatives, but he didn't mention a brother. Finally, he sucked his front teeth with his tongue and asked what was going on.

"You've been arrested for a rape," Shea said. She read him his Miranda Rights and he sullenly agreed to talk to her.

"I ain't raped nobody."

"Actually…" Shea opened her notebook and pulled out several reports. "You and another guy raped a few women."

"What other guy?" He raised his eyes to look over the reports.

"I don't know that yet. The women have only identified you so far," Shea lied. She pulled out his photo line-up and she showed him the copy where the victim had circled his photo.

"That's not right." He shook his head and played with a tiny barbell that pierced his eyebrow.

Shea had him account for his whereabouts on the nights of the rapes and listened to him vehemently deny his involvement. This took almost an hour. She heard a soft knock on the door and she excused herself. When she went into the hallway she found Jack waiting for her.

"You're a sight for sore eyes." She squeezed Jack's arm.

"I was talking to Dan and he kind of filled me in. You've been busy," Jack said.

"I have been, and you don't even know the half of it yet." She grinned at him.

"What do you need to me to do?" He looked at her outfit but didn't comment.

"Can you go with the gang unit to the group home and supervise the search warrant? The main thing I'm looking for is information on the brother, but also stuff from the victims. They rob them *and* rape them," she said.

"I'll get right on it. They're saddling up in the trailer. You want them to leave Dan here, right?"

"Yeah. Thanks."

Shea went back in the interrogation room and told Edgar they were serving a search warrant on his house at that moment. He looked at her blankly. There was a choice she had to make. Some rape suspects responded well to an understanding tone and minimizing their responsibility for their actions, but this guy was acting like a hardcore gang member. He wasn't budging on any of it. Shea decided to try a different tactic.

"Okay, the rape stuff is really not my thing. It's just that when you used the ATM before you shot the cop we have a picture of you from the bank," she said quickly and clearly. His face flashed recognition and surprise before it transformed into a stony mask.

"I didn't shoot a cop," he said.

"You had the lady's purse in the car with you, didn't you? That's why you couldn't risk having the policeman approach your car. Or I should say Mary Jones' car. One of her cars, or was that her boyfriend's car?" She couldn't go too far afield, or he'd know for sure she was speculating.

"That wasn't me," he insisted. He crossed his arms.

"The lady whose ATM card you used identified you as the person who raped her. She remembered the tattoo on your fingers." Shea nodded to his hand.

"But, that doesn't mean I shot anyone." Score. Small, but now they were getting somewhere.

"I guess I don't follow you. The ATM surveillance photo sure looks like you."

"A lot of people look like me," he said.

"Are you saying you might've given her stuff to someone else?" Shea asked him. "You don't want to go down for an attempted murder of a police officer if you didn't do it. The rape is no big deal compared to that." She kept the pressure on him; now he had a choice to admit to one crime in order to deny the other.

He chewed the side of his mouth. "I'm not a rat."

"Of course not, but someone put you into the mix, didn't they?" Shea asked.

"I didn't do nothing." His eyes were twitching.

"Edgar, we have your DNA, you've heard of that, right? Your DNA was found in the lady's car. You aren't going to be able deny the rape. You've been identified. Have I asked you who the other guy was?"

"No."

"No. But, I know about the other guy, too. Don't I?"

"I'm not a snitch."

"I know. You said that. I bet the other guy is older, and I bet he told you that you're a juvenile and that nothing would really happen to you. That happens a lot. Older guys have the younger ones take the fall," Shea said. "Did you shoot the police officer?"

"No."

"Did the other guy?"

Edgar put his head down. Shea sat silently with Edgar for a few minutes. She was tired. This kid wasn't going to give up his older brother. Shea weighed her options. She could go on with the farce that Caesar had not been identified, but one way or another the arrest of Edgar Padilla was going to get back to Caesar. He'd know it was just a matter of time before they came for him.

Shea kept her interrogation up for another half-an-hour with no success. Finally she closed her notebook and stood up.

"I'm going to go call Mary Jones. They should've tossed your room by now." Shea left him and hurried to the tape room where she watched him on the video monitor. He buried his head in his arms on the table.

"What do you think?" Shea asked Dan.

"I don't think he's going to give up his brother."

"Can you keep an eye on him?" Shea asked.

She pulled out her police radio and listened to the base frequency to hear if the gang unit had made it to the location. She requested her partner on the simplex frequency.

"Hey, we're in." Jack told her.

"Roger," Shea said. "Landline me when you get a chance."

"Give me five," Jack said.

"Roger." Shea walked over to her desk. She brought the sleeve of Chad's jacket to her nose and breathed in the salty smell of the ocean. She closed her eyes and thought about him lying naked in his bed. She felt her stomach flip over and she could almost feel his mouth on her neck again. The phone at her desk clanged and she grabbed the receiver.

"Hey," she said.

"Okay, we tossed his room. According to the woman who runs this joint--"

"Mary Jones."

"Right. She says that they have an aunt in Pacoima. She thinks that's where the older brother might be. I sent two units over there. In this guy's room we found a credit card with the name—

hold on, Sarge where's the credit card?—okay, Delia Lanier?"

Shea flipped through her reports. That was the name of one

of rape victims that Detective Ellingsworth thought the Padilla

brothers were responsible for.

"Bingo," Shea said. "That's one of our rapes."

"He also has a bunch of cash. It might be hard to prove it's

from the rape victims. Are there any clothing descriptions? Wait,

hold on." Shea heard him talking to an officer in the background.

Jack came back on the line.

"Shea, you're not going to believe this, but I'm looking at

newspaper articles of Chloe Diaz's murder. Sergeant Jackson found

them in a shoe box in his room."

"Holy shit," Shea said. "Can you bring in Mary Jones? I want

to press her."

"Yeah, of course," Jack said. "She's being pretty

cooperative."

"There's a little boy there that they call Zero. He might tell

you something. He talked to me the day I was there."

"Right, partner," Jack said. It was good to have him back.

Shea went into the interrogation room and sat down across from Edgar. He held his hands apart as if to say, "what?"

"They were in your room," she told him. "They got the credit card of one of your victims."

"Shit." Edgar looked up at the ceiling.

"Why did you have a newspaper article about the murder of a female police officer at a party at the Odyssey Restaurant?" He looked at her quizzically. Shea wondered if he truly did not know about it. Caesar could have stored the articles in the shoebox without him knowing.

"I don't know about that," he said.

"Is everything in your room yours?"

"Most of it."

"Did you share your room with someone?" Shea asked. His face colored.

"Edgar, I already know the answers to the questions I am asking." He kept his head down and then abruptly jerked it up, like a wild horse spitting out a bit from its mouth.

"Then why are you asking me if you already know?" he shouted. His eyes were filled with tears.

"I want to know if you're being honest with me or not. Because at some point you are going to want me to believe you didn't shoot the cop during the traffic stop, and you're going to want me to believe you didn't murder the female cop at her party," Shea told him quietly. "I can only believe you if you are telling the truth up until those important parts."

"I didn't kill no lady cop." He rubbed his eyes roughly.

"Who do you share a room with?"

"My brother, Caesar." Edgar was fighting back the tears.

"Good, okay Edgar. That was the truth. Thank you." Shea moved her chair around the table and put her hand briefly on his arm.

"Where's your brother right now?"

"I honestly don't know. I haven't seen him for a month," Edgar said.

"Is he your full brother?"

"Huh?"

"Do you have the same mother and father?" Shea asked.

"Same mother. Different fathers."

"What's his father's name?"

"Gonzalez."

"What's your father's name?"

"Lopez."

"Where does Padilla come in?" Shea asked, writing all of this down.

"My mom's name." He sighed and looked at his hands.

"When they first placed you guys, it said you were placed with your grandfather on your father's side."

"My dad's dad. My dad was killed. Caesar's dad and all his family were in Mexico. He never knew his dad," Edgar said.

Shea said a silent "shit." Family in Mexico was not a good thing. Caesar was probably already there. There would be no extradition on a death penalty case.

"Does Caesar speak Spanish?"

"Just a little," Edgar said.

"Caesar got you in to all this freaky stuff with the women?" Shea downplayed the criminal act of rape with softer, less volatile words.

"Yeah. I used to just go along and lookout for him. Then...well, I..."

"Did he kind of force you to do it?" Shea asked. Deflect the blame and admit to the crime was a common tactic of hers.

"Yeah, he'd call me names. The first time he told me to do it, I didn't want to. The lady was like, old, and I didn't want to. He put the gun to my head, and he told me to do it or he would shoot me." It didn't matter to Shea whether this was true or not, it mattered that he was on a roll, he was talking.

"Did that make you mad or scare you?"

"Both. He's crazy. He coulda shot me. You don't know all the stuff he'd do." Edgar was chewing his lip.

"To you? Like when you were younger?" Shea asked gently. Edgar nodded and then said he didn't want to talk about it.

"He's just crazy."

"Well, he sounds like it. Did you know he was going to kill the lady cop?" Shea used his words.

"No, no, I didn't know nothing. He didn't tell me nothing. Just after he wanted me to get rid of the gun, and I'm like why? What did you do? We never shot nobody we raped, why do I need to get rid of the gun? And he is like, well I shot someone, so you gotta take it and dump it somewhere."

"Did he say who he shot?" Shea said. He could've been talking about killing a gang member.

"He showed me the newspaper and I was like, fuck, why'd you do that?"

"What did he say, exactly?"

"He just said he blasted the bitch and it was at a big cop party. I already knew about the other cop he shot and that was with his same gun."

"Where did you dump the gun?"

"I threw it off the Santa Monica pier." Shea was startled at the mention of the place she was just at a few hours ago.

"How did you get there?"

"I drove."

"Was anyone with you?"

"No. Hell no. I didn't tell no one. He would kill me," Edgar said. "Is he going to know I talked to you?"

Shea hated this part. She knew if she told him the truth he would stop talking.

"Not if I can help it," Shea said encouragingly. "Where is Caesar right now?"

"I don't know. I was glad he was gone, to be honest with 'chu. I didn't want any more trouble. He already killed a lady, I knew if we went out hunting for bitches he'd kill one with me with him, and then what?"

"I understand. Why do you suppose he killed the lady cop at the party?"

"Probably was trying to get some from her. He didn't say anything about why."

"Why did he shoot at the officer that pulled him over that day?"

"It was like you said. He had the one lady's purse with him. He thought the cop would arrest him. He was way wasted that day, too. We used her money to buy rock, so he wasn't even thinking straight."

"What did he do with the car?"

"He burned it up in Little Tujunga."

"Does he have a girlfriend?"

Edgar laughed and shook his head.

"Friends?"

"Everyone hates him. No one likes him. Everyone thinks he's

crazy. He'd tell people that when our mom got out of prison he was going to rape her. No one wanted to be around him," Edgar said.

"He'll never hurt you again," Shea said. Edgar's gang persona was completely gone. He was shaking in his chair.

"He's crazy," Edgar repeated.

"Mary Jones said he has an aunt in Pacoima."

"It's not an aunt, it's a place he used to go to buy from. Sometimes they let him stay there."

"Is there a chance he's there now?"

"Maybe, but I don't know." Edgar said miserably.

"What kind of gun did you throw in the ocean?"

"Beretta 9mm."

"Where did he get it from?"

"I don't know. He had it for a long time. We shot it before up in the Tujunga Canyon."

"It was the one he used on all the rapes?" Shea asked.

"Yes. It's the only one he had."

"Was it loaded when you threw it in the ocean?"

"I don't know. I never checked. I went there in the middle of the night, and I took it from my pocket and threw it fast. No one saw."

"When was this?"

"The day after the lady cop was killed."

"Why was he working at the Odyssey Restaurant?"

"The counselor at school got him the job. He did it because he could break into people's cars on his breaks. He'd spit in people's food too, he liked that." Edgar shook his head.

Shea added another scenario to the night of the Christmas party. Chloe had interrupted a burglary from motor vehicle.

"Are you hungry?" Shea asked him.

"A little."

"I'm going to get you a candy bar. Could you find the place in the Canyon where you guys shot the gun?" Anticipating that finding the gun would be difficult, maybe she could at least find some casings.

"I think so. I kinda gotta use the bathroom."

"Hold on. I'll get an officer to take you." Shea put her hand on his shoulder as she left the room. She ran back to the tape room. Dan met her with a high-five.

"Out-fucking-standing!" Dan said.

"Tape running? Everything okay, it's on tape?" Shea looked past him to the monitor.

"Yeah, I flipped the tape when you went in the last time. Oh my God!" Dan ran his hands through his hair.

"Will you take him to the bathroom?"

"Yes, yes," Dan said. "I'll even buy him *two* fucking candy bars."

"Thanks, Dano."

"That was so good. That was so cool," Dan said. She ran to her desk and picked up her radio and asked Jack to come up on the frequency.

"Where are you?" Shea asked.

"En route back to the station. Ten minutes."

"What's the status of the units on the other location?" Shea said.

"They should be door-knocking right about now."

"Okay, tell them it's not an aunt's house, it's a crack house."

"Rog. See you in a few," Jack said.

Shea picked up the phone and paged Detective Lancaster. He called back quicker than he had the first time. "Edgar Padilla, the younger brother, rolled on Caesar. He said Caesar killed Chloe Diaz and that he disposed of the murder weapon for him."

"What?" Lancaster said.

Shea briefed him on the interrogation.

"Is this all inside Miranda?"

"Yes. He waived."

"On tape?"

"Video and audio," Shea said.

"What's the status of the suspect now?"

"We have a unit door-knocking a possible location in Pacoima, but he has family in Mexico and Edgar hasn't seen him for a month."

"Shit, okay. I have to call my partner. I'm on my way there. I live in Santa Clarita, so it won't take me long. If they get Caesar, no one Mirandizes him."

"Of course," Shea said.

"I'll see you within the hour."

"I'll be here." Shea hung up. She turned up her radio to see if she could hear any information on the gang unit's status in Pacoima. Jack came in through the back door, carrying paper bags filled with property seized from Edgar's room.

"I couldn't bring Mary Jones back with me. There's no one to watch the kids." Jack dumped the bags on his desk. He looked at her.

"You have that "king shit" look about you...did you break him?"

Shea nodded and told him the story.

"Congratulations!" Jack said. "This is some serious police work you did. You solved it, Shea. You fuckin' solved it. Chloe *was* murdered. You solved the OIS, a bunch of rapes. God, there's going to be no working with you now."

"I wish you were with me."

"Well, if I was, we might've been working *our* cases. You got caught up in this because I wasn't here," Jack said.

"I think the boys in the group home are going to have to be interviewed thoroughly. This crazy guy might've molested them, too."

Jack's radio chirped. "W22 are you on the air?"

Jack grabbed his radio, "That's Hector. Go ahead for W22."

"W22, this is W38, suspect in custody." Shea fell back into

her seat and closed her eyes.

"W38, roger, good work."

"Rog. En route back to the station. W40 is going to search the location." Jack keyed his mike twice and sat down across from Shea. She held out her hands and he slapped them.

"RHD's coming in. No one can talk to him," Shea said.

"That sucks. So much for the cherry on top."

"It doesn't matter." Shea shook her head. "I'm too happy and too tired to care."

"Do you want me to book the other one, so he's not in here when his brother arrives?"

"Would you?" Shea asked. "I'll start the arrest report."

"No worries." Jack got up from his desk and went to get a booking approval form.

Shea called Chad and he answered on the first ring.

"You were sleeping," Shea said.

"Li'l bit," Chad said.

"Chad, I got him. The brother rolled on the suspect. We have the suspect in custody."

"That's awesome. I guess it's worth you bailing on me in the middle of the night. That's great."

"It is. I just wanted to tell you. I'll let you go back to sleep."

"When you get a chance, call me back, I want to hear all the details."

"I'm going to be here for hours." Shea twisted the phone cord in her fingertips.

"Okay, get back to work. Shea…"

"Yeah?"

"I'll talk to you later." They hung up. Jack returned with his booking approval.

"Lt. Wonderful?" he asked, nodding at her phone.

"No," Shea said. "I met someone."

"You *met* someone?" Jack smiled at her. "Is that why you look like you slept in your clothes?"

"Yup." Shea nodded.

"Man, I take a little time off for a baby and I miss everything. Who is he?"

"He works narcotics."

"And you like him?"

"I like him. I like-like him." Shea grinned at Jack. "If you were a girl, I'd tell you some amazing details."

"If you were a *guy* you'd tell me amazing details," Jack

countered. He began filling out the booking approval. "What's this

guy's name again?"

"Chad."

"Chad?" Jack looked up from the booking approval form.

"Oh, no-Edgar Padilla." Shea started laughing.

"Shea, when we're done, I'm buying you breakfast and

you'll tell me the amazing details, but for now…can I get you to

focus on the case at hand?" Jack said.

Hector and Jimmy came back into the detective squad room.

"We put Caesar in a holding tank, but he's going to have to

be booked on the 13th floor," Hector said, referring to the medical

facility of the Los Angeles County jail.

"5150?" Shea said.

"I don't know if he's crazy, but he's definitely on something.

He was just slobbering in a back room. The place was filled with

dope and idiots. One dipshit tried to reach for a sawed-off shotgun

he had stashed under the cushions of the couch. Another guy tried to

bail out of a second story window. We called in some Foothill units.

Lots of assholes are going to jail this morning," Hector said.

"We found three keys in plain sight. We'll get a warrant for a better search. There's gonna be dope everywhere," Jimmy said.

"RHD is en route," Shea said.

"I don't think he can be interrogated. He is way out-of-it," Jimmy said.

"I owe you guys at least a case of beer. Thank you," Shea said.

"Beer or Scotch?"

"Both, you guys get both and some chips. I'm going to go take a look at him," Shea said to Jack.

She went over to the patrol side of the station. She walked to the row of holding tanks. Caesar was handcuffed to a bench. He was shirtless and in boxer shorts. He was very thin and frail-looking. It was hard to believe he had waged such violence in the last few months. He swung his head up and looked at her dizzily. He stuck out his tongue and licked his lips. Shea touched the glass and walked away.

She intercepted Detective Lancaster at the back door of the station.

"Hi," he said. He shifted his notebook and shook her hand. "Steve Lancaster. I think we talked the night of the party."

"Yes, briefly. Your guy is in the first holding tank. He's pretty out-of-it. He's under the influence of something."

"No one talked to him?"

"No one talked to him," Shea said.

"Okay, point me to the coffee. When my partner gets here, you can brief us both at the same time."

"All right." Shea took him over to the coffee pot and handed him a Styrofoam cup. Lancaster set down his leather notebook. Shea noticed the embossed Robbery Homicide emblem on the front in gold.

"My desk is over there." Shea pointed across the room. He told her he needed to make some calls and he set up shop at an empty desk near hers. Curt came in the back door with another detective that Shea assumed was Steve Lancaster's partner. Lancaster greeted them both and the three joked and chatted with each other. Curt was wearing a golf shirt and Dockers slacks. It was the most casual attire Shea had ever seen him in. He walked over to his desk with the two RHD detectives following him.

"Hey, Shea. Have you met Lenny Nelichek?" Curt asked. Shea introduced herself to the older detective.

"Why don't you give us all a rundown of what's happened, Shea. Start with how you put all of this together." Curt pulled up two chairs for the RHD detectives. Shea picked up her notes and moved closer to the group. As she spoke, Detective Nelichek took notes. Lancaster just listened.

"What made you go the restaurant to find Padilla? I don't get that," Lancaster said.

Shea remembered her dream about the Christmas party and decided that bordered on ridiculous in present company.

"It was just a hunch. Maybe he worked there and confronted Chloe that night."

"The younger brother's being booked for the Foothill rape?"

"Yes, but there are at least two other rapes that can be filed on him," Shea said.

"We can book Caesar for rape and you'll have time to investigate the homicide. We can book him for the attempted murder on Ornelas too," Curt said.

The RHD detectives agreed that was a good idea. It was

unlikely that Padilla would be able to make the astronomical bail that several counts of rape and attempted murder would hold.

"Let's see how screwed up Padilla is," Lancaster said. Curt told them where the tape room was and handed them a blank audiotape. "We might not even need that if he's as bad as the officers are saying."

The two detectives left the homicide unit and Shea went back to work organizing her paperwork.

The RHD detectives quickly surmised they wouldn't be able to interrogate Padilla, so a unit drove him to LA County jail, 13th floor, to book him for as many charges as Shea could articulate— with the exception of Chloe's homicide. Detective Lancaster told Curt they would be writing the press release on Monday morning.

By early afternoon, it was just Jack, Curt, and Shea left at the station. Jack finished writing the property report and leaned back in his chair.

"Are we ready to call it?" Jack said.

"I think so. I finished the rape reports. I've been here since three." Shea said wearily.

"You want to grab breakfast? Well, lunch I guess now?"

"Yeah, Curt, do you want to join us for lunch?"

"You two go ahead. I'm going to finish this personnel complaint they assigned me three months ago," Curt said. "Turn in your greenies before you leave."

"My overtime for this month's going to be crazy." Shea filled out her green overtime slip.

"That's another reason why I had to come back to work. A week without overtime is a serious problem," Jack said.

"Where're we eating?"

"Somewhere I can buy a bottle of champagne," Jack said.

"Champagne?" Curt looked at them over the top of his glasses.

"We're celebrating. I know it's going to be months before she gets a commendation, if RHD will ever write one. And this was some crazy-ass police work that deserves to be properly celebrated. That, and we are celebrating my baby and what else, Shea…oh yeah, a new romance?" Shea gave Jack a dirty look.

"Is that why you're in jeans and a wrinkled shirt?" Curt gestured to Shea's outfit.

"Remind me to never tell you anything again," Shea said to

Jack. She tossed her overtime slip into Curt's in-box.

"Well, I'm all for it. Did you notice, Jack she did not get in a fist fight with the RHD guys? This is a kinder, gentler Detective Reed. She appears…what is the word I'm looking for…happy?" Curt said.

"That's new, huh?" Jack put his overtime slip on Curt's desk as well.

"If you're looking for champagne, you know the Odyssey has a great all-day Sunday brunch," Curt said.

"That'd be too weird," Shea said.

"I think it'd be perfect. Come on, I'll meet you there," Jack said.

"You just want to go there because it's half-way home for you."

"It's either that or the golf course. We could get a burger and a warm beer. You pick."

"All right. Odyssey, but I still think it's a creepy place to celebrate," Shea said.

"Shea, if RHD isn't writing a commendation, I'll do it right away. The gang unit shouldn't have to wait around for something to come out of downtown." Curt got up from his desk, holding his empty coffee cup. He put his hand lightly on her upper back between her shoulder blades, "You did a fantastic job."

Chapter 19

In the parking lot back at the Odyssey, Shea looked out over the San Fernando Valley. A marine layer had left a hazy mist, making it hard to see very far. She got out of her car and stretched. Jack pulled in next to her and jumped out of his SUV. He was bouncing on his toes.

"You know that Lancaster guy, we were in the can and he said I was lucky to have you as a partner. He called you 'tenacious.'"

"Hmm. He never said shit to me."

"They never will. Come on." He grabbed her by her sweat jacket and pulled her along.

"You really don't think this is weird to drink champagne at the place where someone was murdered?"

"Of course it is, but that's us," Jack said. "We still eat the donuts on Victory and look what happened there."

Jack had tossed his sports jacket and tie in the car, but they still looked like an odd couple. The hostess seated them at a table near the window and handed them menus. When the waitress appeared, Jack ordered a bottle of champagne.

"What are we celebrating?" The waitress asked in a sugary

voice.

"You don't want to know," Jack said. The waitress giggled and told them she'd be right back.

"She's going to think we're celebrating something really crude."

"Yeah, yeah. I know what I'm having." He shut his menu and put it on the edge of the table.

"Let me guess…something steak-related." Shea put her menu on top of his. "Tell me about the baby."

"She's different from her sister. She cries non-stop. Kaylee was easy to get on a schedule, but this one's fussy," he said. "Sam's so tired."

"I thought you were going to be off a lot longer."

"Her mom's coming on Monday. Sam really needs better help than me. I apparently get too distracted for her taste. She lost her mind because I was supposed to put a load of wash in the machine and I ended up outside because the dog had gotten into the trash and had diapers all over the lawn."

"Sounds fun."

"It's crazy at my house. I'm glad to be back to murder."

"How is Sam physically?" Shea said.

"She's okay. Second time around, so she knew what to expect." The waitress returned with the champagne and poured their glasses. She took their orders and left.

"Okay, seriously..." Jack raised his glass for a toast, "Congratulations. You did an awesome investigation."

"Thank you." Shea clicked her glass to his and took a long swallow.

"Tell me about the narco guy," Jack said. Shea felt herself blush and she smiled – a guy she could talk about! She told him how she met Chad and about their encounter with the robber in Rampart. She left out the make-out session in Elysian Park. Then she told him about her date with him on Saturday, again leaving out the salacious details.

"So, he's younger then you?" Jack said.

"Yes. I know. It's ridiculous."

"Guys do it all the time. Shit, Sam's seven years younger than me," Jack said.

"Well, it's like a whirlwind thing. I don't know how this is going to work out long-term."

"What about the other guy?" Jack didn't call Andrew "Lt. Wonderful," and Shea appreciated that.

"I told him I was going to start dating other people. I can't just keep doing what I've been doing forever." Shea drank a long sip of champagne and Jack refilled her glass.

"What if he leaves his wife now? What would you do?"

"I really doubt that'd happen," Shea said.

"But would you dump the new guy?" Jack asked.

"I don't know. Not right now. I mean, you know how it is, this is the stage when things are perfect." Shea smiled.

"I think I can remember that stage."

By the time finished their meal, they had consumed the entire bottle of champagne. She felt more sleepy than drunk. They ordered coffee and sobered up while gossiping about people at work, Jack complaining about having his mother-in-law moving in with them, and discussions about the upcoming preliminary hearing they had to get prepared for.

"Okay, now give me the amazing details. I've sat patiently through how interesting 'narco boy' is, how pretty his eyes are, etcetera. I think I'm entitled to the juicy details," Jack said.

"First of all, you are not *entitled* to anything." Shea laughed. "You just haven't had sex in a few months and you want to live vicariously through me."

"Is that so wrong?"

"Okay, he's really good in bed," Shea said.

"You're gonna have to do better than that," Jack said. He paid the check and Shea put cash down for the tip.

"He's really sexy. He has this amazing torso. I think because he surfs and bike rides. Anyway he's skinny and muscular and…"

"This isn't going to work. You start discussing his genitals and I'm going to throw up," Jack said. "Why don't you have sex with a girl and tell me about that? I think that might work for me."

They walked slowly back to their cars.

"Thanks for coming in today. I'd still be there if you didn't come in."

"You're welcome," Jack said. "You okay to drive?"

"Yup. The coffee woke me up." Shea unlocked her car door. "You know why Caesar was working here? He liked breaking into cars on his breaks."

"Terrific. Shit, maybe you solved some BFMV's, too."

"You're right. I'll tell the auto guys on Monday. They'll be happy to get a few clearances," Shea said.

"I wonder if Chloe interrupted a BFMV," Jack said.

"There's a chance he wanted to rape her. He might've confronted her in the bathroom where I saw the blood. Or maybe she recognized him. Hector said she was doing her own investigation to try to identify who shot Ornelas."

"The bottom line is that no one will think she killed herself now. That's worse than it not getting solved. Having everyone think you killed yourself."

"That was a stupid theory anyway. She shoots herself and then one of her friends finds the gun and takes it? That was so farfetched," Shea said. "I think it was a convenient theory because they weren't solving it."

"Well, it's a fantastic investigation. I better get home." Jack left her and walked over to his car.

Shea got in her car and drove home. She was close to falling asleep as she made the final turn into her sister's driveway. When she got to her door, she almost missed a card under her welcome mat. She pulled it out and unlocked her door.

It was one of those long-winded printed cards that summed up someone's innermost feelings, requiring them only to sign their name. It was from Andrew. He added that he came by and she wasn't home. He loved her and hoped to see her soon.

Shea tossed the card on the television set, pulled off her clothes, and climbed into bed.

She slept hard. When she woke up, she was in a pool of drool on her pillow. She crawled out of bed and took a shower. Her inner thighs were sore, her calves were sore, and she felt like she had been on a narrow bike saddle for one hundred miles. When she got out of the shower and looked in the mirror, she saw a purplish hickey on her neck and wondered if it was visible yesterday. She determined that it wasn't, as Jack would've taken a lot of pleasure in pointing it out. She decided to wear a turtleneck and hoped the day wouldn't get too hot.

After she was done getting ready for work, she sat down on a single bar stool she kept near the kitchen counter to enjoy her final cup of coffee and the Metro section of the *LA Times*. Her home phone rang. She reached across the counter and picked it up.

"You're home." It was Andrew.

"I am."

"Can we meet for coffee? I'm about ten minutes from the Starbucks." They had met there many times before work.

"Ah, I really need to get into work. We arrested the guy who murdered Chloe Diaz yesterday."

"*That's* where you were." She thought she heard relief in his voice. "I came by your house on my way home from San Diego about noon."

"I got your card."

"Come meet me. Just for a minute. I want to hear about your case."

Shea wanted to tell him. Impressing Andrew Thorpe with her police work had started in the academy.

"Okay, I'll see you there." Shea hung up. She gathered her bag, gun belt, and went out the door.

Andrew beat her to Starbucks and ordered for her. He surprised her by leaning over and kissing her cheek as she approached him. He was wearing a black suit, a yellow tie and a crisp white shirt. He was impeccably groomed, as usual, and Shea could smell his aftershave. Shea smiled to herself, thinking about Chad in his jeans and his tumbled blond hair.

"Tell me about your case," Andrew said. Shea had told the story so many times now that she had it broken down to an outline format. Andrew surprised her for the second time by leaning across the table and kissing her again. She looked around the café.

"You're pretty and smart, and I'm crazy about you." He smiled at her. "You belong in RHD, Shea. I keep telling you that."

"Oh, Andrew, you know it's a club. A lot of qualified guys don't get in because they don't have a 'sponsor.'" Shea sipped her coffee.

"Whatever. Hey, I have news for you. I'm leaving OIS," he said.

"Where are you going?"

"I got a lieutenant II spot in Metro. 'D' Team."

"You're going back to SWAT? I didn't know anything about this," Shea said.

"I know. It happened kind of quickly. And we haven't seen much of each other recently."

"You must be excited."

"The most fun I ever had on the job was in SWAT. Plus, my hours will be so crazy again that I'll be able to see more of you." He reached across the tiny table and squeezed her hand.

"It's going to be a hectic week. I might be the one filing the rape cases. I have to get a hold of the Foothill sex detective. And we have a pre-lim on Wednesday."

"You need to take some time off soon, I think," Andrew said. He stood up and they walked out to their cars.

"I'm scheduled for a September vacation this year," Shea said.

"That's a long way off. What about a long weekend? I know you need some rest," Andrew said.

"I'm okay as long as they make caffeine." Shea tipped her coffee cup at him.

"You look beautiful. I love it when you wear black. I'll never forget that black dress you wore, the one with the lace and no back. Ah, that was such a great night," Andrew said. He was referring to her birthday weekend in Palm Springs last year.

Shea pulled back her hair and showed him the pearl earrings he had given her that night.

"The first time you wore those, you were naked."

"Thanks for the reminder." Shea gave him a wave and headed for her car.

Shea's morning was as hectic as she thought it would be. Curt dragged her into a meeting with the lieutenant and captain, and she briefed them about her investigation. She met with the sex detectives to let them know which rape cases she thought were attributable to the Padilla brothers. She got a hold of Detective Ellingsworth, and they decided they needed to present the rape cases to the district attorney's office together. Before Shea's phone could ring again, Curt tapped her on her shoulder.

"I just got off the phone with RHD," Curt said. "The Chief is doing a press conference in front of Parker Center at noon. RHD's announcing they'll be arresting Padilla for Officer Diaz's murder. You're invited to attend the news conference."

"I'm not going."

"You are, and so is the lieutenant. He'd like some face time with the Chief and the media," Curt said.

"I have to go with him?" Shea whispered.

"No, you don't have to ride with him. Tell him you have to serve subpoenas afterwards or something," Curt said.

"I'll go with you," Jack said.

"Thanks, but..." Shea was exasperated. "I have so much to do, Curt. I've got to--"

"You're going to the press conference," Curt said. "You deserve the accolades."

Parker Center was teaming with activity. News vans were parked illegally in front of the building with their periscopes shooting into the sky. The media-relations officers were setting up the podium and scurrying around. Jack couldn't find any parking spaces next to the building, so they parked a block away. By the time they made it the front of Parker Center, Shea was hot and sweaty in her turtleneck and blazer.

"Our lieutenant's already here." Jack pointed to their boss talking to the lieutenant in charge of RHD. Other detectives Shea did not recognize were milling around. Shea saw Detective Lancaster in the middle of the group. She also recognized Chloe's ex-husband, looking solemn and sour. She was mortified to see William Shea standing next to him, whispering in his ear.

She moved behind Jack so William couldn't see her. Sworn and civilian Parker Center employees lingered in front of the building on their way back from lunch to see what the fuss was about. Shea and Jack found a place in the shade and observed the crowd.

"I can't believe he's still on the job. He was a classmate. What a geek." Jack leaned into Shea and pointed to an officer in a suit on the periphery of the press conference. "I think he works Planning and Research." Shea listened, but her attention was drawn to the handsome man coming out of the glass doors of Parker Center. It was Andrew. He made a direct line over to Shea.

"Detective Reed. I heard there was a press conference and I knew you'd be here. After all, weren't you the one who solved this thing?" He smiled at her and then turned to Jack. "Andrew Thorpe."

Jack shook Andrew's hand and introduced himself. Shea was sure that Jack knew exactly who Andrew was in that instant.

"She solved a murder, several rapes, and an attempted murder all in a week," Jack said.

"That's what I've heard." Andrew smiled at Shea and she

pulled at her turtleneck. She was steaming hot.

She looked over Andrew's shoulder and saw Walter Smith in the crowd. He tipped his head to her and smiled before he went over to talk to Lancaster and Nelichek. The Chief's staff came out a few minutes before his arrival and Shea knew the press conference would begin soon.

The Chief walked out the door and stopped to talk to the lieutenant in charge of Homicide Specials. Then he went to the podium. He was wearing a suit and looked more like a detective than a police chief. His inner circle was composed of the same vultures that picked at the corpse of the previous chief, Daryl Gates. It would only be a matter of time before another coup was launched on the sixth floor of Parker Center.

"Good afternoon, ladies and gentlemen. We're here today to make a great announcement. Robbery Homicide detectives have identified a suspect in the murder of Officer Chloe Diaz." One of the RHD detectives moved an easel closer to the Chief with a large booking photo of Caesar Padilla.

"Caesar Padilla's in custody on unrelated charges. He's responsible for several rapes in the San Fernando Valley, and he's the suspect in an officer-involved shooting that resulted in Valley

Officer Sean Ornelas losing most of his ear—a few inches over and

there would've been two slain officers. LAPD has taken a violent

and brutal man off the streets. I'm going to turn this over to

Lieutenant Woods who'll fill you all in on the investigation."

The Chief moved to the side. The RHD lieutenant shook his

hand and placed his paperwork on the podium. Several detectives

stood behind him, looking like a civil service choir.

"Nothin' but a group grope," Jack whispered to her. "A

buncha bobbleheads standing behind the main bobblehead."

Shea listened to the well-written press release. Other than, "a

lot of good police work was done by several members of Valley

Division," there was no mention of her or the gang unit. The

lieutenant named Lancaster and Nelichek as the hard-working

detectives who worked tirelessly for months to bring this suspect to

justice.

Andrew leaned in and said, "I heard it might go this way. The

powers-that-be thought they needed to improve the image of RHD

because of OJ and all of that."

Shea nodded and stared out onto the street. She knew she

shouldn't have come. Shea saw a group of undercover narcotics officers approach the crowd. She felt a groan in her throat and sure enough, Chad was in the group of scruffy young officers. He caught her eye and lifted his hand to wave to her.

Jack turned and looked at her with one eyebrow raised. Shea felt like her head was filled with Pachinko balls bouncing behind her eyes. Her heart was pounding so loud in her ears that it drowned out the lieutenant. All she needed was for William Shea to yell "hello namesake" across the crowd.

"Let's go," Shea told Jack.

"Stay the course," Jack whispered back. "It's finally getting interesting."

"For you!"

The lieutenant was taking questions from reporters, calling some of them by their first names as if he was the president. Shea had all that she could handle. She turned to leave and bumped into Walter Smith. He motioned for her to follow him.

They walked over to the fallen officer's memorial near the front of the building.

"You did a fantastic job and everyone knows that," Walter

started. Shea was mortified to feel her eyes well up. "Lancaster was impressed. Don't let this silly press conference take away from any of that. This is just image rehabilitation. You and those gang officers are going to get a great commendation, if I have to write it myself."

"Thanks," Shea said thinly.

"I have a sense you were on to something that night you called me at home. But you do know that they were looking at Padilla as a top suspect from the get-go." Walter smiled and then he chuckled. "Or that's the story."

Shea looked at him. It was a disloyal thing for him to say, but she felt validated by someone she had grown to admire.

"I didn't want to be here. It's not about recognition, you know." Shea wiped the corner of her eyes with her fingertips.

"Detective Reed, there are a lot of factors that go in to being a big-city homicide detective. Adroitness, tenacity, the ability to be absolutely comfortable taking credit and to be comfortable not getting any." He touched her arm lightly. "I hope we get a chance to work together again." He smiled at her and went back to his colleagues.

Shea turned around. She saw Jack and Andrew talking. She

walked quickly over to them. The press conference was officially over and reporters were talking to the investigators individually.

"Can we get out of here now?" Shea asked. She looked around, but she didn't see Chad or any of the other narcotics officers.

"What did Walter want?" Andrew asked. Shea was completely off balance. He had kissed her twice in public and now was speaking to her in such a familiar way, it would be clear to Jack that they knew each other intimately. Andrew didn't seem to care.

"Just said it was a good investigation."

"He's a nice guy. Smart too," Andrew said. "I guess the show's over. It was nice meeting you, Jack."

"You too, Lieutenant."

"Call me Andrew. Bye, Shea." He winked at her and went back into Parker Center. Shea turned to Jack speechless.

"Holy shit." Jack chuckled and ran his hand through his hair.

"No kidding," Shea said. "Can we please get out of here now?"

"Anyone else you want to say hi to?"

"Absolutely not, thank you." She tugged on his jacket sleeve. "Let's go."

"Reed, Rainier." Their lieutenant jogged after them.

"Hey, L.T.," Jack said.

"I was really hoping they would acknowledge the good work our division did," he huffed.

"That's the breaks," Jack said.

"I need to get back. I'm presenting the rapes to the DA tomorrow morning, so I have a lot to do," Shea said.

"Of course. I won't hold you up. I just don't know why they wanted us down here," he said. "I guess to witness the shift-shaft for ourselves."

"Never too busy to hold the curtains open for RHD, Lieutenant," Shea said as they walked away.

They didn't speak until they were on the Hollywood freeway heading back to the Valley.

"So that was--"

"Yes."

"And the guy in the baseball hat that waved to you was –"

"Yesssss." Shea rested her head on the passenger window.

"Man, it's like working with a soap-opera queen. The drama."

"There was no drama," Shea said in a frosty tone.

"There's potential for drama," Jack said. Her cell phone rang and she dug it out of her jacket pocket.

"Were you wearing a turtle neck 'cause I gave you a hickey?" Chad asked as soon as she said hello.

"Yes," she said.

Jack rolled his eyes at her and mouthed, "Drama."

"We had a meeting at PAB. I didn't know you're going to be down there. Hey, how come they never mentioned you?"

"I guess my contributions weren't as significant as I thought."

"Oh, don't go all martyr on me now. I gotta go. I just wanted to say hi and tell you that you're really pretty when you're pissed."

"I'm not pissed," she said, in the same tone she had denied the drama accusation.

"You were at the press conference; you have a very expressive face. Okay, I seriously do have to go. Bye, Shea Lynn," he said her name sweetly. It made her smile.

"Bye," she said and hung up.

"The young one or the old one?" Jack said.

"Oh God, why did I tell you anything?"

"21 Jump Street or The Suit?"

"Jump Street." She laughed in spite of herself.

"I knew it."

"What did Andrew say to you?"

"He asked if you were taking care of yourself. He thought you pushed yourself too hard. It was as if he knew that I knew. And I really didn't. I mean, I figured it out, but I thought he was more careful than that."

"He has been, up until today."

"He's smooth. I bet he doesn't rattle easy."

"Yeah," Shea said.

When Shea got back to the station, she went up to her locker. In a plastic tray on the top shelf of her locker, she pulled out four uniform buttons and put them in her blazer pocket. When she reached her desk, she placed the four buttons in a row next to her lamp. She went back to finishing her reports on the rape.

Chapter 20

The homicide unit met at the municipal golf-course bar after work. Curt felt they needed to celebrate the arrests and commiserate over the press conference. Shea made a quick detour to the liquor store to buy a case of beer and a bottle of scotch for the gang unit. Usually the gang officers would meet the homicide unit over at the bar; but they were working a cruiser task force and wouldn't be end-of-watch until 2:00 a.m. After she transferred the liquor from her trunk to Hector's pick up, she headed to the bar.

The television above the bar was blaring when she walked in, broadcasting the news conference. When it was over, the detectives saluted the TV by raising their beer bottles.

"If Shea was still my partner, I can guarantee this whole mess wouldn't have happened. I'd never permit her to be involved in any case that had anything to do with RH and D," Vaughn said.

"'Permit me?'" Shea laughed and was ready with her retort, "Working with you was like living in a Dirty Harry movie. You were Harry Callahan and I was – what's her name, his female partner- with my conservative suit, sensible heels…trailing after Harry."

Vaughn flicked his cigarette, "Didn't she die in that movie?"

"Asshole." Shea shook her head.

"What do you think happened that night? Do you think she recognized Padilla?" Curt said.

"I honestly don't know," Shea said.

"It's just crazy," Jack said.

"Did she ever say anything to you?" Shea asked Vaughn.

"She'd ask how the OIS investigation was going, but she didn't try any theories on me."

"Vaughn, are you sure she never mentioned anything? Hector said that she wanted to talk to him the morning of the Christmas party about the shooter, but he didn't have time."

"No, nothing." Vaughn shook his head. He abruptly stood up and then sat back down on the bar stool.

Shea knew her old partner and something wasn't right.

"Prostate problems, old man? Thought you had to piss, but it was a false alarm?" Curt said.

"Well, it's over now." Shea thought about the picture of the men in her unit tucked at the back of Chloe's trophy photos. "Whatever else was going on with her will just be buried, too."

"She – Chloe…sort of…ah…" Vaughn started.

"Did she have a thing for you, Vaughn? I thought she sort of hit on you at the party." Shea took a drink from her beer. *There.* If he had something to say, here was his opportunity.

Vaughn drank his beer as if she hadn't said anything. Finally he ground his cigarette into an ashtray and looked at her.

"At the party…she and I went in that grotto thing…and she gave me head." He turned his hands palms up. Jack and Curt stared at him.

"Shit, Vaughn…they must've swabbed her mouth!" Curt said.

"No, no. I didn't come. She stopped; she was just being a tease. And the blood you found in the bathroom? Well, while she was…while we were uh…together, she got a splinter in her knee. She was headed that way to clean up. She must've been killed right after that. Shea, I'm sorry. I wanted to tell you. I swear to God."

"You'd've road the top of the damned suspect list, Vaughn." Curt shook his head. "What the hell were you thinking?"

"Well, I'm pretty sure I know what he was thinking, boss. When was the last time you passed up a blow job in a grotto?" Jack said.

"I can't remember the last time I was in a grotto." Curt took a swig of his beer. "As for the blow job, can't say I remember much in the category either."

Jack and Curt continued their banter about the lack of oral sex in their marriages and Vaughn leaned over to Shea, knocking his beer bottle into hers.

"I'm sorry, kid. I knew you told RHD about the blood and it would've complicated the hell out of things...especially if you hadn't solved it."

"I'd be putting money on your books for Marlboros at San Quentin if you had. RHD would've nailed your ass," Shea said. "And partner rules, Vaughn. Shit. Trust me for a change."

"I do, kid. I always have." He gave her a smile and she knocked her bottle back into his.

"Well, I just hope this shuts up her stupid ex-husband. He can't claim there was a big cover-up now," Curt said.

"He'll still continue with his fifteen minutes of fame. Probably sue the Department for not arresting Padilla sooner," Jack said. "He was at the press conference and he had that puke, William Shea with him. But at least he didn't talk to the press."

"When people lose someone they love, do you notice how they have to have a campaign or something? They lead the charge for a new law or a safety regulation. Like the baby that got its head caught in the baby swing a few weeks ago. That mom's leading some big campaign to outlaw baby swings or something," Shea said. She wanted to divert the conversation away from William Shea.

"Yeah, that's true. I think it makes them feel like they're doing something, like they're not powerless," Jack said.

"I heard the mom on the baby swing thing's actually a suspect," Curt said.

"No kidding!"

"Munchausen's by proxy," Curt said. And just like that, Chloe Diaz and her murder faded from their discussion. As the sun set and the last of the golfers wandered into the lounge, the homicide unit was aggravated to see the infamous, acquitted double-homicide suspect, OJ Simpson, enter the bar. A gaggle of Asian golfers followed him.

"I thought he was going to move to Florida," Curt grumbled.

"He can't play at any of his private courses anymore," Vaughn said. They watched as the golfers took pictures with him.

"Give me a nine iron, right now," Shea said. "I swear I'm just drunk enough to get away with smashing in his melon skull."

"Diminished capacity?" Vaughn offered.

"You can't kill him in our own division. Our stats are too high as it is," Curt said.

"But it'd be a clearance. We arrest Shea after she kills him," Vaughn said.

"I gotta get home. I can't drink with guys from USC." Jack stood up.

The rest of the unit agreed it was probably time to call it a night. They threw bills on the table and walked out of the lounge without looking back. They grumbled that they were going to have to find another dive to drink at, since they preferred drinking with un-prosecuted criminals.

Chapter 21

With Chloe's case behind her and dates with Chad in front of her, Shea's days passed quickly. She dipped into her bloated accumulated overtime bank used the time off to have some fun. She went on dates, dates like a regular girl. Chad was the prom date, the boyfriend who kissed her at the top of the Ferris wheel; he was the father of her children, and the man with the smile waiting at the end of the aisle. He was all of those things she *could have* had, but somehow missed along the way.

When Chad invited her to the Renaissance Faire on the outskirts of LA civilization, Shea told him she had never been and had no desire to sit in a car for a two-hour drive for the opportunity to walk around in the dirt, looking at mental patients dressed like Queen Elizabeth and munching on turkey legs.

Despite her protests, Chad picked her up on a Saturday morning in May and they headed east on the 10 freeway in his El Camino. Shea was wearing a sundress she bought last summer, but never had an opportunity to wear. She pulled her hair back in little clips and let the rest tumble down her back. She felt girlie and a little silly. Chad drove with his hand under her dress, placed firmly on her thigh.

After they parked in the massive parking lot, they walked a quarter of a mile before they got to the entrance. Shea was really sorry she had chosen to wear a dress and new sandals, as opposed to jeans and tennis shoes. Her feet hurt and her inner thighs were chafing in the heat. A woman in full 16th century garb took their money. She was the third woman Shea had seen wearing a corset laced so tight her boobs bulged over the material of her dress, like overloaded ice cream cones.

"Now I see why you like it here. It's a breast fest," Shea said.

"Yeah, and most of the ones you'll see today are natural. It's like spotting endangered species in the forest." Chad led her into the fair.

They wandered through the exhibits and watched the demonstrations of sword-making and glass-blowing. Chad bought them extra-large beers and they found a seat on a worn grassy knoll. They watched the people, in costume and in regular clothes, strolling on the path below them. It was a warm, sunny day, and as close to perfect as Shea could imagine. She was lying with her head in Chad's lap while he stroked her hair. There was a trio of musicians near them playing ancient instruments.

"So, it's not as bad as you thought, right?"

"No. I like the flute music. Very romantic," Shea said with her eyes closed.

"Romantic, huh?" Chad drank the rest of his beer.

"Yeah, or relaxing. I'm not sure which," Shea said.

"Hey, I forgot to tell you, we're working a buy bust detail in your neck of the woods all next week. Maybe we can get together for a Code-7, that is, if you ever take a break for lunch." Chad got up and pulled her to her feet.

"I do. That would be great, there's a good Mexican place not far from the station." Shea dusted off the back of her sun dress.

"Good. I want you to meet my partner, Darcee." Chad grabbed her hand. "Come on, there's more to see."

They wandered through the jewelry section, holding hands and looking in the cases. Chad brought her over to a small exhibitor's booth. The jewelry was handcrafted and unusual.

"I love this guy's stuff," Chad said. The artist was showing another couple some earrings.

"I like all the vines on the rings," Shea said.

"I think I'm going to buy you a promise ring." Chad bent to look in the case.

"Oh really?" Shea laughed. He looked up at her and she could see he was serious. "A promise of what?"

"Don't you know what promise rings are for? Love, all of that stuff." He stood up and looked over at her. "I love you, you know."

A breeze rustled the canvas roof of the booth. The artist moved over to them and asked Chad if he could show him anything. Chad said yes and pointed to a silver ring, with vines etched into it.

"This is one of my favorite designs. It works for both men and women." He pulled out a wooden tray with several rings on it. Shea watched them as if she was having an out of body experience. She barely noticed when he held her left hand out and the jeweler slipped on the ring.

"Ah…" She took it off and put it on her right hand. The jeweler and Chad exchanged looks.

"It's really pretty."

"I think so. I have others with the vines and semi-precious stones," the artist said.

"I like this." She held out her right hand and admired the ring. "But, I don't –"

"Shhhhh." Chad said. He pulled out his wallet.

"The fit is good?" The jeweler took her hand.

"Yes, I think the fit is good."

Chad followed him around to the other counter and paid for the ring. Shea waited outside the booth.

"Today is your lucky day!" A woman, dressed as a peasant from the Renaissance, declared in a phony Cockney accent. All of her bare skin was covered in tattoos.

"What?" Shea pulled her hand behind her skirt.

"You have a dragonfly on your shoulder." The woman pointed a black-polished fingernail at Shea's right shoulder. "It means you're soon to marry, my lady."

"Really?" Chad came up beside her. The dragonfly flew off her shoulder, its iridescent blue wings catching the sunlight. "That's a sign."

"Indeed, squire." The tattooed, reincarnated, peasant woman blew a kiss to them and disappeared into the crowd.

"Chad, thank you," she said, showing him her hand.

"It's pretty." He pulled her hand to his mouth and kissed her fingers and ring. "It's just a promise that I'm not going anywhere. The right hand is the perfect place for it."

Shea wrapped her arms around his neck and he held her tightly. They swayed together and she told him she loved him, in her mind, but not out loud. Chad bought two more beers and a plate of chocolate-covered strawberries. After the second beer, Shea told him she needed to go to the bathroom. She left him with a kiss.

Shea used the Port-a-Potty and afterwards ran back to the jeweler.

"You're back. Does the ring fit okay?" The jeweler asked.

"It's perfect. I want to buy the larger one like this – "

"For your boyfriend?"

Shea's head bounced up. She was warmed and surprised by the concept of a "boyfriend."

"Yes." Shea pointed to the ring she wanted and he told her if it didn't fit to bring it back. It matched the design on her smaller ring and felt huge in her hand. Shea paid for the ring and ran back to Chad.

"Where did you go?"

"I just had an errand to run."

"An errand? You made a call, didn't you?" Chad looked at her purse.

"No, no. I didn't make any calls," Shea said. She opened her sweaty palm. Chad looked at the ring and then at her.

"Is it too corny? You don't wear rings?"

"I can't believe you did this." He picked it up out of her hand.

"Chad, I'm not usually impulsive...but, I love you too," Shea felt the words tumbling out of her mouth like a minor landslide.

"A promise?"

She helped him put it on his right hand. She kissed his hand like he had kissed hers.

"I don't know what it's a promise of, except that I love you," she said, feeling more confident with the concept. Her heart was pounding in her chest. Chad pulled her to him and hugged her.

"This is the sweetest thing anyone's ever done for me."

Chad slipped the ring off his right hand onto his left ring finger.

"I ain't nearly as skittish as you, my dear."

Back home that night, Shea laid in bed holding her hand up and a looking at the ring. She didn't wear any jewelry when she slept and she pulled off the ring, placing it on top of a couple Michael Connelly novels on her nightstand. She rolled onto her side and stared at it. What the hell did this small piece of jewelry really represent?

The next morning she woke up, went for a run, took a shower and it wasn't until her second cup of coffee that noticed she wasn't wearing the ring. She sat down on her bed and slipped it onto her left hand ring finger. What would that be like? She quickly took it off and put it on her right finger. A sharp knock was followed by her door opening and Shannon came into her apartment in her red silk robe and carrying a narrow white box of waxy chocolate donuts.

"I'm fasting."

"Fasting? Why?"

"Isn't it obvious?" Shannon grabbed her zaftig stomach and flopped down on Shea's bed.

"That isn't healthy."

"Really? Would you like to lecture me on health?"

"No." Shea slid her thumb under the flap of the Hostess box and opened it. They used to live off of chocolate donuts and Ding Dongs.

"I saw the cute hippie boy here yesterday. What's going on with him?" Shannon rolled onto her side and propped her head up with her right hand.

Shea took a bite of a donut and showed her the ring.

"What?" Shannon grabbed her hand. "That's pretty. Is it an engagement ring? Why is it on your right hand?"

Shea finished chewing and said, "It's a promise ring. I know, I know."

"Look at you, all grown-up making a puppy-love commitment." Shannon reached for a donut, sniffed it and put it back. "One hundred calories just smelling it."

"Remember how Dad would lecture us about how bad these were for us?"

"While he drank his Delaware Punch and vodka." Shannon laughed. "Remember how no matter what started the lecture; it'd always end with a dissertation on Karl Marx?"

"Or Lenin. Dad's go-to guys."

"So, what are you gonna do with the married one? You gonna break it off with him?"

"I gotta figure this shit out. If I don't, I'm going to end up living here for the rest of my life and we'll end up like the two spinster sisters in 'Whatever Happened to Baby Jane.'"

"Speak for yourself, Bette Davis."

"We're already half way there. You live with three cats and I live in your basement." Shea finished the rest of her donut and went to the refrigerator to find something to wash it down with. She checked the milk carton and the date had expired. She poured the curdling milk in the sink and got drink of water.

"The difference is I'm single but *want* to be married. You on the other hand..." Shannon got up and took the upside down milk carton out of the sink. "Fear domestication."

Shea's phone rang before she could come back with a smart reply. She answered it as her sister grabbed a donut and headed out of the apartment with a wave over her shoulder.

"Hey, Shea." Andrew's voice was familiar and unsettling at the same time.

"Hi."

"You got anything going today?"

"No." It would be today. She would end it with Andrew today.

"We just finished a repelling exercise up at Universal. Yours truly still has it. I'm the only one who went Australian. Face first."

"You mean – walking down the outside of a building?"

"Uh-huh. Anyway, can you meet me in Studio City?"

"Yeah..."

Andrew gave her an address and she quickly found a pen.

"That's where I live now. Come on over."

Chapter 22

Shannon was heading to the house with the newspaper and her half-eaten donut when Shea came up the stone steps to her car.

"Where are you going? Was that the youngster on the phone?" Shannon said.

"No. It gets weirder by the minute. Andrew moved out, I guess. He's got a place down the hill." Shea unlocked her car door.

"So, you're breaking up with him right?"

"I don't know."

"Oh shit, poor hippie boy…thought he gave his promise ring to a nice girl." Shannon popped the last of the donut in her mouth.

"Thanks for the support." Shea jumped in the car.

"You don't need support; you need a swift kick in the ass!" Shannon said as Shea backed out of the driveway.

Shea had no problem finding the apartment in Studio City. It wasn't far from the building where she had spent her teenage years, but miles away in terms of income needed to afford the rent. The apartment Andrew moved into was only a decade old, a bleached white stucco monstrosity with a tiled roof and exotic landscaping. It was the San Fernando Valley meets Morocco. Shea stood at the heavy security gate, looking at the list of tenant's last names. It was too soon for Andrew's name to be placed on the list. She pressed the number he gave her over the phone and after a few seconds she heard his voice.

"You're here," Andrew said and she heard the gate buzz. She pushed it open and entered a courtyard with an empty glistening swimming pool. It seemed the more people paid in rent, the less they used the pool.

Andrew opened the door before she could knock. He was wearing jean shorts and a faded blue Hawaiian shirt. Shea couldn't remember ever seeing him in shorts or a casual shirt. Shea ran her hand over the stubble on his cheek. He grabbed her around the waist and pulled her to him. She buried her face in his shoulder and breathed in his familiar, masculine scent. Maybe she was beginning to recognize him.

"I still can't believe this," she said.

The apartment was empty, with the exception of several suitcases and a cardboard box. A drop holster with his .45 caliber pistol was on the kitchen counter and his rifle bag was tucked underneath where a bar stool might be someday. The rest of his

SWAT gear was in the dining area.

"I've only been here a few days myself."

Shea wandered around the small apartment. In the bedroom she saw an inflatable mattress on the floor. It was hooked up to what looked like a bicycle pump. The only furniture in the apartment was a bed. *How appropriate.*

"I was trying to get this thing inflated. Every time I sleep on it, it loses air. I went by a mattress store, but they couldn't deliver for a week and I wasn't going to sleep on the floor." He began pumping it with air. Shea leaned against the wall and watched him. Once the bed was filled, he sat down on the edge and looked up at her.

"What? What's wrong?"

"It's just, so...so fast."

"I doubled my deposit so I could get in here before the first of the month." Andrew reached for her hand. "Aren't you happy?"

"I don't know. I'm in shock." Shea pulled her hand away from his. "We haven't even talked for a week and the last time we did, we fought."

"Do you remember what we argued about?" Andrew asked.

"I dunno," Shea said. "The usual."

"I could tell you were done. I was going to lose you if I didn't do something. It's been a bad week. Anyway, I don't want to get into that right now. The point is, I told you I'd leave and I did."

"Why didn't you talk to me about this…before you made this decision?" She wanted to add, *before you left your wife and three kids, why didn't you make sure I would still be here?*

"Talk to you? That's all we've been doing for the last year is talking about this." Andrew stood up abruptly and Shea stepped back. His eyes were on hers and there was nowhere to hide.

"Half my pension, my children, my house, and my wife," Andrew said. Shea nodded. "For you. Just to be with you, Shea."

Shea felt lightheaded; maybe she had forgotten to breathe. He reached out and put his hand on her neck in a very gentle c-clamp. An increase in pressure and she'd go unconscious, more pressure and he'd crush her windpipe.

"Do you love me?"Andrew said.

Shea nodded. She did. She had always loved him.

The next morning Shea nearly rolled off the air mattress as she hit the alarm on the clock radio next to the bed. She got her balance and looked over at Andrew sleeping. He was naked, sheets in a twist around his ankles. Even in sleep, his body was tense and prepared for an instant response to danger. She traced the scars from his old bullet wounds along his shoulder and leg. A department legend.

What was she going to do? Her life had changed twice in one short weekend. Her fingers lingered on the raised scar tissue, like a brand, on his right shoulder.

"Lower," Andrew said, with his eyes closed.

"Mmm. I gotta go home and change for work."

Andrew took her right hand and brought it down from his shoulder, across his tight stomach to his cock. Shea ran her hand from the base to the tip, hard, just like every other part of his body. Chad's ring caught the morning light through the window as she leaned down to take him in her mouth.

Shea sat at her desk in an empty homicide unit. Curt was in a supervisor's meeting and Jack and Vaughn had gone to the academy for monthly qualification. She welcomed the solitude and she buried herself in paperwork for the upcoming preliminary hearing for

Caesar Padilla. She was getting ready to call Detective Ellingsworth

at Foothill Division to see if she would drive the rape victim to court

next week, when her phone rang.

"Good Morning, Valley Homicide, Detective Reed, can I

help you?"

"Very professional. This is William."

"Who?"

"Your godfather."

"Oh, listen, I'm really busy-"

"I know you are," he interrupted. "It's important, otherwise I

wouldn't have called you at work."

"What's it about?"

"I don't want to do it over the phone."

"Is it about my Dad? Shannon?"

"No. I'm down the street, at a House of Pancakes."

"Really, I don't have time."

"Or I can come to the station."

"Okay, okay. I'll be there in five minutes. But, I warn you

William, I'm not in the mood for family drama and I'm not going to

confirm any juicy LAPD gossip for you either." Shea hung up and grabbed her car keys.

William was standing outside of his car, talking on his cell phone and gesturing wildly with his hands. He put up an index finger to Shea as she approached and she listen to him bark orders into the phone. He snapped the cell phone shut and stuck it in a little holder on his belt.

"That was a private eye who's working a case for me. What a moron. I thought he'd be good, he's retired RHD."

"We lost another one to the other side." Shea pressed her lips together tightly.

"My side pays better." William reached out and held her shoulders. "Okay, do you want breakfast?"

"No! I don't have time for this," Shea said pulling away from him.

"I'll get to the point. You know I'm consulting with the ex-husband."

"What are you talking about?" Shea shook her head.

"Chloe Diaz's ex." William took off his aviator sunglasses and wiped them against his shirt.

"Okay?" Shea knew he was being coy about his information.

"He was going through her things and found a box."

"William, the police have been through their house. The case is closed, by the way."

"I know that. It doesn't have anything to do with the case. It has to do with you." He placed the glasses back on the bridge of his nose.

"Me?"

"Yes. He found a box of photos. Some of them he recognized. He's a photographer and he was getting her into it, too."

"Get to the point." Shea had a bad feeling about what was coming next. If it was a picture of Vaughn, then he had lied to her again. What would that mean? What had he gotten himself into with Chloe?

"So, he was showing some of the pictures to me. And I recognized a guy."

"What? From where?" Shea was trying to think of a time when William would have been in contact with her homicide unit.

"From your sister's driveway."

Shea felt confusion give way to dread. William pulled a Polaroid photo out of his shirt pocket as if it was a winning lottery ticket. He handed it to her and she flipped it over.

"I thought you should know."

Andrew was standing in a bathroom, in front of a sink, nude. His right hand was up, palm facing the photographer. His expression registered surprise. Same bullet scars she had just drawn her fingers over that morning.

"I have an amazing memory for faces. I didn't recognize anyone else. I was kind of hoping Chief Gates would be in the collection, but no such luck. Just some young guys. Most seemed to know their pictures were being taken, but this guy...he got caught unaware. I figured you should know what you're getting yourself into."

"Is this the only picture of him?"

"Yes."

"Did you make copies?"

"No, of course not! My God, I wasn't planning on blackmailing anyone!" He feigned indignation.

"Thank you." Shea put the picture in her blazer pocket and turned to leave.

"Do you want to talk?" He began to follow her. Shea turned

around, her eyes on fire. William took a step back when he saw her expression.

"No, I do not." Shea got in her car and grabbed her cell phone from in between the seats. She waited until she pulled out of the parking lot and away from William's view. Andrew answered on the first ring.

"Hi honey, I can't talk right now."

"Andrew, I need to see you."

"Okay, but I'm on my way to a call-out in your division. We got a barricaded suspect, big-boy shit. I'll call you as soon as I'm done."

He hung up on her. Shea screamed in her car and pounded her fists on the steering wheel. Her mind was racing. How did he know Chloe? Shea felt like she was going to vomit. She grabbed the phone and dialed Chad's cell phone. There was no answer, so she waited for the voice mail to kick in.

"Chad, it's Shea. I need to talk to you. Can you call me? Can we meet somewhere? Call me."

Chapter 23

The homicide unit was gathered in front of a portable television perched on a file cabinet next to Curt's desk. As Shea approached she could see the image on screen was from the vantage of a news helicopter. The banner at the bottom declared it was 'breaking news.' The helicopter reporter was explaining to the anchor they couldn't get closer because it would interfere with police tactics. She tossed her car keys on her desk and walked over.

"Let me guess, SWAT dogs in action," she said.

"It's up on our border with Foothill." Vaughn said, not turning around.

"The suspects are barricaded in a liquor store," Curt said.

Jack had his ear to his radio as he watched the television.

"211 went bad. Looks like they might've killed a cop and are holding another one hostage," Curt continued.

"What?"

"The watch commander came back here and told us it's no one from our division. Maybe narco," Vaughn said.

Shea looked at Jack and he put the radio down. She turned and hurried back to her desk with Jack right behind her.

"Chad... he was working a buy bust out here, Jack."

"Call him, Shea. Call him, maybe he'll answer." Jack scrambled his hands over her desk to pick up her cell phone and held it out for her.

"I did. He didn't answer." Shea stared blankly at the phone in Jack's hands.

"What is it?" Curt walked over to her desk.

"A guy she was seeing, he's working narco..." Jack said.

"Well, there's no reason to think it's him. Narco has a hundred officers," Curt said.

"He was working a buy bust in the valley today," Jack said.

"We still don't know anything. You can't go looking for trouble now, Shea."

"We could head over there...our team would process the scene when this is finished." Shea picked up her car keys.

"Whoa, wait a minute. If that's your friend in there you're not going anywhere near that crime scene," Curt said.

"I'll keep her out of trouble, boss." Jack grabbed his jacket.

"See that you do. Stay outside the perimeter until this things resolved!" Curt called after them.

Jack and Shea were in their unmarked Crown Victoria speeding north through the San Fernando Valley.

"I don't know how we're going to get past the perimeter, Shea. It'll be locked down tight," Jack said.

"Just get close." Shea flipped through the dials of their police radio trying to find the frequency SWAT was communicating on.

Jack stopped the car in front of yellow police tape that stretched across the street. He jumped out to talk to middle-aged patrol officer. The officer's sunglasses were mirrored and his face was expressionless. Shea watched Jack point to her and then back to himself and then a firm finger in the officer's chest. The officer smirked, but backed up and lifted the crime scene tape over his head. Jack jumped back in the driver's seat and gave a little wave to the officer as they drove under the yellow tape.

"You're Deputy Chief Reed. This is an officer-involved shooting and I'm heading the investigation and you're my bitch boss. He seemed to buy the last part. The command post's just a little farther. Are you sure you want to do this?" Jack said. "Because, the SWAT guys aren't gonna just let us in and give us some coffee, you know."

"They will."

"No, they won't. Are you crazy?"

"Andrew got the lieutenant II spot. He'll be there."

"Shit. Okay." Jack slowed as the approached the command post. "The CP is in the car lot over there. In the trailer."

It looked more like a junkyard than a car lot. Jack parked on the street outside the lot.

"We've got to go in around the back, okay? Listen, you stay with me. Understand?"

"Yes, of course." Shea was feeling numb.

Andrew was bent over a map, pencil in this mouth, when they opened the car dealership's trailer door. Khaki fatigues, tac-vest over a black t-shirt, and his drop holster strapped to his right leg, he looked formidable and completely comfortable in the middle of a crisis.

The interior of the trailer was one large room with several old metal desks and posters of Corvettes taped to the walls. It smelled like a combination of burnt coffee and motor oil. A Metro officer stopped them as soon as they crossed the threshold.

"It's okay, officer," Andrew said, meeting them at the door.

"You guys shouldn't be here. This is a tactical situation."

"I know. We know." Shea stumbled to find the right words and tone. "We'll have to – we're responsible, as divisional detectives, to handle to the crimes associated with this…incident…and processing the crime scene."

"Yeah, but we'll call you when we're finished."

"Ah…I thought since it *is* our division…I could just watch you work?" Shea tried to turn her mouth into a smile. Andrew looked at her for a moment and then around the room.

"Okay, but this is our CP. You two have a seat over there and stay out of everyone's way."

"We'll do, sir," Jack answered for them both and pulled her over to a desk in the corner. He yanked an old swivel chair out from under the desk and shoved her into it. Shea held her hands together to keep them from trembling.

There was so much radio traffic she was having a hard time understanding what was being said. Officers were talking over one another and someone would inevitably tell the others to get off the frequency. Shea couldn't get a feel for what portion of this incident they had walked in on; the SWAT officers were moving quickly, talking on radios, writing notes, looking through binoculars at the liquor store kitty corner from their command post.

The trailer door burst open and a heavy man with a white beard, earrings in both his ears and an unbuttoned baseball jersey over a wife-beater, pushed inside holding his badge in front of him. The Metro officer who stopped Shea and Jack got on the radio and yelled to the perimeter officers to keep people out of the command post.

"Westerbrook, Narco!" The man's voice was forceful and hoarse. "That's our UC van parked in front of the liquor store!" He was beet red and spitting as he talked. Andrew looked up from his map.

"Pete?"

"Oh, fuck Andrew, I didn't see you. Andrew, my guys are in there. My fucking guys are in there!"

"Get him a chair," Andrew told the Metro officer. "This is Sergeant Westerbrook."

"What's going on, Andrew? What the fuck is going on?"

"We've got two suspects, male blacks, one looks like a teenager according to the wit. We might have two down and a live hostage. Here's the thing...the wit thinks one of the deceased is a cop."

The officer pushed a chair over to the sergeant just as his knees began to buckle.

"We don't know anything for sure, Pete." Andrew put his hand on Sergeant Westerbrook's massive shoulder.

"Just tell me what you know, Andrew."

"The wit was walking in, stopped at the doorway, saw a black guy, not the suspect, yell 'police.' Not in uniform, she said he looked like a bum, but she thought she saw a badge when he pulled out his gun. Everyone starts shooting and she bails." Andrew paused, but Sergeant Westerbrook spun his index finger around in a circle, he was ready for more information.

"We think the clerk is dead or wounded. He's not in play. The hostage's a white kid. Patrol officers responded to the 211 and one male black drags this kid halfway out the door, in a chokehold, with a semi-auto to his head, yelling for them to back off. They do and he takes him back inside. The officers who responded said the kid looked like a tweeker."

"It's Darcee Washington and Chad Hanson. We were going

to do a buy bust in the park. They were late. That's their van in front of liquor store." Sergeant Westerbrook pointed out the window, his big sausage fingers shaking. *Darcee Washington.* Shea remembered Chad telling her he wanted her to meet his partner, maybe for lunch today. Now Darcee was likely dead.

"Are they white, black or what?" Andrew was writing in his notebook.

"Oreo team. Chad's white. Darcee's black."

"Okay, Chad Hanson's got blonde hair, shoulder length, looks like a tweeker?" The SWAT sergeant standing next to Andrew was taking notes also.

"Yeah, a speed freak. He can buy dope from anybody."

"Hanson's alive. He's probably who the responding officers saw. We don't know the status of Washington," Andrew said. "Pete, is Hanson armed?"

"Well, he wouldn't have his badge on him. Or his ID. He was going to buy today. Darcee was part of the arrest team. If Chad has a gun, it'll be a two inch. He has an ankle holster. I think he wears it on the outside of his right ankle."

"The suspects might not know he's a cop," Andrew said to his element leader.

"That could work to our advantage," the officer said.

"And to Hanson's. Okay, let's get this going. Where's our negotiator?" Andrew pulled out his radio. "Pete, you can stay, but don't – "

"I know the drill, Andrew." Pete Westerbrook fell back in the chair. "Darcee just got married. His wife's pregnant. Andrew, they're just young cops. Like we used to be."

"We'll get 'em out, Pete," Andrew said.

Chapter 24

With the SWAT hostage negotiator, Kevin Cross, in place next to Andrew, the plan to make contact with the suspects was ready to unfold. Shea sat on the edge of her chair, elbows on her knees. In seconds she would know what was going on in that liquor store. She'd know if Chad was alive. She closed her eyes, remembering the man who screwed his 9mm into a robber's forehead in Rampart. If he wasn't hurt, he could get the best of his captors, she was sure of that.

"Okay, everyone, when we make this call it has to be dead quiet in here," Andrew said. "This will only work on speaker if everyone is completely quiet."

As the element leader dialed the number, Officer Cross took a deep breath. Jack put his hand on Shea's shoulder and gave it a little squeeze. After ten rings, someone answered.

"Talk!"

"Who am I talking to?"

"Who da fuck is this?"

"My name is Kevin Cross. LAPD. Your turn." He scribbled something on a small pad of paper.

"Call me 'T'."

"You in charge, T?"

"Yeah, me and my boy." There was talking in the background and Shea struggled to hear what was being said. Finally she made out the second voice, 'We don't want no shit like Rodney King."

"What's your friend's name?" Kevin Cross exchanged glances with Andrew.

"Why you gotta know all dis shit?"

"So I know who is who."

"You can call him...Pyro."

"Okay, anyone else in there with you guys?"

"We got ourselves a little peckerwood, caught slippin' in the ghetto."

"What's his name?" Cross said.

"Fuck." More mumbling in the background that Shea couldn't understand. Finally she heard, "What the fuck's *your* name?"

"Chad Hanson." Shea gasped at the sound of Chad's voice and Jack gave her shoulder another warning press.

"He says his name's Chad. Can you tell he's a white boy or what?"

"Is he okay?"

"Yeah, he's a little shook up. Got hisself all up in the mix here."

"Okay, anyone else in there?"

"Just some dead folk."

"You're sure?"

"Oh yeah."

Shea stole a look at Sergeant Westerbrook. His right eye was twitching uncontrollably. Shea knew it would take all the self-control she and this old narcotics sergeant could muster to sit still while this operation ran its course.

"Okay, T...we don't want anyone else getting hurt, not Chad...not Pyro...not you either."

"I saw what ya'll did to Rodney King. We ain't playin' that way. Now, here's our demands."

"Okay, I'll listen to your demands, but we'll have to negotiate a little."

"We want the Reverend James Booney here right away. He'll

see to it no brothers are killed by you racist motherfuckers."

"Just so you know, T...I'm black. I'm no racist. I can see about getting the Reverend Booney here, if he's in town. Okay, now you gotta do something for me. Let me talk to the white kid."

"Oh no."

"I got one of my guys finding the number to the Reverend right now." Cross rolled his eyes at Andrew. "I'll always keep my end of the bargain. How about you? If you won't let me talk to the white kid, let me send in some paramedics for the hurt guys."

"They ain't hurt, they DEAD!"

Sergeant Westerbrook put his head in his hands.

"Okay, then we're back to the white kid. Put him on for a minute. I need some proof he is alive."

"Hold on." It sounded like the suspect covered the phone and he repeated his version of what Kevin Cross said. Shea thought she heard Chad's voice in the background.

"No, I lied about the name. I gotta warrant. I don't want to talk to them..."

"You're gonna talk to them and show them you're alive...*for now*. You keep talkin' about that fuckin' warrant and I'll kill you myself."

"Yeah?" Chad said. "Yeah? Hello?"

Shea looked at Jack. His voice was hoarse. It sounded like the voice of a man who was forced to talk with a gun at his head. Jack nodded at her and put his finger to his lips. Had she said that out loud?

"We're gonna get you out of there buddy, do they know you're a cop?" Kevin Cross said calmly.

"No. I'm not hurt."

"Good, good. Is the exit to the rear viable?"

"No. I'm not hungry, Jesus Christ. I'm sick."

"You got a gun?"

"Just a little."

"Both guys armed?"

"Yeah. They want that Reverend guy to come."

"Are they high?"

"Need to be. Bad day."

"Your partner gone for sure?"

"Yes sir." Chad's voice cracked.

"They have his gun, too?"

"Yes. Can you tell my mom I love her?"

"Hold fast, son. We'll get you out of there."

The suspect must have grabbed the phone from Chad, there was more muffled talking and the suspect was back on the line. Shea took a breath for the first time since she heard Chad's voice. Her chest was so tight it hurt to breathe.

"Satisfied?" T was back on the phone.

"Yeah, T. Thank you. I'm going to give you my phone number, so you can call me back when you need to." Kevin Cross gave T the number and a false assurance he'd call back when he heard from the Reverend Booney. T hung the phone up with a slam.

Andrew was looking through a pair of high powered binoculars at the liquor store.

"Smart kid," Andrew said.

"He is," Sergeant Westerbrook said.

"Could you get eyes on him?" Kevin Cross said.

"Yeah, and Rudy says he's got a good view when they come up to the counter. They went back to the storage area now. This kid married, too?" Andrew asked Westerbrook.

"No."

"Oh. He's got a ring on his left hand."

"He's got a new girlfriend. I don't know her name. Shit, someone should notify her. She works Valley Homicide."

Andrew lowered the binoculars, but didn't turn away from the window.

"What did you say, Pete?"

Chapter 25

Shea watched Andrew's back as he put the binoculars down on the desk. He didn't turn, he didn't look at her, he just kept working.

"Lieutenant Thorpe, a unit on Osborne Street says he's got the clerk's wife and daughter with him. They don't speak much English," a Metro officer told him.

"Tell them to get her to Foothill Station, get a translator, get a *ski* of the store, find out if there's a shotgun behind the counter, etcetera," Andrew said. A schematic of the location would give the SWAT officers information they could use to make an entry.

"Kevin, get those assholes back on the line and find out if they've got a television set in there," Andrew said.

Access to a television would determine how Andrew directed his team. Shea hoped for Chad's sake they didn't have a TV or radio in the store.

"Roger." Kevin Cross dialed the number.

"Whaddup?"

"Is this T?" Kevin asked.

"Yessss."

"Do you have a TV in there?"

"Hold on." The phone was away from his mouth again. "They wanna know if we got a TV in here. No. We ain't got one."

"Okay. Well, the Reverend's on TV. He's in New York City. We can't get him out here." Kevin Cross said so smoothly that Shea was beginning to believe him herself.

"Fuck that!"

"I know, but that wasn't under my control. So, let's see how we can get this thing resolved."

"The Reverend was gonna guarantee our safety, man."

"I can guarantee that. No one wants anyone else to get hurt. Not you or your partner. Look, we've been talking man-to-man here, right? You've been keeping up your end of the bargain, and I respect that. I respect you."

"Good. Good, you had better."

"Straight up, T. Now look, you're in a little trouble here, right? Can your partner hear us talking?"

"No."

"Maybe he got you tied up in something you weren't planning on. You didn't plan on killing anybody today, right? You was just gonna hit a liq and go."

"Keep talking."

"So, maybe we can work something out here. You hearing me? Brother, someone in there killed a cop. I can let the district attorney and the judge know that you were cooperating and this whole thing just got out of hand. That's the way it went down, right?"

"I gotta go." And the line went dead.

"Put the snipers on the roof of the donut shop," Andrew told his element leader. "They should be able to get a site on them from there."

"He's in good hands," Jack whispered. Shea nodded. The team was working together as if Andrew had been their boss for ages, in concert and tight.

"I think we can put the emergency assault team in the narco van. It's right in front the store. If the suspects come out, or we need to go in a hurry, we're right there," Cross said.

"I agree, but we don't want them getting hinked up."

"I don't think they can even see the van when they're in the back of the store. The team could enter on the side door on the van easily."

"Is it unlocked?" Andrew picked up the binoculars again.

"Doesn't matter. I got keys to all the rides we use," Sergeant Westerbrook said.

"Let's do it."

SWAT team members crept on roof tops, low-crawled and scurried between cars until everyone was in the positions Andrew directed. Andrew was looking out the window, his back still to Shea.

"My concern about going in with flash-bangs is-" the element leader started.

"David-10, David-10, green Honda Accord heading south – " Andrew keyed his radio, trying to warn a unit on the street of an approaching car. How did a car get inside the perimeter? Had it been there all along and missed by responding officers?

"What the hell!" The element leader followed Andrew's line of sight.

"Clear the frequency!" Someone yelled over the air.

"It's a fucking lay-off car!" Andrew tried again to get the message out over the air.

Shea and Jack stood up. She craned her neck to see out the

window. The car was creeping down the street, the driver wearing a red bandana pulled up to his eyes. Either the suspects had left their partner waiting around the block for a quick getaway or this guy was trying to perform some sort of rescue or diversion.

Andrew tried a third time to warn his officers on the air but the officers were stepping on each other over the frequency.

"Goddamnit!" Andrew flew out of the trailer, officers in his wake. Sergeant Westerbrook ran to window. Shea pushed past Jack and he tried to grab her by the back of her blazer, but she was too quick. She made it to the open trailer door in time to see the driver of the Honda pull a sawed-off shotgun from his lap and point it out the window at an officer who dove behind a short retaining wall.

Shea's hand instinctively went to her holster, but she was in no position to take a shot. SWAT officers in helmets and flak jackets with rifles at their shoulders were moving in between the cars in front of her. Someone yelled orders to drop the gun. Jack yanked her inside as the driver hit the brakes, coming to stop in the middle of the intersection between the CP and the liquor store. Jack reached out to grab the trailer door as Shea tried to get a glimpse of Andrew. The door slammed on her view as she heard the first blast of the shotgun and the SWAT officers return fire.

"Get down, get down! Rounds'll go through these walls!" Jack yelled to Sergeant Westerbrook over the gunfire. Westerbrook crouched just below one of the windows, trying to see out, his academy-issued blue steel revolver in his hand.

Not since New Year's Eve in Rampart Division had Shea heard that much gunfire, that close. Shea bent at the waist and dashed across the trailer to Sergeant Westerbrook. He looked at her for the first time, his blue eyes were wide and bloodshot, his mouth moved to say something, but no words came out.

"Sarge, come on. We can't help just yet," Shea said to him. Jack was by her side and they guided Westerbrook to the back of the trailer. Like sideways hail, the wall where they had been standing was under assault with projectiles. Shea watched as the glass spider webbed and she fell to her knees.

"Fuckin' shotgun pellets. They haven't killed him yet," Jack yelled over the din.

They hunkered down behind a desk.

"It's bullshit. Bullshit!" Sergeant Westerbrook's meaty hand clutched his revolver. "We're stuck in here like school kids."

"We've got no vests and I'm guessing you've got six rounds to your name," Jack said.

"Six rounds I'd like to put in the head of the bastard who killed my officer!" He was breathing heavily.

There was a pause in the gunfire and Shea could hear officers yelling commands. She strained to recognize Andrew's voice.

"Stay still," Jack said.

Shea's shoulder was pressed against the metal desk and she was sandwiched between the sergeant and Jack. More commands from outside, more yelling. None of it sounded like Andrew.

"Go, go, go!" Someone yelled. It sounded further away. Shea couldn't stand it anymore; she stood up and could barely see out the window from the back of the trailer.

"They're going inside," Shea said. Westerbrook was her ally; he used her arm for leverage and stood up as well. Jack couldn't stop both of them; they raced over to the cracked window in time to see a line of SWAT officers invading the liquor store. A flash-bang exploded and there was a bright burst of light and smoke visible through the store windows.

"Shea, just get out of the window." Shea could barely hear

Jack. Her heart was pounding in her ears, Sergeant Westerbrook was breathing like he was about to have a heart attack, and then there was gun fire in liquor store.

Shea scanned the street and saw a black man lying face down in front of the green Honda. Blood pooled at his head and disappeared from her view, probably trailing into the gutter. Where was Andrew?

Another lull in the gun fire hung over the three of them like a net. Shea put her hand on Sergeant Westerbrook's heaving back. It was wet with sweat.

"It's like the riots. Watts and this last one." Westerbrook shoved his gun in a paddle holster under his shirt. "You two probably only remember the last one."

"You okay, Sarge?" Jack said.

Shea watched as officers begin to move from their cover.

"It's done. It's over," Shea said.

Suddenly the shrill scream of a fire engine siren blasted through the trailer. All three peered out the window to see a fire engine and a rescue ambulance barreling down the street. That meant word had gone out that it was safe for the LAFD to approach.

Sergeant Westerbrook bolted for the door, his baseball jersey blowing behind him as he scrambled down the metal steps of the trailer. Shea tried to follow him, but Jack anticipated her move and he gripped her arm.

"Not just yet, partner." Jack pulled her back to the window.

"I think it would be okay if we out there," Shea said.

"Hang on."

Two RA units stopped in the middle of the street, next to the van. Paramedics spilled out and opened the rear doors. The paramedics ran into the liquor store, carrying orange trauma kits that looked like giant fishing tackle boxes. Firemen rushed stretchers in behind them.

"I'm done." Shea turned to the door, but Jack stepped in front of her. She put her finger in his chest. "Jack, I swear to fuckin' god, if you don't get out of my way – "

He grabbed her finger and locked eyes with her. She was breathing hard.

"We stay out of the way," Jack said. She nodded and ran around Jack to the door. Shea swept the scene – where the hell was Andrew? A third RA unit screeched to a stop in front of the car lot.

Shea stopped at the bottom of the metal stairs.

A team of firemen were wheeling Chad out of the store on a stretcher. She could see his blond hair for a moment, but a paramedic clamped an oxygen mask on his face as they eased the stretcher over the curb. Another medic ran beside the stretcher, hands on Chad's chest. They loaded him into the RA, but before the doors shut, a paramedic reached a hand to Sergeant Westerbrook and pulled him aboard. Seconds later the ambulance was heading lights and sirens north bound.

"Do you want to stay and find Andrew or follow the RA?"

Shea was already sprinting to their car.

Chapter 26

Over the next hour, hospital was overrun with narcotics officers, detectives, press relations personnel and the Chief's staff. Shea stood with her back to the wall, holding a cup of lukewarm coffee. She was drained, but didn't want to sit. She barely noticed when Jack took the cup away from her.

"Hey, Andrew's here," he said quietly.

"Is he okay?"

"Yeah. He's talking to the Chief outside."

"I don't care." It was easy to say that now that he was accounted for and unhurt.

"I just thought you'd want a heads-up," Jack said. "I called Boots, he's on his way. Our division isn't doing the crime scene. RHD is going to handle it."

"Did you see all the blood, Jack?"

"You know that doesn't mean anything." Jack began to list different types of wounds and their propensity to bleed heavily or not, but Shea stopped listening. Two narcotics officers clutched each other, one sobbing. Jack said something about getting her a fresh cup of coffee and she was vaguely aware he walked away.

"Are you okay?"

Shea recognized Andrew's steely, low voice. She didn't turn to look at him.

"Let's go somewhere and talk," he said. "I got word that they're going to be in surgery for awhile. Come on."

Andrew took her by the elbow and led her outside. She followed him woodenly through the parking lot to a small grassy area that looked like a place hospital workers might go to steal a smoke. He wasn't wearing body armor and his black t-shirt clung to his torso from sweat. She noticed a rip in the knee of his pants. He brought his hand up to rub his eyes and she saw a gravelly abrasion stretch the length of his forearm. She was about to ask what happened when Andrew began to talk.

"I'm really sorry," he said. "I see you've got the same ring as Hanson."

Andrew reached for her right hand. She yanked it away and shoved her hands in her blazer pockets, the Polaroid pressed against her knuckles.

"He's going to be okay. So is Cross. Just a graze wound from one of the shotgun pellets."

Before Shea could respond to the news about Kevin Cross, Andrew continued.

"Why didn't you tell me about Hanson? Why didn't you say anything? How long has this been going on?" His questioning was making her blood bounce in her veins.

"I guess you figure I'm not entitled to know…or it was okay to cheat on me, because I was married –"

"Cheat on you?!" Shea finally found her voice.

"That's what I'm talking about. Maybe you felt –"

"Did you cheat on me?" Shea could feel the carotid artery throbbing in her neck.

"Shea." Andrew sighed, as if this was too worn a topic to discuss. "If being married was cheating…"

"Did you ever cheat on the woman you were cheating on your wife with?"

"What are you talking about? I know you're upset, but you aren't making any sense."

Shea pulled the Polaroid out of her pocket and stepped back so he couldn't grab it. She held it up for him to see. His face didn't change expression, but his cheeks burned red.

"So, you slept with Chloe Diaz?"

"Where did you get that? How long have you had it?" He reached for it, but she was too quick. He folded his arms and looked around the parking lot.

"It was forwarded to me by someone who found it in her house. I got it this morning. That's why I called you." She put it back in her pocket.

"Lower your voice," Andrew said.

"You're a sociopath, you know that?" Shea said. "Do you know that you were just one of many naked men she took pictures of? She had a whole album of dumb clods who posed for her."

"I didn't pose," Andrew said. He turned away from her. She ran around him so she was facing him again.

"You want to quibble about the word 'pose'? Tell me how your naked ass ends up in this picture."

"And you tell me how you exchanged rings with a guy while you were begging me to leave my wife," Andrew countered.

"I never *begged* you to do a damned thing."

"Lower your fucking voice, Shea." Andrew said.

"I told you I was going to date other people."

"You came into my command post and watched as I got this piece of news. If anyone is a sociopath, it's you."

"Really? I'm the sociopath?"

"Did you have my dick in your mouth just a few hours ago? Did you get off watching us rescue your boyfriend?"

"I didn't intend any of that. When I heard Chad might be...I just went." The soft skin under Andrew's eyes flinched at the mention of Chad's name. He was silent for a moment.

"Okay," Andrew finally said.

"'Okay?'" *What the hell did okay mean?*

"What do you want me to say? It's all my fault?" Andrew asked.

"How-did-you-end-up-in-this-picture?" Shea waved it in front of his face again. With great speed, Andrew clamped his hand around her wrist and pushed it down to her hip.

"If we are going to do this here, you *are* going to control yourself," he said with deadly calm. He released her wrist. "I met her at the OIS. She was..."

"What?"

"Outrageous. She..." Andrew drew in a deep breath. "She

made a crazy proposition and...it just...was a one-night stand. She opened the bathroom door and she had a camera."

"Weren't you worried RHD would find your picture with everyone else's?"

"Not really. I saw the other pictures. Steve kept me in the loop."

"Lancaster shared confidential information about the *murder of a cop* with you?" Shea tried not to shout.

"Stop. I mean it. You're way out of line."

"I'm out of line?" Shea's voice rose again. She knew the officers hanging around in the parking lot had been subtly watching the SWAT lieutenant in fatigues arguing with the detective in heels. Now they actually turned their heads and stared openly.

"Shut the fuck up, Shea. Are we done with this conversation?"

"No. One more question. And you have to answer it. I swear to God," Shea said. "What stupid line could the girl say that would make you go with her?"

Andrew held up his hand. "She said, 'what would it take to get a lieutenant in bed with me tonight?'"

"That's the big outrageous line?"

"No. She had just been in a shooting and she was just...brazen. I know now that she wasn't stable. But at the time, she just seemed tough and I have a weakness for tough girls." Andrew almost smiled at Shea, but then quickly changed his mind. He looked up at the sky.

"Okay. I said that she'd have to let me fuck her in the ass."

Shea stared at him. "Do you know why you like tough girls? You like them because you like to humiliate them. It's a challenge. You're the one with the problems."

"Okay, doctor. Thanks for the diagnosis," Andrew said and Shea slapped him. There was a gasp from the choir of detectives and officers. They were out of hearing range, but witnessed the slap and watched as the lieutenant's hands curled into fists.

Two detectives ran across the parking lot and broke them up.

"Hey, hey!" Jack wrapped his arm around her shoulders. He was using all of his strength to control Shea's arms as he dragged her away from Andrew. She looked over her shoulder to see Andrew throw off Curt's hand. Andrew's fists were still clenched.

Motherfucker!

"I'm going to kill him."

"Not in front of half the department." Jack guided her past the officers and back into waiting room. Jack asked the officers who there if they could get some privacy. They were initially put out, but after seeing Shea's face, they quickly left. Jack pushed her into a chair.

"You're like trying to shove a cat into a bag. What happened? Was he giving you a hard time about being with Chad?" Jack said.

"Oh, yeah. Until I showed him this." Shea pulled the picture out of her pocket and handed it to Jack.

"I don't get it."

Curt burst in the room. He saw Shea and shook his head in wonderment.

"What the hell is going on? You slapped a lieutenant?" Curt said. "I tried to calm Thorpe down, but he just tore off in his car. Did you interfere at the CP? I told you not to go past the perimeter."

"No, no that's not it," Jack said.

"Who is he to you? Is he the married guy you were seeing?"

"Yes," Shea said.

"Jesus, what a scene. This wasn't a good place to have a domestic violence dispute," Curt said.

Jack handed the picture to Curt. He looked at it and shook his head.

"Chloe Diaz took that picture," Shea told them. It took a moment to register. "It was found in her house. I got it today. Don't ask how. What you guys don't know, or maybe you do...maybe everyone is in the loop but me...anyway, Chloe liked to take compromising pictures of guys. There were a bunch in her locker and apparently more at her house."

Curt handed the picture back to Shea and sat down across from her. Jack ran both hands through his hair and then left his hands at the back of his neck.

"Wow," Curt said.

"No wonder you hit him," Jack said.

"Hey, kid." Curt rested his hand on her knee. "There's some news on your friend."

"What?" Shea looked up.

"He made it through surgery. He's going to be unconscious for quite a while. I think we should all go over to El Presidente and get some tequila. Vaughn's going to meet us over there."

"I think I should stay."

"I know. But it would be better if we get out of here. It's just down the street and we can all be back here in a flash. The head nurse in ICU has my cell number and I think she likes me. Okay?" He shook her knee. Shea drew in a deep breath and followed them out of the hospital.

The El Presidente restaurant was just a few blocks away from Holy Cross Hospital. It was late afternoon and mostly empty. Vaughn was sitting in a circular booth in a dark corner of the bar. When Vaughn saw Shea he slid out of the booth and hugged her tightly. The lump in her throat progressed immediately to tears.

"Can I get you guys something?" The waitress asked, interrupting the hug.

Shea wiped her eyes and slid to the middle of the booth. Curt told the waitress they wanted a round of tequila shots and a pitcher of beer. Shea blew her nose in a napkin and dried her eyes. The waitress returned and placed all the liquor on the table. They reached for the shot glasses simultaneously. The tequila burned her throat, but it felt good.

"Can we bring Vaughn up to speed on the other developments?" Jack asked Shea.

Shea shrugged and tossed the Polaroid onto the table as Curt poured her a glass of beer. Vaughn looked at the picture and listened as Jack gave him the basic story.

"Whoa," Vaughn said. He was still looking at the photo. "Thorpe is Lieutenant Wonderful?"

"Probably the wrong alias now," Jack said.

"We could've saved you a lot of trouble, Shea, if we knew you were seeing him. That's like picking a bull from the killer pen." Curt bumped his shoulder into hers.

"Yeah, yeah," Shea said.

"How did she end up with Andrew? Did he tell you?" Curt asked.

"Yeah, the night of the OIS. She came on to him and apparently made him an offer he couldn't refuse."

"I knew it." Vaughn picked up the picture and snapped it with his fingers.

"What?" Shea said. He handed the photo back to her and she put it on the table, face down.

"I saw them talking in the break room after I interviewed her. They were just standing too close, you know? But, I know him. I know his reputation," Vaughn said. "Then was leaving, I saw them by her car. She was squeezing in between hers and another one, trying to unlock her door. Well, he was right behind her and then she backed into him. He grabbed her and just held her to him. That was it. He let her go. Shit, he saw me and gave me a wave."

"Oh..." Shea sighed. "I feel so stupid."

"I didn't know he was the guy you were seeing, otherwise I would've told you, Shea."

"I know."

"Shit." Curt refilled Shea's empty glass and motioned the waitress for another pitcher. They drank their beers in silence.

"Just so you can all stop worrying, I'd like to say I didn't have sex with Chloe Diaz *or* Andrew Thorpe," Curt said. Everyone laughed and Jack tapped his glass to Curt's.

"I thought I was the only one who was left out." Jack chuckled.

Curt's cell phone rang and he took the call. After a series of "uh-huhs and yeahs" he snapped the phone shut and looked around the table. Shea knew what was coming, it was the same evaluation he gave them all the night of Chloe's murder. Who was sober enough to play?

"Okay, we got ourselves a double on Chatsworth, near the 405. Who is good to go?"

Shea reached in her bag and popped a peppermint Lifesaver in her mouth.

"I am," Shea said. "Come on, partner."

50053821R00280

Made in the USA
San Bernardino, CA
12 June 2017